Classic Restaurants

of

NEW ORLEANS

ALEXANDRA KENNON

FOREWORD BY WALTER ISAACSON

AMERICAN PALATE

Published by American Palate
A Division of The History Press
Charleston, SC
www.historypress.com

First published 2019

ISBN 9781467142830

Library of Congress Control Number: 2019947300

Notice: The information in this book is true and complete to the best of our knowledge. It is offered without guarantee on the part of the author or The History Press. The author and The History Press disclaim all liability in connection with the use of this book.

The author and The History Press assume no responsibility or liability for any damages that might be experienced resulting from the recipes included in this book. As always, care should be taken when cooking using raw eggs and open flames.

For my mother, Ellen Kennon, whose excellent cooking and taste have made me a lifelong gourmand, and who always pushes me hardest to reach my goals.

For my father, Kenwood Kennon, who told me I could do anything when I grew up, and truly believed it.

In many ways, this book is the product of both of their love and support.

Contents

Foreword

New Orleans has an ever-changing and innovative food culture, but it is anchored by a dozen or so old restaurants that helped to establish the DNA of the city's cuisine. These beloved institutions reflect the city's French and Creole roots, with some flavorings of Cajun and Spanish and Italian styles. They have formed the foundation on which each new wave of immigrants has built when they added their own ingredients to the local gumbo pot of cooking styles.

This book is a wonderful tale of cultural influences but also a paean to the role of families in upholding great institutions. At these restaurants, the owners do so with great style and also an understanding of the role of theater.

It also reminds us of the importance of honoring both preservation and progress. Even as New Orleans bustles ahead as an innovative and creative twenty-first-century city, it has been able to nurture its roots and respect its venerable institutions. In that way, New Orleans's food is like its jazz: always improvising but remembering to remain true to its traditions.

The tales in this book are inspiring and savory ones. They remind us that whatever our endeavors, it's important to pursue passions with love and good taste. And also, by the way, the book is a lot of fun—just like a meal in one of these restaurants. *Bon appétit*!

WALTER ISAACSON
history professor at Tulane, best-selling biographer
and former managing editor of *TIME* magazine

Acknowledgements

This book is the culmination of not only my own efforts but also, truly, of an entire city's. I absolutely could not have completed this project were it not for the patient and dedicated assistance of many. I will attempt to provide due credit, knowing that to adequately thank everyone who took time from their own lives and projects to contribute to this book would be impossible.

Infinite thanks to Joe Gartrell, my acquisitions editor at Arcadia Publishing and The History Press, for reading my work from hundreds of miles away in Charleston and taking a chance by asking me to write this book. He provided a much-needed sounding board of wit and positivity throughout the entire process and made me truly feel like a small-town Louisiana girl could be an author. Thanks as well to Senior Editor Ryan Finn for his attentive care in editing and to everyone at The History Press who put work into crafting the book you hold now.

Thanks to the many cracker-jack public and media relations gals and others who represent the included restaurants and fielded my many e-mails, scheduled interviews, dug up old photographs and so much more: Elizabeth Muir, Samantha Cusimano, Meaghan Donohoe Regan, Simone Rathlé, Abby Mayo, Caitlin Strother, Stella Chase Reese, Nancy Weinstock, Katie Ostrowski, Liz Bodet, Dominique Ellis, Lindsey Saucier and Carrie DeVries Pavlick. Thank you for trusting a probably naïve-seeming twentysomething to interview some of the most important members of your companies and providing enthusiastic assistance along the way.

Thanks to all of the chefs, restaurateurs, waiters, maître d's, bartenders, oyster shuckers and more who graciously took time away from their own very busy lives to talk to me about what they do for inclusion in this book: Leah Chase, Ralph Brennan, Slade Rushing, Ti Martin, Tory McPhail, Chris Montero, Katy Casbarian, Tommy DiGiovanni, Augie Spicuzza, Doug Hopper, Rick and Lisa Blount, Mark Latter, Thomas Robey, Arthur Brocato, Mark DeFelice, Thomas "Uptown T" Stewart, Jimi Setchim, Rita Pastrano, Jay Nix, Justin Kennedy, Michael Tannen, Melvin Rodrigue and Philip Lopez. Not only could this book not exist without them, but New Orleans could not.

Thanks to Rhiannon Enil and Liz Williams at the Southern Food and Beverage Museum, Rebecca Smith at the Historic New Orleans Collection and Laurie Philips at Loyola University's Monroe Library for being research goddesses and providing assistance gathering materials for this project.

Thanks to all of the culinary historians who have been covering the New Orleans food scene much longer than I have, particularly the authors of all of the historic restaurant cookbooks referenced; their work was indispensable for this project.

Thanks to all of my teachers and professors from throughout my education, particularly Karen Douet, Dr. Rodney Allen, Dr. Laura Hope and Michael Giusti. Without the skills and lessons gained from each of them, I would not be half the writer or researcher I am today—I might not be a writer or researcher at all.

Thanks to James Fox-Smith and the folks at *Country Roads* magazine for publishing my articles and photographs that allowed The History Press to find me in the first place and for always encouraging writers to venture off the beaten path.

Thanks to James Corbyn, Angela Monroe and Mark Aspiazu, owners of New Orleans Secrets Tours, who not only trusted me enough to take me on as their company's first hired guide back in 2016 but also put up with my incessant schedule change requests while I completed this project. Much of my knowledge of New Orleans history is owed to them.

Thanks to all of my friends and family for their never-faltering support— you know who you are, and I love and appreciate all of you.

Thanks to my best friend, Paige Skidmore, for hyping me up even when I most doubted myself.

Thanks to my partner, Dominic Rivera, not only for proofreading and testing recipes but also for maintaining my sanity throughout this process with his loving, calm support.

And thanks to Strider, our boxer–pit bull mix, whose funny faces and snuggles were truly the backbone of this entire endeavor.

Introduction

Three Hundred Years to Simmer

*I think traditions in New Orleans are celebrated in the here and the now more
than they ever were before, because as the city evolves, especially since Katrina,
people are worried we could potentially lose some of those traditions that we have.*
—Katy Casbarian, co-proprietor, Arnaud's Restaurant

When New Orleans made its tricentennial in 2018, it was also
named number one on the *New York Times* list of "Places to Go."
Approximately 18 million visitors are welcomed annually to the Crescent
City, and the commonality among nearly every one of them is that they
come to New Orleans to eat. Shrimp remoulade, gumbo, pecan-crusted
trout, po-boys—these are just a few of the overwhelmingly extensive and
delicious culinary experiences one can have in the Crescent City. For those
who live in New Orleans, food is an obsession—we're the type of people
who plan what to eat for dinner while still enjoying lunch. New Orleans
is one of the only cities in America that can claim to have developed its
own cuisine and maintained it through its evolution over the course of three
hundred years. These are the stories of the typically immigrant families
who forged a symbiotic relationship with their adopted city—making a new
home and a livelihood for themselves and their children while contributing
the culinary DNA of their homeland to the ever-diversifying New Orleans
cultural landscape.

Even if New Orleans did not brand itself excessively with the fleur-de-lis,
most discerning visitors would still be able to conclude fairly easily that the

city was founded by France. Although little of the original French colonial architecture survived the fires and hurricanes that plagued settlers in the 1700s, French influence remains strong in many other ways, perhaps most notably in New Orleans's cuisine. Glance at the menu at one of the older restaurants in town, like Antoine's or Galatoire's, and French mother sauces and other heavily accented dish names abound. The initial attempts of René-Robert Cavelier, Sieur de La Salle, to settle the land near the mouth of the Mississippi River for Louis XIV in 1684 failed miserably when he ended up too far west in Matagorda Bay in present-day Texas before his men mutinied and killed him. In 1698, France sent Pierre le Moyne, Sieur d'Iberville, and his brother, Jean-Baptiste le Moyne, Sieur d'Bienville, to make another go of it, and the colony of Louisiana—with the port city of La Nouvelle Orleans its not yet shining jewel—was born.

While the French would have a profound and lasting impact on Creole cuisine that remains one of the most evident influences today, it is crucial to note that meals were being served and eaten on the land between the crescent-shaped Mississippi and what would later be named Lake Pontchartrain for thousands of years before European settlers ever arrived. In 1700, still years before the French sent enough men and provisions to properly establish Nouvelle Orleans, six distinct Native American nations and the different tribes within thrived in present-day Louisiana. According to Louisiana Culinary Ambassador Chef John Folse's *Encyclopedia of Creole and Cajun Cuisine*, they were the Caddos, Tunicas, Atakapas, Natchezes, Muskogeans and Chitimachas.

From what archaeologists are able to gather, Native Americans in Louisiana often utilized "earth ovens" for cooking. A hole was dug in the ground, and heated clay objects were added as desired to raise the temperature and cook what was inside. As Folse pointed out in his *Encyclopedia*, Louisiana earns the nickname "Sportsman's Paradise" today in part thanks to the same bounty enjoyed by its original residents: whitetail deer and duck were some of the favorites, but also some less popular fare by today's standards such as bison, pigeons and raccoons. Turtle soup, now a decadent Creole favorite with sherry used to enhance the flavor of the turtle, was originated by the Native Americans—they would often serve the dish in the turtle shell itself. Many Native American dishes and techniques would be appropriated and adapted by European settlers into Creole cuisine.

Admittedly, the term *cuisine* is a stretch to describe the food eaten in the earliest colonial days of the city. Certainly in New Orleans's early days, no chef was paying mind to what flavor profiles might most delight his audience's taste buds. Food was prepared and eaten when and if it became available—if it happened to be palatable, that was a happy yet extraneous detail secondary to the fact that it would keep you alive. Only later, as the city grew and prospered and came into its own as a port, would Creole cuisine as we know it begin to simmer.

With Native American and French roots thoroughly submerged in the pot, New Orleans was traded from France to Spain in 1762. This change in ownership was a result of the Treaty of Fountainbleu to end the Seven Years' War in Europe, as well as, partially, French King Louis XV and Spanish King Charles III's relationship as cousins. Both monarchs hailed from the House of Bourbon, which would result in the street name most visitors and locals incorrectly assume comes from the liquor rather than a royal family.

The Spanish culinary influence in time began to gradually become incorporated into Creole cuisine. Some even say that the Creole adaptation of the French mirepoix known as the "Holy Trinity" can be traced all the way back to Spanish colonialism. While the French were fond of using the classic mirepoix of onion, celery and carrot as a base for many dishes, the Spanish palate preferred the zesty green bell pepper to the blander carrot. Perhaps the reasons why the "Holy Trinity" of onion, celery and bell pepper was established is this simple, but like most history, it is likely much more complex. Chef Paul Prudhomme, who is credited with introducing the Cajun cuisine he grew up with in his hometown of Opelousas to New Orleans and popularizing it, is also credited with giving Louisiana's iconic blend of seasonings its Catholic name. When garlic is added to the mix, people in Louisiana often refer to it as "The Pope." Louisiana is a Catholic state, after all, and this is reflected in our food.

It is also relevant to this book that shortly after Governor Don Alejandro O'Reilly solidified Spanish control by having a group of French rebels executed in New Orleans, he granted the Acadians who settled modern Arkansas permission to resettle along the Amite River in Louisiana. The Acadians were French Catholics originating from present-day Nova Scotia who resettled in Louisiana after being exiled when Britain took over Canada in 1763. "Acadiana," as they called the land in southwest Louisiana where they settled, is made up of twenty-two parishes (counties) today. Their cuisine reflects a more rural influence than its Creole counterpart: cured meats and ample spices were utilized partially as a technique to preserve the food. Red beans and rice was a staple because a pot could easily be left to simmer while chickens were fed and laundry was done. Jambalaya came about because any ingredients that happened to be available could be incorporated into the versatile dish. Spicy and smoky sausages, like andouille and boudin, are also common, not just for the flavor but because they would help preserve the meat through hot summers. It is only due to a laissez-fare attitude toward pronunciation that the word "Acadian" was eventually shortened to "Cajun." But it would not be until about two hundred years after the Acadians were exiled to Louisiana from Canada that their cuisine would travel to New Orleans, notably with Chef Paul Prudhomme when he moved to New Orleans from his home in the Cajun town of Opelousas.

While French, Spanish and Native American are some of the predominant cultures that affect Creole cuisine, other influences are crucial to note as well. While the exact makeup is frequently debated, John Folse makes a good argument that seven nations make up Louisiana's primary cooking styles: Native Americans, France, Spain, Germany, England, Africa and Italy. It has also been argued by many others that in New Orleans in particular, elements of Caribbean cuisine have also worked their way into Creole dishes. "Who's to say that it will not continue to evolve, incorporating aspects of the Asian, Middle Eastern, or Latin American cultures that now thrive here, or perhaps of those that have not yet arrived?" Folse posits. "I truly hope it does. It is exactly that kind of adaptability and change along with a strong sense of history that makes Cajun and Creole cuisine so exciting, so fun to prepare and so delicious."

Like the cuisine they feature, the classic restaurants of New Orleans are also tasked with honoring Creole traditions while respecting the fact that Louisiana's food, by its very nature, must evolve and change. Different elements of Creole cuisine are featured differently depending on the restaurant, the chef and their backgrounds. Antoine's and Arnaud's, for example, were founded by Frenchmen, and thus their menus to this day largely reflect the French style. At Dooky Chase, on the other hand, Leah Chase incorporated bolder African flavors, what she and others refer to as "Creole de Couleur." Pascal's Manale's menu is decidedly Italian-leaning. Since Paul Prudhomme led the kitchen at Commander's, Creole and Cajun have made a harmonious pair there. What all of these restaurants have in common is that they, in some way or another, contribute to the diverse and unique culinary landscape of New Orleans.

One theme that you will hopefully observe throughout this book, one that is as important to New Orleans as its cuisine, is family. Each of these restaurants has been maintained for so many years because of devoted family members carrying on a legacy, sometimes out of genuine passion, sometimes out of obligation and more often than not out of both. "It has been the family owners, rather than the individual chefs, who have carried the tradition of New Orleans restaurants and influenced their evolution," John Wilds wrote in *New Orleans Yesterday and Today* (1983). Chefs are crucial, perhaps today more than ever, but it is up to the owners to guard the traditions that make their family restaurants unique.

A common philosophy I observed throughout many of these restaurateurs is the comparison of running a restaurant to working in the theater. "But it's like a play—the show goes on. The dining room is a stage, and the whole wait staff has to perform," David Gooch of Galatoire's observed. "Two shows a day," referring to lunch and dinner, commonly echoes between Ti Martin and Lally Brennan at Commander's Palace. Germaine Wells, Count Arnaud's daughter, who left the vaudeville circuit to run her father's restaurant after his death, also frequently made the comparison, and Katy Casbarian, who co-owns Arnaud's today, agrees. New Orleans in general has a flair for the dramatic, and if anyone maintains that reputation, it is these restaurateurs. While food is paramount, style of service must also be maintained over the generations. Whether that is a waiter in a tailcoat suggesting a wine pairing or a po-boy wrapped in butcher paper being handed over a counter, service remains a crucial part of the experience at each of these establishments.

The restaurant owners featured in this book are not merely restaurateurs—they are, by necessity, preservationists. Their institutions have, in many cases, remained constant features of the New Orleans culinary scene for more than a century. This presents the challenge of maintaining favorite menu items and classic atmosphere, while simultaneously evolving with the times enough to appeal to younger customers and streamline service using modern technology. Another massive challenge these restaurant owners face is often in the structure of the restaurants themselves. Particularly in the French Quarter, the building that houses Tujague's dates back to the 1730s; almost all of the buildings housing Antoine's are more than two hundred years old. The Napoleon House is a National Historic Landmark dating back to 1814. Arnaud's has the greatest volume of upkeep with thirteen buildings, all historic. In addition to running a restaurant, these restaurateurs are tasked with the upkeep of very old and consequentially very high-maintenance buildings. Expansion in the French Quarter is, for the most part, entirely out of the question, with restaurants often making due with incredibly limited kitchen space.

Following Katrina, when Parkway and Angelo Brocato's in Mid-City retained more than five feet of floodwater and other restaurants across the city experienced extensive damage, the owners of these historic eateries, often setting aside their other losses and the overall devastation of the experience, prioritized reopening their restaurants and feeding the people of New Orleans. These restaurants are inherently woven into the culture of the city, and in returning to serve New Orleans after Katrina, they helped solidify that nothing, natural disaster or otherwise, would weaken that bond. While gas lines were down in certain New Orleans neighborhoods for months after the storm, each of these dining institutions returning to their former glory in a way signifies that the incredibly bright light of culinary influence from New Orleans can never be extinguished. This is in large part thanks to its devoted restaurateurs and chefs ensuring that the gas lamp remains burning.

Chapter 1

Antoine's
(1840)

One of the many characteristic traits of New Orleans' social existence is the excellence of its temples to the culinary gods. And if a canvass were taken among the many visitors who have come to this delightful city, and tasted of its gastronomic delicacies, it is safe to presume that the palm would be awarded to Antoine's Restaurant.
—Times-Picayune, *1902*

It is fitting that America's oldest restaurant owned continually by the same family exists in a city so preoccupied with both food and kin. To say that Antoine's opened in 1840 as a restaurant in the sense that restaurants are understood in the modern era, however, is misleading. Antoine's evolved into the classic dining institution that exists today as the city of New Orleans developed its notion of what that should entail—thus setting a precedent for Creole fine dining still thriving in its own right nearly two centuries later.

A restaurant does not remain within the same family lineage for 179 years due to mere happenstance. Generations have worked shrewdly and tirelessly to ensure that Antoine's remains in the legacy of its namesake: current CEO and owner Rick Blount's great-great-grandfather Antoine Alciatore.

Antoine Alciatore was born in Alassio, Italy, in the year 1822 and at a young age moved with his family to Marseille, France. His father, Joseph Alciatore, was a wool merchant, trading materials to tailors, with an impressive array of aristocratic clients, among them the highly regarded chef Jean-Louis Françoise-Collinet. At his father's request, young Antoine began apprenticing under Collinet at the Hotel de Noaillles, where the chef taught him the technique for making Pommes de Terre Soufflées, or souffléd potatoes, which Collinet is credited with inventing.[1] During Antoine's apprenticeship, the hotel received a visit from notable French politician Charles Maurice de Talleyrand-Périgord, along with his highly respected cook, Chef Marchand. Sixteen-year-old Antoine was granted the opportunity to cook Talleyrand's roast beef himself. Talleyrand preferred his beef rare, so Antoine named the preparation to Talleyrand's liking "Fillet de boeuf Robespierre," after his father's description of the French revolutionary Robespierre's face being peeled back prior to his beheading.[2] Beef Robespierre would remain on the menu at Antoine's Restaurant all the way until the 1960s.[3]

His tutor, Chef Collinet, arranged for Antoine to be appointed cook at the notorious fortress Chateau D'If, where the Count of Monte Cristo is famously imprisoned in Dumas's novel. Having perfected his craft, and tiring of overseeing the preparation of prison food, young Antoine left the unforgiving European economy of the early 1800s for America, joining countless other immigrants in boarding a ship for New York City and the prospects awaiting across the Atlantic.[4] One of them, a young Alsatian girl named Julie Freyss who was traveling with her parents to settle in New York, would eventually become Antoine's wife.[5]

New York City did not suit the young chef's European sensibilities, however. Speaking almost exclusively French, Antoine was continually told that he would be far better suited in the other major American port down south, the more Francophile and Francophone New Orleans. So, after only a brief stint in the Northeast, Antoine made his way to New Orleans in 1838,[6] five years later sending for his fiancée, Julie, to join him. Upon her arrival, they were shortly married, eventually having seven children total.[7]

After arriving in New Orleans at eighteen years old, Antoine completed a short stint working in the kitchen of the highly regarded St. Charles Hotel and then wasted no time in opening a hotel-restaurant, or *pension*, of his own.[8] The concept of a restaurant existing exclusively for dining was practically unheard of in America in 1840, so in keeping with the business model of the time, Antoine's initially offered lodging attached to the small restaurant.

The first iteration of Antoine's was situated on St. Louis Street at the intersection of Exchange Place Alley in the French Quarter, and its menu was incredibly compact compared with the extensive options that would appear in the future. In fact, rather than providing a written menu, Antoine would concoct specials based on what meat or vegetables he was able to obtain that day. Reflecting Antoine's training, these of course included French classics,

Antoine's exterior today. *Alexandra Kennon.*

along with dishes Antoine invented himself utilizing ingredients available in 1840s New Orleans, such as the wildly popular Dinde à la Talleyrand, an elaborate dish featuring the newly domesticated American turkey, named for Antoine's earliest celebrity client.[9]

Wildly successful with indulgent New Orleans locals and travelers alike, Antoine's Restaurant quickly outgrew its modest original location. By 1857, Antoine had purchased a larger building at 713 St. Louis Street, an address that would within another generation be recognized worldwide as Antoine's Restaurant.[10]

As successful as the restaurant Antoine Alciatore created was, Antoine's could not remain in the hands of its founder forever. In 1877, Antoine was diagnosed with a fatal case of tuberculosis. Not wishing his wife and children to witness his deterioration, and yearning to be buried in his home country of France, Antoine returned to Europe, telling his wife, "As I take boat for Marseilles, we will not meet again on this Earth." He was correct, as he died just a few months later at the age of fifty-two. His wife, Julie Freyss Alciatore, outlived her husband by more than thirty years, her eighty-fifth and final birthday party garnering a loving social writeup in the *Times-Picayune*:

"Gran'mere" Alciatore, radiantly happy, was sitting by the great white-frosted birthday cake with its eighty-five candles. She had been sitting there throughout the evening when the guests of the reception at "Antoine's" came to her to offer congratulations and wish her many happy returns. But when the lusty voices of her children and friends and her children's friends and friend's children struck first into the "Marseillaise" and then into "The Star-Spangled-Banner," sitting was not to be thought of. Gran'mere Alciatore stood up—stood up as straight as she would have stood when, as a slim girl, she became the wife of "Antoine."[11]

Although in keeping with the times the lineage of Antoine's Restaurant is predominantly male, it is worth noting that when the founding Alciatore made his final departure back to Marseille, he left control of the restaurant in the hands of his wife. Julie took the helm of Antoine's for nearly a decade, meanwhile tutoring their son Jules, who at the age of eleven expressed the most interest in the restaurant of any of the children, in the skills necessary to maintain the business before sending him at age seventeen to train in the fine kitchens of Europe as his father did. Jules apprenticed in many of the great resort cities of his time, including Vichy, Karlsbad, Nice, Trouville, Bordeaux and Paris.[12] When Jules returned to New Orleans, he served as chef of the highly regarded Pickwick Club until 1887. Only when Julie deemed her son completely prepared did she summon him back to Antoine's to carry on his father's legacy.[13]

During this transitional period, a prominent planter and frequenter of Antoine's named Pierre Bienvenu Roy traveled to New Orleans on business, bringing his daughter, Althea. Shortly after their visit, Jules, having become smitten with the Acadian girl, traveled to her family's plantation in the town of Royville (today Youngsville, outside Lafayette) to court Althea for her hand in marriage. He obtained it, and on April 1, 1894, the *Times-Picayune* wrote of the wedding, "Rev. Father Mignot, Vicar of the St. Louis Cathedral, officiated, and the ceremony took place in the handsome and brilliantly-lighted parlors of Antoine's Restaurant, on St. Louis Street. Rare exotic plants, festoons of evergreens, wreaths of fragrant flowers in endless profusion were artistically arranged in elegant decorative style that is very appropriate and pleasing."[14] Jules and Althea Alciatore had three children: Mary Louise, Jules and Roy.[15]

During his tenure as owner of Antoine's, Jules is credited with creating many signature dishes, such as the appropriately rich Oysters Rockefeller. The now-famous dish was purportedly invented as a result of the kitchen

Huitres à la Rockefeller.

Oysters baked in their shell with such rich ingredients that the name of the multi-millionaire was borrowed to indicate their value.

Oysters Tipperary.

Something new for the epicure.

Will be imitated as his other creations

But: Its a long. long way to duplicate it.

Tomates Frappées à la Jules César.

Iced stuffed tomatoes for hot weather, creating a sensation to the palate as if one were suddenly elevated to the ethereal regions.

Bisque d' Ecrevisses à la Cardinal.

A soup made of crayfish boiled in white wine and subsequently pounded into a pulp with an addition of cream, aromatic herbs and vegetables.

Truite Saumonnée Rupinicoscoff.

Salmon-trout prepared according to the famous Moscovite chef Alexandrovitch Rupinicoscoff, whose recipe was given to Jules on the condition that its composition never be divulged.

Terrapin à la St. Antoine.

A tide-water diamond-back tortoise fed for weeks in a private pond on a special diet, to impart the particular flavor so characteristic when cooked and served in its own shell.

Jules Alciatore's description of dishes. *Antoine's Restaurant.*

lacking enough imported snails for the usual escargot fare, prompting Jules to create a rich sauce of green herbs and vegetables (but notably no spinach), baked atop oysters on the half-shell. The Oysters Rockefeller recipe remains a guarded family secret to this day, although many have attempted to replicate it.[16] Jules also took advantage of the increasing variety of produce available, putting creative vegetable dishes on the menu like "tomates frappées à la Jules César," for which he would stuff cold tomatoes with crabmeat ravigote, since tomatoes were undergoing a surge of popularity. Jules is one of the first chefs in America to utilize avocados, offering a similar dish involving halved avocados filled with shrimp in a ravigote sauce. One of the more elaborate dishes Jules concocted was Pompano en Papillote, wherein the fish was baked in a paper container in honor of the famous hot air balloonist Alberto Santos Dumont, who visited New Orleans the year of the dish's advent.[17]

Jules's era of ownership is also of particular interest, because from 1919 until 1933, the Eighteenth Amendment prohibiting the sale of alcohol threatened to dampen—or rather, dry up—typical New Orleans festivities. Jules was crafty, however, and was able to circumnavigate the strict law of the time. Regulars at Antoine's who came to dine during Prohibition received an innocuous-looking coffee cup containing a key that could be used to open a hidden door at the back of the ladies' washroom to reveal a full bar in what was at the time the carriage house. The guest would fill their coffee cup with their liquor of choice, and if other diners questioned where they obtained the illegal spirit, they were to reply, "It is a mystery to me." This room of Antoine's restaurant, now used for dining and featuring Prohibition-era newspaper articles on the walls, is referred to as the "Mystery Room" to this day.[18]

Jules is responsible for garnering international acclaim for the restaurant. When he died in 1934, his obituary in the *Times-Picayune* noted, "Imperishably linked with the words 'New Orleans' throughout the civilized world are the names of the dishes and drinks Jules Alciatore invented."[19]

When Jules was ready to retire and hand off Antoine's to the next generation, his daughter, Mary Louise, was occupied with her family and small children, and his eldest son, Jules, was already well established as a linguistics professor at Tulane, studying romance languages. Despite initially not being particularly enthusiastic to become a restaurateur, young Roy was the next logical link in the chain of family proprietors. But like his father and grandfather, Roy first had to put in some time experiencing the restaurants of Europe firsthand before he was given control of the family business.[20]

In 1923, Jules took Roy to the famous kitchens of France to give him a taste for how classic French cuisine was to be prepared and served. Throughout this decade, Jules gradually passed the duties of operating the restaurant on to his youngest son. This ensured that when Jules finally died in 1934, Roy was very much prepared to take ownership of Antoine's.[21]

Like his father, Roy was passionate about garnering fame for the restaurant, creating new dishes and enticing celebrity diners. During Roy's tenure, the boarding aspect of the business was shuttered, allowing Antoine's to finally come into its own as solely a dining institution. He expanded the restaurant, added several dining rooms and closed the Japanese Room upstairs following the bombing of Pearl Harbor in 1941; it would remain closed until 1985 (today, a to-be-announced Mardi Gras krewe is in discussions about converting the room for their purposes). Rooms Roy added also include the

Above: Mystery Room today. *Alexandra Kennon.*

Left: Pamphlet distributed by Jules Alciatore, second-generation proprietor of Antoine's. *Antoine's Restaurant.*

NTOINE'S IS TO NEW ORLEANS WHAT DELMONICO'S WAS TO NEW YORK OR THE CAFE ANGLAIS TO PARIS.

The home of good cheer.

The home of Fine Cooking.

The place where trouble and tribulations are left behind.

It is the place "par excellence" for the gourmet, because there is always something new for the refined senses.

New dishes, new seasoning, new presentation of eatables.

What you can get elsewhere you can get at Antoine's.

But, some things you can get at Antoine's you cannot get elsewhere, because they are special concoctions of the culinary art, prepared under the master's eye.

Dishes are created, or new ways of serving old ones are discovered almost weekly.

Eating at Antoine's is like getting a new start in life.

You go in with the blues and leave with rosy impressions.

76693

1840 Room, built in celebration of the restaurant's centennial in 1940 to honor Antoine's rich family history; and the Rex Room, established in the 1930s as a private dining room ornately decorated in honor of one of New Orleans's longest-standing Mardi Gras krewes, the Krewe of Rex, and its kings.[22] In addition to the Carnival royalty that frequents the Rex Room, the Duke and Duchess of Windsor also famously dined there before attending the Rex and Comus Balls on Fat Tuesday in 1950.[23] Another room Roy established was the Escargot Society Room, for the society of distinguished culinary enthusiasts of which Roy was a member; his grandson Rick is also a member of the organization. Today, fifteen distinct dining rooms make up Antoine's Restaurant, which is able to potentially seat up to seven hundred guests.[24] Dining rooms range in size from the Tabasco Room, also known as the "Last Room," which seats a maximum of six diners but more frequently just two—as it is reportedly where the most marriage proposals in New Orleans take place—to the Japanese Room, which could seat up to two hundred prior to its World War II closure.[25]

Roy made a point of inviting all manner of famous actors, musicians, politicians and more to Antoine's and utilized these appearances in his

The 1840 Room, dedicated in the year 1940 for Antoine's centennial to honor the restaurant's founders. *Alexandra Kennon.*

Left: The Rex Room, established in the 1930s for the Krewe of Rex, one of the city's oldest Carnival krewes, in the 1970s. *Antoine's Restaurant.*

Below: The Rex Room today. *Alexandra Kennon.*

advertising. He is credited with beginning the trend of requesting signed photographs of notable clientele to display on the walls of the dining rooms and continued Jules's trend of printing pamphlets titled "Souvenir du Restaurant Antoine." Roy utilized the booklets primarily for touting the impressive individuals who have dined at his establishment. Categories include Notables, Nobility, Aviation, Celebrities, Sports, Opera and Music, Stage, Cinema and more—each with an extensive list of names that would doubtless have been impressive to readers of that time.[26] A few individuals who have dined at Antoine's whose importance remains more relevant today include Presidents Kennedy, Nixon, Roosevelt and countless more; founder of the FBI J. Edgar Hoover; General George Patton; Pope John Paul II;

Above: Antoine's Annex today. *Alexandra Kennon.*

Left: President Roosevelt with Roy Alciatore. *Antoine's Restaurant.*

and actors ranging from Katharine Hepburn to Whoopi Goldberg and the Marx Brothers. The list seemingly goes on infinitely, having the potential to fill multiple pamphlets. Because of Roy, many of these impressive diners' experiences at Antoine's are immortalized on the walls for visitors to appreciate to this day.

Antoine's menu before 1930.
Louisiana Menu and Restaurant Collection, Louisiana Research Collection, Tulane University.

Antoine's menu after 1940.
Louisiana Menu and Restaurant Collection, Louisiana Research Collection, Tulane University.

Roy concluded his centennial marketing booklet with his summation "Food Favorites of the Famous," in which he applauds his late father's signature dish: "I shall begin by saying that of all the famous New Orleans dishes, Huitres en coquille à la Rockefeller is beyond question the 'plat' which has met with universal acclaim by visiting celebrities."[27] Roy invented many dishes for the restaurant himself as well, telling a reporter in the 1930s that they were capable of preparing more than one thousand dishes at Antoine's, many original to members of the Alciatore family. Thanks to Roy's enthusiastic efforts at garnering attention for Antoine's, business thrived throughout the Second World War, with lines often stretching down St. Louis out to Bourbon and Royal Streets.[28]

In addition to being a brilliant marketer and restaurateur, Roy was fascinated, and consequentially skilled, with high-frequency radios. Voice radio had not yet been invented, meaning Roy would transmit messages via Morse code. An avid wine connoisseur, Roy was responsible for adding the 165-foot-long, twenty-five-thousand-bottle-capacity wine cellar that can be seen through a small labeled window on Royal Street. Utilizing the technology to curate his impressive wine collection, Roy would tap out Morse code messages to Europe using high-frequency radio to check on grape harvests for various vintages. According to his grandson Rick Blount, who uses the comparison that today his grandfather might have qualified as a "computer nerd" given his obsession with technology, until his death Roy had a ham radio with a massive antenna protruding from his home on Canal Boulevard that he used to transmit messages as far away as South Africa, Europe and Asia. To credit Roy's "geekiness," as his grandson refers to it, his interest in radio technology gave him a global connection, allowing him to not only cultivate the contents of Antoine's now fabled wine cellar but also garner worldwide attention for his family restaurant.[29]

Noted novelist of the time Frances Parkinson Keyes wrote a murder mystery novel set partially in the 1840 Room that was published in 1948 as *Dinner at Antoine's*. This, too, contributed to the restaurant's notoriety and eccentricity, earning a place in the top ten on the annual *New York Times* fiction list that year. Even Bugs Bunny paid homage to Antoine's in a 1951 cartoon titled "French Rarebit," wherein Bugs finds himself in Paris, coveted by two chefs who want to cook him. Bugs makes an escape by offering a complex recipe for "Louisiana Bay-Back Bunny Bordelaise," which he attributes to Antoine's in New Orleans.[30]

In the mid-1960s, Roy's nephews and sons of his sister, Mary Louise Alciatore Guste, Roy Guste and William (or "Billy") Guste Jr.—both attorneys, with Billy later serving as Louisiana attorney general—stepped in to assist their uncle in updating bookkeeping practices. When Roy Alciatore passed away in 1972, leaving only his daughter, Yvonne Alciatore Blount, as direct heir, those two nephews became general managers of Antoine's.[31] Lacking the ability to devote enough time and energy to the venture, they eventually handed control of the restaurant to Roy Guste's son, Roy F. Guste, a chef classically trained in the traditions of the restaurant's founder. He is also a culinary historian, having authored twelve predominantly Creole cookbooks, including *Antoine's Restaurant Since 1840* (1978).[32] In pursuit of his writing career, Roy F. Guste stepped away from his role as proprietor and chef of the restaurant in 1985, ceding control to his cousin Bernard "Randy" Guste, who would manage Antoine's until 2004.[33]

THE CURRENT GENERATION

During the period when Roy Alciatore's nephews owned and managed the restaurant, Roy's grandson Rick Blount was employed at Antoine's when he was as young as thirteen. By the time he was in college at Loyola University, he was an assistant manager, and upon graduating, he sat down with his cousins Roy F. Guste and Billy Guste to discuss his future at the restaurant. The Gustes prioritized the many descendants bearing their own last name, however, and Rick was told that a future there did not exist for him. His cousins used the analogy that he was like a "bull in a china

Rick and Yvonne Blount.
Antoine's Restaurant.

shop," a description he would later laughingly acknowledge might have had some truth to it. Instead, Billy Guste Jr.'s son, Randy Guste, managed Antoine's until 2004.[34]

In 2005, the Gustes were faced with financial difficulty, and Rick and his mother, Yvonne, bought out their shares of Antoine's Restaurant. The alleged "bull in a china shop" of his younger days was now CEO of Antoine's and, as Roy Alciatore's grandson, a fifth-generation proprietor.[35]

In buying the family restaurant, Rick had more of a project on his hands than he initially realized. His cousins had made minimal reinvestments into the business, which was made evident by damaged and out-of-date equipment, broken air conditioning, issues with the structure of the building and on goes the list. This meant that when Hurricane Katrina hit shortly after Rick became owner, the otherwise devastating storm had somewhat of a silver lining: the walls that fell down due to wind would likely have collapsed on their own accord regardless, and now they had the opportunity to make those repairs with the help of insurance.[36]

Of course, there was a much darker side of Katrina for the restaurant: Clifton Lachney, who had waited tables at Antoine's for decades before becoming maître d' at the age of seventy, drowned following the levee breach along with his son in his home. The surviving staff members were spread out among fourteen states, many of their homes damaged beyond repair.[37]

A simultaneous curse and blessing bestowed by Katrina was the extensive damage to the legendary wine cellar Roy Alciatore had established. The glaring downside was that the power failure ruined sixteen thousand bottles valuing close to $1 million in the prolonged heat, many of which were rare vintages Roy had shipped from Europe as early as the 1930s. The insurance policy on the collection covered the original bottle price, meaning vintages worth thousands today might have only garnered a few dollars or even cents from the insurance claim.

The unexpected positive outcome, according to Rick's wife, Lisa, who has a background in the wine business, was that the "clean out" provided an opportunity to update and improve the collection. "Many of the older wines procured by Ricks grandfather Roy may have been brought over from Europe in unstable conditions," Lisa said. Today, high-end wines are shipped very carefully in temperature-controlled containers; in Roy's time of transporting wines from Europe via boat in the 1930s, this was difficult at best, meaning that some of the older wines from Roy's collection could potentially have been tainted by heat long prior to the 2005 storm.[38]

"Also, the wine world has really changed since Roy's time," Lisa noted. "Wine consumers now can drink great wines from all over the world. Current world-class producers from places like Napa Valley were just starting up in the 1930s. Same thing for places like Argentina, Chile, South Africa, Australia and other European countries." Following the storm, the contents of the cellar were updated to reflect the broader global tastes of modern wine aficionados. That said, in honor of Roy, Antoine's still maintains an extensive assortment of French wines in particular.[39]

After repairing the damage caused and revealed by Hurricane Katrina at the end of August 2005, Rick Blount had partially reopened Antoine's Restaurant before the start of the new year, despite the fact that he was losing money in the process. "So many people would just close up shop, or open a smaller restaurant, but I think what we really realized is what Antoine's meant to New Orleans," Rick said. "What a symbol of 'We're still here, and we're gonna plow on through!'"[40]

Signs in front of Antoine's Restaurant on St. Louis Street. *Alexandra Kennon*.

Since then, Rick and his massive team at Antoine's have made some updates of their own. In 2009, a former dining room at the front of the building on St. Louis Street was converted into the Hermes Bar, named for a relatively contemporary Mardi Gras krewe whose memorabilia is displayed in the space. The Hermes Bar allows for guests to enjoy a drink or a meal more casually than the typically more extensive "Haute Creole" service guests receive in the formal dining rooms.[41] At Lisa's urging, the restaurant has also adapted the use of technology like OpenTable for making reservations, something Rick initially thought surely could not work with their more old-fashioned system, since it was, and still is, customary for regular customers to have assigned waiters.[42]

Another new development came at the end of 2018, when the Blounts hired Rich Lee as their new executive chef. This allowed the longest-running chef in the restaurant's history, Michael Regua, to retire after forty-seven years in the kitchen at Antoine's. Lee hopes that he will be at Antoine's until his own retirement as well. "Just driving in, I'm still in awe of coming in and being able to work here."[43]

Moving forward with a restaurant whose charm is rooted so much in its family history, legacy is of utmost importance to the Blounts. Between Yvonne Blount's six children, thirteen grandchildren and great-grandchildren

Hermes Bar, added in 2009. *Alexandra Kennon*.

Antoine's executive chef, Rich Lee, who was hired at the end of 2018, when former executive chef Michael Regua retired after forty-seven years. *Alexandra Kennon*.

beyond that, it is doubtless that some descendent of Antoine Alciatore's will step forward to carry on the family business. Rick hopes that when he is ready to retire in the next nine or ten years, the logical sixth-generation owner will be clearer. In the meantime, he is still having fun despite the 24/7 commitment and hopes to continue to improve Antoine's so the next generation of ownership—whoever he, she or they might be—can continue to succeed for many more decades to come.[44]

Recipe from Antoine's

Pompano Pontchartrain

Antoine's current chef, Rich Lee, developed this modern version of Pompano Pontchartrain (or, more broadly, Poisson Pontchartrain), an Antoine's original dish that has remained on its menu since the late 1800s. Much like a shrimp scampi, the simple dish is intended to highlight quality seafood.
Yields: 4 servings

Fish
4 7- to 8-ounce pieces of pompano, skin on
salt and white pepper
1 teaspoon cottonseed or canola oil

Sauce
6 teaspoons butter
½ cup sliced green onions
1 teaspoon chopped garlic
1 ½ cups white wine
3 tablespoons lemon juice
6 ounces lump crab meat
1 tablespoon chopped parsley
salt and white pepper

Season pompano with salt and white pepper. With the pan on medium to high heat, place oil in the skillet and the pompano skin up in the pan. Cook for about 3 to 4 minutes on each side to lightly brown the fillet and crisp the skin. While the pompano is cooking, sauté butter, green onions and chopped garlic over low-medium heat until onions are soft.

Increase heat to medium high and add white wine and lemon juice. Sauté for 2 minutes and then add lump crab meat and chopped parsley. Sauté for 1 minute and season to taste with salt and white pepper. Spoon over pompano fillets.

Recipe courtesy of Executive Chef Rich Lee and Lisa Blount at Antoine's Restaurant.

Chapter 2

Tujague's

(1856)

New Orleans is famed throughout the world as a place for good food. The reputation that this city enjoys in all corners of the earth for its good cuisine was not gained in a few years, nor in a generation. It came as a result of the unusual ability of chefs of the old-time restaurants, such as Tujague's, located at 823 Decatur street, corner of Madison street.
—Times-Picayune, *1938*

Like many Creole dining institutions, the story of Tujague's Restaurant begins with a French man on a boat in the Atlantic with hopes of finding prosperity in Nouvelle Orleans. Set apart from the tradition of being trained in the refined arts of French cuisine, however, there was Guillaume Tujague, the skilled butcher who founded New Orleans's second-oldest dining institution in his name.

Already a culinary destination and bustling port, New Orleans offered ample work for butchers in the 1850s. In 1852, Guillaume arrived from his hometown of Mazerolle, France, and set up shop in the section of the French Market designated for butchers. Shortly after opening, he returned to France to wed his betrothed, Marie Abadie, returning with his new wife and opening Tujague's in 1856, first at 811 Decatur.[1] Guillaume had a large, ornate mirror shipped from Paris that same year, having served 90 years in a Paris bistro before its move and another 160 years at Tujague's; greatly characterized by time, that mirror remains behind the Cypress stand-up bar in its current location today.[2]

Bartender Gregory Fonte brandishes Sazerac Rye. Besides the plastic cups, little has changed in 150 years. *Alexandra Kennon.*

The original location of Tujague's at 811 Decatur Street was in proximity to another esteemed restaurant of the time with a notably similar business model, Begue's Exchange. Following Begue's suit, Tujague's offered a leisurely and substantial "butcher's breakfast" targeted at the French Market workers hungering for a second breakfast by eleven o'clock in the morning and tourists seeking a luxurious booze- and food-fueled experience they could not find elsewhere. Begue's "butcher's breakfast," cleverly imitated by Tujague's, is arguably the earliest iteration of brunch. Because Begue's never seated more than thirty guests at a time, turned-away guests would inevitably meander down the block to Tujague's, which enjoyed the overflow of business.[3]

The *Times-Picayune* ran a column in 1925 describing the clientele of both Tujague's and Begue's through a retrospective lens: "Many say that in the early eighties Mme. Begue's was the most prominent among the French style restaurants. Wealthy planters, men lucky at gaming and others of means would often come to breakfast at ten or eleven o'clock in the morning and not leave until three or four in the afternoon. But that was when the red wine flowed....In the same vicinity is Tujague's, which

Tujague's bar in the early twentieth century. *Tujague's Private Collection.*

was established in about the same period, and which in later years became a favorite meeting place for prominent horsemen—somewhat on the stag order, but serving ladies, too."[4]

The hallmark of Tujague's throughout time, remaining a staple long after the final butcher's breakfast was served, is the *table d'hôte* menu: a five-course *prix fixe* including hearty staples of shrimp in red remoulade and boiled brisket with horseradish sauce. Dock laborers, French Market workers and, of course, butchers favored the predictably filling menu. As historic as Tujague's itself, the *table d'hôte* menu was described by the *Times-Picayune* in 1956: "There is no menu card at Tujague's. Instead, there is a selection of dishes for each day of the week. The only dish which remains constant is the slice of boiled beef or soup meat, with hot mustard sauce."[5]

Madame Begue's Exchange on Decatur, 1900. *Library of Congress, Detroit Publishing Company.*

Having overseen the operations of his namesake restaurant for fifty-six years, Guillaume died in 1912, leaving ownership of Tujague's to his sister and brother-in-law, Alice Tujague Anouilh and her husband, Etienne Anouilh. Etienne quietly purchased the building located at 801 Decatur Street from the owner in France, where rival restaurateurs the Begues had operated their business for almost forty years, with the intent of relocating Tujague's into the former Begue's building. Etienne died not long after the transaction, after which Alice sold the business of Tujague's to John Castet and Louis de Barbierre, with a scandal emerging from the fact that Castet had been a longtime bartender at Begue's. The other partner, Louis de Barbierre, had for multiple years been a bartender at Tujague's. The pair likely met as a result of Louis's brother, Charles, working with Castet behind the bar at Begue's. In 1914, with the First World War looming, Tujague's Restaurant moved with its new ownership into Begue's former building, and Begue's restaurant was relocated nearby on Decatur.[6] Shortly after, part of the ownership of Tujague's would change hands again, from

Tujague's after relocating into the former Madame Begue's space at 823 Decatur. *Louisiana Menu and Restaurant Collection, Louisiana Research Collection, Tulane University.*

Louis de Barbierre to Philip Guichet, who would act as Castet's business partner for decades to come.

Begue's former bartender and Tujague's new proprietor, Jean-Dominic Castet, later known as the more anglicized John Castet, was a French immigrant like Guillaume Tujague. Philip Guichet was born in the nearby town of Guichetville, Louisiana (not far from Raceland, in LaFourche Parish); both moved to New Orleans shortly after the turn of the century with hopes of making their names there.[7]

Taking ownership of Tujague's restaurant provided each with those means of success, particularly because the restaurant was now thriving in the space that formerly housed its rival, Begue's. The *Times-Picayune* looked back on the benefit of this move in a 1935 article: "When [Tujague's] moved into Madame Begue's place years ago, Tujague's inherited some of the steady frequenters of Madame Begue's, some of which, to this day, have been patronizing this place for as many as fifty years." The former Begue's building where Tujague's currently resides at 823 Decatur dates back to the 1730s, allegedly having served as a Spanish arsenal long before the Begue family obtained the space.[8]

While John Castet and his wife took charge of the kitchen, Philip Guichet headed the legendary bar. This, of course, was a hurdle during Prohibition, which was ratified in early 1919, not long after Guichet and Castet took ownership. It can be gathered that with the help of Guichet, Tujague's regulars still managed to imbibe during visits to the restaurant. In 1931, Philip Guichet was tried for serving absinthe to a customer after being caught by a Prohibition officer. This prompted a raid, leaving officers dubious when no other liquor was found.[9]

As the pains of Prohibition ended, those of the Great Depression were just beginning. During the Depression, certain loyal waiters continued to serve a cast of devoted local regulars without wages. Still, the occasional celebrity tourist would make his or her way in for a meal, as well. In 1935,

John Castet and Philip Guichet behind the bar. *Tujague's Private Collection.*

Tujage's welcomed director W.S. Van Dyke for breakfast on his visit to New Orleans for Mardi Gras.[10]

Guichet's bar program brought Tujague's national acclaim, particularly in the 1950s. In 1956, Guichet took second place in the Early Times National Mixed Drink Competition for the state of Louisiana, comparable to today's Tales of the Cocktail, held at the Roosevelt Hotel. His drink was the whiskey punch, made with orange flower water and an egg white and topped with nutmeg. The drink, along with seven others crafted by Louisiana bartenders, went on to compete in New York City and is said to have gone on to win first place nationally.[11]

The Grasshopper—the famed chocolate-mint dessert drink that remains Tujague's highest-selling drink today—is believed to have very similar origins. Restaurant historian and *Louisiana Eats!* radio host Poppy Tooker, who wrote *Tujague's Cookbook*, published in 2015, says that the drink garnered second place at a similar yet unnamed cocktail competition also in New York City in 1918 just prior to the passing of Prohibition laws; she asserts that Grasshoppers were available "one way or another" at Tujague's throughout the 1920s.[12]

John Castet's wife, Clemence Castet, was also a valuable asset to the business as a chef and hostess, drawing much attention and praise for her culinary skills, as well as her bon vivant personality. She personally

Philip Guichet receiving an award for his Whiskey Punch at the 1956 Early Times National Mixed Drink Competition. *Tujague's Private Collection.*

received frequent coverage in the *Times-Picayune*, which noted once, "The restaurant is proud of the fact that Madame Castet often brings the dishes to the table herself, and that each meal is topped with cafe noir served in thick liquor glasses."[13]

Not only was Madame Castet a darling of the press, but her large black-and-white cat, Baby, seems to have been loved by the media as well. A 1955 *Times-Picayune* bulletin referred to Baby as Tujague's mascot and pleaded for information regarding the whereabouts of the tomcat, which had briefly gone missing.[14] Never fear: Baby would return to Tujague's and make other news, particularly when the restaurant celebrated its centennial in 1956 and another local celebrity cat, Prettypuss, attended the party as Baby's guest: "When Prettypuss arrived Saturday night he was greeted not only by Baby but by Mme. John D. Castet, who was wearing more orchids than he had ever seen on one person."[15]

Guichet and Castet agreed that when one of them died, the other would buy out his shares and continue operating the restaurant. John Castet passed away in 1958, leaving Guichet and his two sons, Philip Jr. and Otis, control of

Tujague's. Guichet survived his business partner by more than fifteen years, dying at the age of seventy-eight in 1975.[16] Otis's son, known as "Noonie," took over his father's duties as manager; thereafter, Noonie and Philip Jr. alternated serving as manager of the restaurant each week.[17]

In 1982, Noonie and Philip Jr. sold Tujague's to brothers Steven and Stanford Latter. While Stanford's plan was simply to rent the property out to whichever business owner was willing to pay the most rent for the Decatur storefront, Steven had a bit more nostalgia toward the aging restaurant. He insisted the legacy of Tujague's remain alive by running the business and eventually purchasing his brother's shares. Philip Guichet's grandson Noonie remained employed as Tujague's bar manager. Steven Latter was the hands-on owner of Tujague's, slinging sarcastic jokes and making sports bets from his beloved Crown Royal throne in the bar, until his unexpected death in his sleep at the age of sixty-four in February 2013. Steven Latter's death threw the future of Tujague's into uncertainty once more.[18]

A SECOND LIFE

Rumors that a retail shop slinging souvenirs in the vein of "Drunk 1" and "Drunk 2" T-shirts could replace the historic restaurant abounded; regular customers rushed to secure what they feared might be their final reservations at Tujague's. Fortunately, Steven's son Mark, who had been only five years old when his father initially bought the restaurant, made the quick decision to continue Tujague's. Mark Latter obtained a long-term lease on the property from his Uncle Stanford—the same building at 823 Decatur that once housed Mme. Begue's.[19] "I literally grew up here," Latter explained. "So growing up here, and being a busboy, the vibe of the place now is more me, the old place was more my dad."[20]

Unlike his father, Mark had plans to update the Decatur grande dame, rather than simply maintain it. Renovating the aging space was Mark's first monumental task: dated, dark wood paneling was removed from the main dining room for the first time in more than fifty years and replaced with crisp, white paint and mirrors to make the most of the space and lighting. The upstairs dining room was renamed and designated for Krewe d'Etat, a contemporary Carnival krewe that satirizes more traditional krewes— Krewe d'Etat is reigned over by a "dictator" rather than a "monarch" like its more old-fashioned peers, for example.[21]

"My goal for Tujague's was kind of bringing it up to the current times. When we took over, it was five-course preset *table d'hôte* menu....We brought the first name chef into the restaurant, our first à la carte menu in the history of the restaurant since 1856 and really just kind of brought it more into the 2000s as opposed to the 1960s."[22]

Recently, Latter brought in Executive Chef Thomas Robey, who was previously employed as sous chef at Commander's Palace, to take charge of the restaurant's time capsule–like kitchen. "Now it's a beat-up old kitchen. I mean, our walk-in floor is made of wood," Robey said. "And it's probably the last one in existence."[23]

In 2012, when his father was still alive and managing the restaurant, Mark had pitched an à la carte menu that provided options beyond the classic five-course *table d'hôte* menu, but the idea was shot down before the menus ever reached the tables. Steven Latter prioritized the preference of his local regulars, whom he perceived wanted Tujague's, and its menu, to remain the same as it always had been. Now running Tujague's himself, Mark implemented the more modern à la carte menu as an alternate option to the elaborate affair of the traditional *table d'hôte*.[24]

Chef Thomas Robey. *Alexandra Kennon.*

Some of the more modern items on Tujague's à la carte menu are goat cheese crêpes with duck and dried cherry confit and braised pork belly in an orange horseradish. Instead of offering a Grasshopper cheesecake as Tujague's did before, Robey created a Grasshopper Panna Cotta. Robey has embraced the chance to update Tujague's aging menu while also appreciating the classics that remain. "I like the classics, I respect the classics. I mean, how can you hate shrimp remoulade?" Robey questioned.[25]

While the restaurant's business has increased, Mark admitted that there was some negativity when he first began implementing changes. "We got a lot of backlash from a lot of people," he said. "But I would say eight to ten months later, they were like, 'This is great!'"[26]

Poppy Tooker referred to Tujague's as "America's oldest neighborhood restaurant." French Quarter regulars would agree with that sentiment: "It used to be you couldn't walk a block in the Quarter without seeing someone you know," David Erath, a longtime regular of Tujague's, told the *Advocate* in 2016. "The Quarter's not like that anymore, but it still feels that way when you walk into Tujague's." While Erath and others agreed that the changes Mark Latter implemented were controversial, they also conceded that the updates were necessary for the longevity of the business. "The locals I know who are still around are happy to see what Mark [Latter] has done with it," Erath told the *Advocate*, "and, probably, if they'll admit it, like to eat there better now."[27]

One commonality between Tujague's under Mark and his father is that the restaurant has retained its family atmosphere for guests as well as staff. "We have waiters who have been here thirty-five to forty years, and they joke that they used to change my diapers and now they have to listen to what I say," Mark laughed. "There's probably about five longtime employees who have literally watched me grow up. So it's definitely a family atmosphere. And even the new employees that we have, we tell 'em when we do orientation, 'We don't want this to be just another job. This is a family place.' And that's how my dad was here, too."[28]

In 2016, Tujague's was inducted into the National Culinary Heritage Register by the National Food and Beverage Foundation.[29] Tujague's may have adapted to the times, but history is still palpable at New Orleans's second-oldest restaurant.

Left: Grasshopper Panna Cotta, created for Tujague's by Executive Chef Thomas Robey. *Alexandra Kennon.*

Below: Tujague's exterior today. *Alexandra Kennon.*

Recipe from Tujague's

Shrimp with Red and White Remoulade

Tujague's shrimp remoulade, which features red and white remoulade sauces, has been one of the longest-standing staples of the Tujague's menu throughout time.

Yields: 6 servings

48 jumbo shrimp, peeled, boiled and chilled
Creole Red Remoulade Sauce (recipe follows)
Creole White Remoulade Sauce (recipe follows)
shredded romaine or iceberg lettuce for serving
6 heads purple cabbage, inner leaves discarded, outer leaves intact to form "bowls" (optional)
fresh parsley, lemon wedges and halved cherry tomatoes for garnish (optional)

Place half of the shrimp and the Creole Red Remoulade Sauce in a large mixing bowl and toss gently to coat. Place remaining shrimp and Creole White Remoulade Sauce in another large mixing bowl and toss gently to coat. Add shredded lettuce to each cabbage head, if using, to form a nest for the shrimp. Evenly divide shrimp with two sauces among cabbage bowls. Alternatively, divide lettuce and shrimp among six chilled salad plates. Garnish with parsley, lemon and cherry tomatoes, if desired.

Creole Red Remoulade Sauce
Yields: about 2½ cups

½ cup finely chopped celery
4 green onions, finely chopped
¼ cup finely chopped parsley
⅓ cup finely chopped iceberg lettuce
½ cup finely chopped yellow onion
¼ cup Creole mustard
2 tablespoons fresh lemon juice
1 tablespoon paprika
¼ cup olive oil
salt
cayenne pepper

Thoroughly combine celery, green onions, parsley, lettuce, onion, Creole mustard, lemon juice and paprika. Whisk in olive oil in a slow drizzle to emulsify. Chill mixture for 6 to 8 hours or overnight. Add salt and cayenne pepper to taste.

Creole White Remoulade Sauce
Yields: about 2½ cups

1 cup Creole mustard
1 cup mayonnaise
¼ teaspoon minced garlic
4 green onions, finely chopped (white and green parts)
¼ cup finely chopped yellow onion
¼ cup finely chopped celery

Combine all ingredients. Chill mixture for 6 to 8 hours or overnight.

Recipe courtesy of Tujague's Restaurant. Also featured in Poppy Tooker's Tujague's Restaurant Cookbook.

Chapter 3

Café du Monde

(1862)

The French Market has evolved over the decades, becoming a center for tourism in the city, but Cafe du Monde's stalwart adherence to tradition seems to be working out just fine. Its relatively unchanged menu signifies many of the things to love about New Orleans: a city rooted in tradition, that enjoys indulgence, and doesn't like things too complicated. Little compares with the joy of sitting in the sunshine with a creamy and bitter cafe au lait and a pile of sticky, powdered-sugar coated beignets.
—Allie Mariano, *NOLA.com*/Times-Picayune, *2017*

While food was obviously paramount in New Orleans in the mid-1800s, coffee was an increasingly beloved commodity as well. The port city's proximity to Latin American planters made for easy access to the aromatic beans, and thus coffee took off in popularity relatively early on in the Crescent City compared to the rest of America. At a time when today's French Market (originally used for trade by the Native Americans) was still referred to as the "Butchers' Market" because of the excess of butchers in the mid-1800s, Café du Monde was born.

By the time of the Civil War, the French Quarter was primarily a working-class neighborhood, with its proximity to the docks allowing residents an easy commute if they worked as laborers loading and unloading ships. While the French Market offers primarily souvenirs and knockoff sunglasses these days, in 1862 it was a more practical market where residents of the French Quarter could purchase necessary meat and produce for their homes and businesses.[1] It was this "Butchers'

Above: Café du Monde in the French Market at night, 1938. *Collections of the Louisiana State Museum.*

Left: Linus Noel offers beignets and chicory coffee at Café du Monde, 1980s. *Library of Congress, photograph by Carol M. Highsmith.*

Market," as it was called—particularly the "Butcher's Hall," erected in 1812 on the Jackson Square end—where Frank Koeniger first opened his coffee and beignet shop. Locals who utilized the market along the river could now sip coffee or enjoy a hot French doughnut before purchasing their necessary groceries.[2]

To this day, simplicity is embraced at Café du Monde: coffee with chicory, either black or "café au lait" (half coffee, half hot milk), beignets with powdered sugar and a select few other morning beverages (like milk and orange juice) are available. Chicory, an addition to coffee popular in New Orleans, is the dried root of the endive plant that contributes an additional earthiness to the bitter morning beverage. Until 1958, the beignets were simply referred to as "doughnuts" but underwent a rebranding that year to embrace the city's French influence.[3]

It is worth noting that while most of the French culinary influence in New Orleans results from the Creole colonists who settled Louisiana from their previous home in Europe, both chicory coffee and New Orleans–style beignets are more accurately attributed to the influence of the Acadians, who made their way to Louisiana after being exiled from their home of Acadia in Canada when Britain took the country from France in 1763.[4] Beignets may not seem like a distinctly Cajun food, but their origins are, in fact, more Acadian than classically French.

In 1930, the Works Progress Administration undertook renovations of the French Market building, adding the colonnade that extends from the roof to provide a covered walkway along Decatur Street. Although Café du Monde's business was a success under its original ownership, the market was still starkly different than the tourist-driven area it is today. The air smelled strongly of fish, and the French Market Fisherman Supply Shop sitting across Decatur from the café confirmed that fish purveyors were the primary patrons on the block.[5]

THE CAFÉ TODAY

In May 1942, Fred Koeniger retired and sold Café du Monde to Hubert Fernandez. Fernandez was originally from Honduras and also owned Fernandez Wine Cellar, which he inherited from his uncle, on the ground floor of the Lower Pontalba Building. Fernandez later sold the wine store in 1972 to allow the family to focus on the extensive commitment that was Café du Monde. Since 1942, four generations of the Fernandez family have had a part in maintaining the iconic café.[6]

Another extensive overhaul of the historic French Market took place in 1975. Prior to the renovations, the French Market operated more or less as a normal city block, but afterward it functioned more as a pedestrian mall with individual stores. According to current owner and Hubert Fernandez's grandson Jay Roman, curbside service was even available for a time when automobiles were first taking off in popularity—families could pull up the car, park in front of the café and have coffee and beignets brought by a carhop out to the vehicle. But as time went on, the demands of increasing tourist traffic to the city ushered in the French Market's transformation. Café du Monde adapted and survived the change easily; other vendors that formerly occupied the block were less fortunate.[7]

While the owners of Café du Monde have been approached about franchising several times over the years, the only other Café du Monde locations existing outside Louisiana today are, interestingly enough, in Japan. The conversation began during the 1984 World's Fair in New Orleans, and members of the Japanese company Duskin pursued the relationship with Café du Monde for several years thereafter, eventually securing the rights to open iterations of the coffee and beignet stand in their home country.[8]

The beignets were first offered in Japan in 1990, when they premiered, appropriately, at the world's fair there. Today, there are twenty-one locations of Café du Monde throughout the country. Apparently, the New Orleans–style beignet stand resonates with Japanese customers, and so they have been successful in Japan for decades. "They love the South, they love New Orleans, they love jazz music," Roman explained to the *Times-Picayune* in 2014. "It was something we didn't really need to educate Japanese consumers about. Almost everybody was aware of New Orleans in one way or another." The Kyoto Station location is even complete with faux street signs, marking the thousands-of-miles-away intersection of Orleans and Chartres Streets.[9]

While Japan is the only place Café du Monde can be found outside South Louisiana, there are now eight locations in the Greater New Orleans area, two of them on the Northshore of Lake Pontchartrain.[10]

After Fernandez's death, his sister, Nora, and two daughters, Silvia and Cynthia, continued to operate his business. Today, Hubert Fernandez's grandchildren Jay Roman and Karen Brenrud, along with Karen's husband, Burton Benrud, are the primary owners of the company that operates Café du Monde. Their children have now stepped in to assist with operations as well, meaning that four generations of Fernandezes have ensured that hot beignets and café au lait are available in the French Market.[11]

Although the 24/7 business of Café du Monde's original location almost literally never stops, the arrival of Hurricane Katrina halted the incessantly bustling café's business for more than ten weeks. "To walk on Decatur Street and not hear jazz playing or smell beignets frying was so sad," owner Karen Benrud said of the difficult time following the storm in her foreword for Peggy Sweeney-McDonald's book *Meanwhile, Back*

Contemporary exterior of Café du Monde from Decatur Street. *Alexandra Kennon*.

Guests enjoying coffee and beignets at Café du Monde today. *Alexandra Kennon*.

A saxophone player contributes to the atmosphere, as is common at Café du Monde. *Alexandra Kennon.*

at Café du Monde. Café du Monde's reopening on October 19, 2005, was celebrated with a large party and banner that proclaimed concisely and happily: "Beignets are Back!"[12]

In 2007, a New Orleans rabbi with a craving for Café du Monde's beignets went about ensuring that the treats were certified kosher. He was successful in his efforts, and the beignets served at the restaurant as well as the box mix were certified just in time to be enjoyed by New Orleans's substantial Jewish community for Hanukkah 2008.[13]

These days, more than ever, just about every visitor to New Orleans does not view their trip as complete without an order of three beignets and a cup of café au lait from Café du Monde. All manner of celebrities, locals and tourists have been to the iconic café and experienced the required powdered-sugar baptism. The simple menu of chicory coffee and beignets has still not wavered in more than 150 years.[14] Based on the hordes of devoted customers who line up daily for just that, it appears that the tradition will continue as strong as the black chicory coffee at Café du Monde for many more years to come.

Recipe from Café du Monde

Beignets

While Café du Monde makes and sells its own beignet mix that is available online, as well as in many South Louisiana grocery stores, it offers the following advice for replicating French Market–perfect beignets in your own home kitchen.

- Combine 2 cups beignet mix with 7 ounces water.
- Mix beignet mix and water with a spoon until fairly soft, like biscuit dough.
- Do not overmix beignet dough, as this will result in tough beignets.
- On a floured surface, roll beignet dough flat.
- Cut dough into 2-inch squares.
- Do not attempt to re-form dough edges into beignets or they will be tough. Instead, fry scrap pieces as they are.
- Fry beignets with oil at 370 degrees Fahrenheit. Café du Monde uses cottonseed oil, although any vegetable oil should do.
- Do not add too many beignets to the oil at once, as the temperature of the oil will drop resulting in flat beignets.
- If beignets do not "puff up" when fried, try rolling the dough out thicker.

Beignet tips courtesy of cafedumonde.com.

Chapter 4

Commander's Palace

(1893)

Commander's is a beautifully-managed, tradition-conscious restaurant with a superior cuisine. It has to be, because the vast majority of the patrons for lunch and dinner are New Orleans people who know fine food and correct service.
—*Lucius Beebe,* Holiday *magazine, 1951*

Commander's Palace sits not far from the site of the former stables for the Livaudais sugar plantation, which existed where the Lower Garden District and Central City neighborhoods are today until after the Louisiana Purchase. After the turn of the century and Louisiana's incorporation into the United States, the former plantation was subdivided and sold to Americans moving to the area whose lifestyles differed from those of the French-speaking Catholic Creoles in the French Quarter. When the neighborhood was first established, it became the city of Lafayette; later in 1852, it was absorbed into the municipality of New Orleans as the Garden District, so named because of the large quarter city block each resident had to devote to elaborate landscaping.[1] Dick Brennan used to joke that Commander's Palace was located in "the dead center of the Garden District," because just across Washington Avenue is Lafayette Cemetery Number One, the third-oldest cemetery in New Orleans.[2]

The curious thing about the founding of Commander's Palace is that for much of its existence, multiple owners were mistaken about the exact year that it first opened. Advertisements and marketing materials from throughout the 1900s, and even a plaque on the side of the building that was present when the Brennan family purchased it in 1969, assert that the restaurant was established in the year 1880. In 2015, the Brennans came across material that made them skeptical of this date, and they hired local research historian Tonya Jordan to investigate. Sure enough, Jordan determined based on building records, the city directory and newspaper archives that 1893 was the true year Emile Commander first opened his restaurant, despite the substantial stack of material and even physical evidence on the wall of the building suggesting otherwise.[3] When current proprietors Ti Martin and Lally Brennan learned of Jordan's discovery, they put their inherent public relations know-how and enthusiasm for hosting grand parties to use and embraced the mistake. Ti Martin quipped about the discovery in a recent interview with the author: "Me and Lally like to have a good time, so we said, 'What the hell?' Let's have a little news conference and invite some dear friends in and just kind of go 'Oops!' and have a laugh on ourselves before anyone else can beat us to it." Ever emphasizing the fun, celebratory atmosphere of Commander's, the decades-long mistake was announced in conjunction with a special promotion in the fall of 2015, featuring specialty "Oops"-themed cocktails and to-go cups.[4]

Contrary to the many articles and advertisements asserting an 1880 opening, Commander's Palace opened for the first time in 1893. The Garden District grande dame's name comes not from any association with the military, but rather from the name of its founding owner, Emile Commander. Emile was of Sicilian descent—his father was Peter Commander, anglicized from his birth name Pietro Camarda, given to him in his birth city of Ustica, Sicily. Prior to Commander's Palace opening, Peter operated a more modest saloon across Washington Avenue, which his son, Emile, managed; today, the Garden District Gallery is housed in the building. In the 1890s, the New Orleans City Council required any business owner wishing to open a barroom to publish a letter of intent in the *New Orleans Item* to gauge the reception of the neighborhood prior to opening. In January 1893, Emile Commander's notice that he wanted to open a tavern at 1403 Washington Avenue ran in the paper, to mixed response—the *Times-Picayune* later indicated that some Garden District residents protested Commander being granted a license to operate a bar on that location. Nonetheless, the city council members in attendance voted unanimously to allow Emile Commander to open a business in his name at the corner of Washington Avenue and Prytania Street, although a great deal was still to come before it would become regarded as the teal-and-white beacon of culinary excellence Commander's Palace is today.[5] Although in its early years under Emile Commander's ownership the restaurant was not as bright in color or reputation as it is today, at the turn of the twentieth century Commander's Palace was already associated with serving fine meals to Garden District high-rollers. According to some, Emile Commander and his wife lived on the first floor of the mansion, operating their restaurant above their quarters on the second floor.[6]

In the summer of 1906, Emile Commander, once reported a "robust and healthy man," fell ill with a cold that most likely progressed to pneumonia. At his doctors' suggestion, Commander boarded a steamer for England, believing that a sea voyage across the Atlantic would cure him. The trip instead gravely worsened Commander's condition, and he was rushed to a sanitarium in northern Wales upon the ship's arrival. Despite his optimistic letters to his wife and family during this period, Commander died within days of arrival in the United Kingdom; his body was shipped back to New Orleans to be interred in his family tomb.[7]

Following Emile Commander's death, his son Pete Commander partnered with another local businessman, Anthony Greco, to continue operating his father's restaurant. Like most New Orleans restaurants to survive Prohibition, the staff at Commander's managed to skirt federal liquor laws during this period, to a degree. But in 1923, federal agents seized forty-eight bottles of beer, a quart of whiskey and a quart of absinthe during a raid at the restaurant—an impressive haul by even legal standards.[8] Legend states that alcohol was sometimes stored at the neighboring Lafayette Cemetery and snuck across the street to the restaurant before the liquor laws were repealed in 1933. Stranger things have certainly happened in order for a New Orleanian to get a drink.

The same year of the federal liquor raid in 1923, elaborate Thanksgiving and Christmas dinner feasts were advertised in the *Times-Picayune* for the cost of one dollar. By the time Christmas came around, Commander's Palace was touting a recently completed remodeling featuring a "beautifully arranged ladies' and gents' dining room."[9] Prohibition might have temporarily hindered the festivities, but they certainly were not going to put a halt to them.

In 1924, Pete Commander and his business partner sold the property and business to another New Orleans Sicilian family: the Giarrantanos. Frank G. Giarrantano and his wife, Rose, lived in an apartment on the second floor while operating the restaurant primarily on the first floor. While Ella Brennan later asserted that the downstairs portion of the building was used to seat respectable families and the like, it is said that certain rooms on the second floor—accessible via a hidden side entrance—were utilized by a more debauched sort: riverboat captains and other men seeking entertainment from the kind of working ladies who were typically relegated to Storyville at the time. Ironically, when Ella Brennan was growing up a few blocks from Commander's Palace at the time the Giarrantanos owned it, her mother used to warn her and her siblings, "Now don't you go in that restaurant."[10] Liquor was not the only thing that often slid by without attracting the attention of local police in the Garden District.

In 1944, with his health in decline, Frank Giarrantano sold Commander's Palace to Frank and Elinor Moran. Giarrantano went on to manage the Mayfair Restaurant at 3633 Prytania Street, the associated bar still in operation today.[11] The Morans placed emphasis on building the reputation of Commander's Palace as an institution of fine Creole cuisine rather than the more sportsman-friendly Commander's of the Giarrantano days. Frank Moran boasted a large oyster bar in addition to extensive *table d'hôte* and à la carte options, particularly highlighting Louisiana seafood. In 1946, the Morans ran an advertorial in the *Times-Picayune* asserting as much:

> *For the many who have regaled themselves at frequent intervals with soft-shell turtle at Commander's Palace, 1403 Washington Avenue, it will undoubtedly be welcome news that the popular uptown eating place now is serving this delicacy regularly. Another sea-food specialty at Commander's Palace is stuffed flounder Commander, a dish many connoisseurs rate as tops in the field. These two specimens of the riches of Louisiana waters and the perfection of Creole cookery are cited as examples of what the Commander's Palace chefs can do with the whole long list of sea foods, not to mention steaks and meat dishes.*[12]

Only four years after the Morans took ownership, the restaurant suffered a severe fire in 1948. Although they considered reopening in a temporary location or even relocating the business, the couple ultimately devoted their energy and funds into restoring the damaged mansion. Commander's reopened around five months after the fire for dinner on September 18 that year. "The building has been completely repaired and looks just as it used to," the *Times-Picayune* noted of the event.[13]

The Morans continued to garner positive attention from the media and patrons alike, developing a reputation as a fine dining restaurant preferred by locals. Under the Morans' ownership in 1951, highly regarded restaurant critic Lucius Beebe said in *Holiday* magazine, "Commander's

Gentlemen and lady in car in front of Commander's Palace on Washington Avenue, 1950s. *Charles L. Franck Studio Collection at the Historic New Orleans Collection.*

is a beautifully-managed, tradition-conscious restaurant with a superior cuisine. It has to be, because the vast majority of the patrons for lunch and dinner are New Orleans people who know fine food and correct service."[14] Amusingly, Commander's Palace also celebrated its "seventy-first" anniversary that year, continuing to perpetuate the myth that the restaurant was first opened in 1880 rather than 1893.[15]

In the spring of 1953, looters broke into a rear window of the restaurant and stole three cases of whiskey and approximately sixty-five other bottles of liquor, the combined value totaling nearly $550.[16] Interesting, considering that thirty years earlier, a similar quantity of liquor was taken from the restaurant by federal agents under very different circumstances. The Morans were not terribly shaken by the loss, and that same year Frank Moran purchased the strip of property adjoining the restaurant with the intent of expanding. His wife, Elinor, created the now legendary garden patio, where her talking mynah bird, Tajar, who was later featured on the show *Candid Camera*, was known to spend ample time conversing with guests around a Koi pond.[17]

"Dining in the grand manner," vintage menu. *Louisiana Menu and Restaurant Collection, Louisiana Research Collection, Tulane University.*

During their period of ownership, the Morans lived in the home adjacent to their restaurant facing Coliseum Street, where Ella and Dottie Brennan would later reside. At sixty-five years old, Frank Moran died after a prolonged bout of an unidentified illness in September 1966.[18] Commander's, by the standards of some local culinary critics, had been slipping in reputation already and continued to decline following Frank Moran's death.[19] The Brennans, having eyed the restaurant for some time, had already made it clear to Elinor Moran that if she were to ever sell, they were interested. In 1969, Elinor Moran came into Brennan's for lunch and told Ella, "I've decided to retire, Ella. I'm ready to sell." Ella arranged for their attorneys to meet, and the deal was complete in under a month: the Brennans bought the restaurant and home behind it and carry on the Commander's Palace legacy today.[20]

THE BRENNAN FAMILY TAKES COMMANDER'S

When Elinor Moran approached Ella Brennan wishing to sell Commander's Palace in 1969, the Brennan family were quick to buy it up. Commander's Palace checked all of the necessary boxes: it was an old establishment favored by locals, situated in a beautiful Victorian mansion and just three blocks from their family homes in the Garden District. "When we first saw Commander's, we were completely won over by its period charm, its fabulous fantasy like Victorian architecture replete with columns, turrets, and delicate, lacy gingerbread trim, and its lush green garden and picturesque patio," Ella remarked in *The Commander's Palace New Orleans Cookbook*.[21]

August 29, 1969, the day the deal closed on the Brennan family purchasing Commander's Palace, happened to be the ninth birthday of Ella Brennan's daughter (and current proprietor), Ti Adelaide Martin. Her mother took her to Commander's for lunch as a special birthday treat that day, and after they were seated, she said to Ti, "We have quite a

Modern exterior. *Commander's Palace.*

birthday present for you. We bought this restaurant today!" Ti still ranks Commander's on her list of "Top 10 Presents."[22]

Elinor Moran and Owen E. "Pip" Brennan Jr. made the joint announcement of the sale, with Mrs. Moran telling the *Times-Picayune*, "Since I have decided to relinquish the ownership and management of Commander's Palace, it is reassuring to know that it will be in the hands of experienced, dedicated restaurant people. I am confident that the Brennan family will maintain the same high standards of restaurant management which my late husband and I have established at Commander's over the years." Pip Brennan told the same reporter, "Our policy will be to maintain that individual character—including the same type of excellent cuisine, superior service and relaxed atmosphere which have made Commander's a favorite with New Orleanians and with visitors to our city. We are happy to have an opportunity to perpetuate the unique quality of Commander's Palace."[23]

While the initial announcement maintained an air of enthusiastic positivity no doubt out of respect to the Moran family, Jack Du Arte, the *Times-Picayune* gastronomy columnist at the time, implied the Brennans had a much more difficult task in taking on ownership of Commander's than they let on. "When the Brennans purchased the old restaurant over four years ago, the place had little direction, a weaning local following, a poorly directed professional entourage and a bad case of poor mouthing by just about everyone," Du Arte wrote. "In other words, the place represented a restaurateur's dream—there was no place to go but up!"[24]

With Owen E. Brennan having died prior to Brennan's on Royal Street opening, in 1973 his three sons and widow decided to seize primary control of Brennan's of New Orleans. The rest of Owen's siblings were fired from their positions at the French Quarter restaurant bearing their family name. Their expertise no longer requested to contribute to Brennan's success, the older generation sunk their efforts into the new task of elevating Commander's Palace to the same status they obtained at Brennan's.[25]

One of the Brennan siblings' first tasks was updating the "dated, dark, and somewhat dreary" décor of the dining rooms. Deep-red carpets were torn up, and dark paneling came down and was replaced with floor-to-ceiling windows in the largest dining rooms. The mission was to transfer the light and festive patio atmosphere to the interior of the building, but Ella decided that she needed something bold and fun outside the restaurant to announce the change as well. Charles Gresham, prominent New Orleans designer and friend of the Brennans at the time, suggested the answer: painting the exterior of the Victorian mansion a bright turquoise with white trim.

Ella Brennan's daughter, Ti Martin, vividly remembered the restaurant being repainted when she was around eleven years old. She rode her banana-seat bike by the restaurant from her nearby home and noticed that sullying the tasteful beige-brown wall was a large test patch of aqua blue paint. "I just biked home and ran in going 'Ma! Ma! Ma! You can't paint the restaurant blue!'" Martin recalled. "And she was like, 'Oh, calm down, it'll be fabulous!' And Aunt Adelaide is there saying, 'It's gonna fade beautifully! It's gonna be great, it's gonna let everybody know we're shaking things up.' And I was horrified, and of course they were perfectly on target. And now you can go to the store and get 'Commander's Blue.'"[26]

While the exterior of Commander's Palace was changing drastically, the style of service was also being updated. At Dick's suggestion, the Jazz Brunch was born. On Saturdays and Sundays, two live jazz bands would meander through the dining rooms playing upbeat tunes; brightly colored balloons added to the celebratory atmosphere.[27]

The first two chefs the Brennans hired to helm the Commander's kitchen were "old-school Europeans," according to Ella Brennan, but failed to truly comprehend the culinary dynamism the Brennans were attempting to

Commander's Palace dining room interior, 1964, before the Brennans purchased the restaurant. *Photo by C.F. Weber, via the Historic New Orleans Collection.*

obtain. Eventually, a local WDSU anchor and friend of Ella's suggested she consider a Cajun chef with whom she had been hosting cooking classes.[28] In a joining of forces that many restaurant historians argue permanently changed the course of Louisiana cuisine, in 1975 the Brennan family hired Paul Prudhomme as the first American-born executive chef of Commander's

Chef Paul Prudhomme
in the courtyard at
Commander's Palace.
*Marty Cosgrove and K-Paul's
Louisiana Kitchen.*

Palace. By the mid-1970s, the farmer's son from the small Acadian town of Opelousas was already the president of the local chefs' association in New Orleans and leading the charge of incorporating more of the Cajun flavors he grew up with into Creole menus. Paul Prudhomme's tenure in the kitchen at Commander's was a revelatory time not only for the restaurant's menu but also for the fusion of Creole and Cajun cuisines throughout New Orleans and beyond.[29]

Between Prudhomme's culinary genius and the Brennans' collective restaurant savvy, Commander's Palace was changing the approach to Creole staples. Dickie Brennan recalled a conversation his father, Dick Brennan Sr., had with the chef in the late 1970s about creating a more Louisiana-centric answer to trout amandine: "Paul, I walk to work every day. I've never walked by an almond tree, but I trip over pecans. Why can't we put pecans on our fish instead of almonds?" And so pecan-crusted fish, a preparation popular today not only at Commander's but also throughout the city, was born with a lifelong restaurateur and a Cajun chef bouncing ideas around a kitchen.[30] Prudhomme's Trout with Pecans was a natural hit with food critics and others, with Du Arte proclaiming, "On my last visit I enjoyed the Trout with Pecans which is so simple and delightful it is hard to imagine. Topped with a rich meuniere sauce, it is one of the city's outstanding fish dishes."[31]

Prudhomme invented numerous dishes in the Commander's kitchen, including his now-famous "blackened" fish. It went on the menu as "seared redfish" because Ella did not care for the word *blackened*, and later, when Prudhomme implemented "blackened redfish" on the menu at his own restaurant, K-Paul's, the formerly undesired redfish became so popular that fishing restrictions were implemented to avoid the species' extinction in the Gulf. Prudhomme's cooking was bold and flavorful; Ella encouraged him to refine and lighten it. The combination was an instant hit.[32]

Ella Brennan referred to this exciting Acadian update to more French-oriented Creole fare as "Haute Creole."[33] Jack Du Arte at the *Picayune* praised Prudhomme's deftness in quickly and skillfully updating the menu and the quality of dishes produced: "About two years ago, Paul Prudhomme was coaxed into the executive chef's post with some startling results. In a matter of months (which is quite a short period for this sort of change), the food coming out of the kitchen began to demonstrate a consistency and flair which had been totally lacking before. Commander's missing link had been located!"[34]

Prudhomme introduced more bold Cajun seasonings and ingredients; the beginnings of his Magic Seasoning Blends he would later sell commercially came about in that Garden District kitchen.[35] Prudhomme placed emphasis on showcasing local bounty as well. While chefs at Commander's in the 1950s had used primarily frozen and prepackaged meats and produce, Prudhomme went directly to local farmers and butchers for his ingredients. Other chefs in the city did not hesitate to follow suit.[36]

In October 1976, national publication *Holiday* magazine held its annual Restaurant Awards in New Orleans, featuring meals at both Commander's Palace and Brennan's. The *Times-Picayune* marveled at Prudhomme's execution of the Commander's event, despite him being injured on his way to the restaurant to prepare the dinner: "Despite the fact that Executive Chef Paul Prudhomme of Commander's Palace injured his knee in an automobile accident on his way to the restaurant to prepare a meal for over 300 guests, he continued working throughout the day. In my opinion, that meal helped establish Prudhomme's national reputation as one of the premier chefs in the country." The Acadian chef also convinced the American Culinary Federation to stage its first Pan American Culinary Olympics in New Orleans in the summer of 1978.[37]

Although Prudhomme's time at Commander's brought the restaurant and himself to local as well as international acclaim, in 1979 he and his wife, Kay, opened their own more casual Cajun restaurant in the French Quarter named for the two of them, K-Paul's Louisiana Kitchen. Prudhomme met Kay Hinrichs, his second wife, while working at Maison Dupuy restaurant—she was a waitress who followed Prudhomme when he left for Commander's and then ran front of house at their new venture, K-Paul's. The couple hired young chef Frank Brigtsen—who had worked under Prudhomme at Commander's and would later open his own award-wining restaurant, Brigtsen's, in the Uptown neighborhood—to help run the kitchen at K-Paul's while Prudhomme was still juggling both his restaurant and Commander's. Today, K-Paul's remains open on Chartres Street with Chef Paul Miller, who is from the same town of Opelousas as the late Prudhomme, at the helm. In 1980, Prudhomme was the first American-born chef to be honored by the French government with the prestigious Merite Agricole Award in recognition of the work he did to adapt and combine Creole and Cajun cuisines.[38]

The demands of running both restaurants understandably wore on Prudhomme, and within a few years, it was suggested that Dick and Ella Brennan hire a much younger but very promising chef who hailed from—surprisingly—Massachusetts. Although the notion of hiring a twenty-three-year-old Yankee was doubtlessly terrifying to the Brennans, in 1982 the decision was made that he was skilled enough to take over as executive chef. Following Prudhomme's tenure at Commander's Palace was none other than a young Emeril Lagasse, just beginning his career long before he would become the Food Network–branded celebrity chef known throughout the country today.[39]

At first, Ella Brennan did not want to risk flying the potential recruit in from the Northeast, as she did not expect to hire the young chef. Eventually, she took the chance and invited Lagasse to come to the restaurant, and he arrived somewhat shabbily to Commander's Palace after the airline lost his luggage. Ella brought her potential hire into the kitchen and asked for his thoughts. Lagasse replied, "Well, it kind of smells like my mom's kitchen," and Ella realized based on his genuine response that he might be "someone special." After Lagasse prepared a meal for Dick and Ella, it was solidified: Commander's Palace had its next executive chef. How Lagasse would suit the Garden District establishment was still somewhat uncertain. After the Brennans made Lagasse an offer, an acquaintance called Ella and proclaimed of Lagasse, "He's full of personality, but he can't cook."[40]

At first Ella was shaken by this, but not long after Lagasse returned to New Orleans and assuaged her fears: "And could he cook! Emeril furthered the evolution of Haute Creole cuisine and expanded on what Paul had been doing with Cajun, but he also brought his French-Canadian/Portuguese heritage—and his own insatiable curiosity—to bear on the menu," Ella said in her autobiography coauthored with daughter, Ti Martin, *Miss Ella of Commander's Palace*.[41]

At twenty-three years old, Lagasse had spent very little time in New Orleans and had a very limited understanding of Louisiana's indigenous cuisines. Fortunately, Ella Brennan was ready and able to impart the knowledge he lacked. A graduate of Johnson & Wales culinary school in Rhode Island, Lagasse possessed the necessary skill set; Ella filled in the gaps in his education in areas such as staple Louisiana dishes and southern hospitality. "He knew what he had learned in school and a little of what he had learned on the job, but he didn't know anything about Creole cooking or New Orleans," Ella recalled in her autobiography. "We had to get that into his head. We sent him to every restaurant in town, and I sat with him by the hour. I fed him books and newspapers. He was like a sponge."[42]

"Dick and Ella were very tough," Lagasse remembered. Each Saturday, Lagasse and Ella Brennan would meet in her home to discuss new developments in food and wine. He began to love Louisiana—its food but also, as importantly, its culture and people. He learned the necessity of respecting culinary traditions in a city as proud of its Creole roots as New Orleans: "New Orleans in the 1980s was a time of strong tradition," Lagasse reflected. "I never disrespected tradition. I always enhanced it."[43]

While culinarians today would certainly agree with Lagasse's statement, Ella Brennan had her reservations upon hiring the oft-described "hothead" young chef. His aggressive personality sometimes clashed with the Brennans' genteel nature, culminating in Ella Brennan slipping Lagasse a folded note during a busy dinner service one night not long after he started. When he had a chance to read it, he discovered it said, "When you wake up tomorrow, leave your ego at home." Perhaps this was Ella's way of letting her new hire know that he had the job but should not forget whose house he was in, so to speak. Emeril would lead the kitchen at Commander's for more than seven years until 1990, when he and his ego left to open his own namesake restaurant, Emeril's, in the Warehouse District.[44]

During Emeril's reign in the kitchen at Commander's Palace, a shift in responsibility among owning members of the Brennan family gradually occurred. In 1997, the remaining members of the older generation—including Dick, Ella, John and Dottie—stepped aside to let their children Ti Adelaide Martin (Ella's daughter), Lally Brennan and Brad Brennan take over the majority of operations. After Ella suffered a heart attack and had emergency double bypass surgery in 1985, Ti returned to New Orleans and the family business from Houston, where she was selling real estate. Lally had entered the restaurant business as a hostess at Mr. B's in the early 1980s; her innate marketing and hospitality skills became apparent under Ella's tutelage at Commander's. According to Ti Martin, she and her cousins were still very much "under the watchful eye of Ella and Dottie Brennan, who live[d] next door—literally."[45]

With another chef having left the kitchen at Commander's Palace with newfound notoriety and a venture of his own, the Brennans were in need of someone who matched Prudhomme and Lagasse's talents to take the helm. Jamie Shannon, hailing from the Jersey Shore, was the logical choice for Commander's next executive chef. Shannon was trained at the American Culinary Institute and had worked in the Commander's kitchen under Lagasse since 1984. He continued to place emphasis on sourcing meat and vegetables that were grown or fished "within a hundred miles of his stove," often hunting or fishing the animals himself. Shannon speaks to the importance of fresh ingredients in his cookbook *Commander's Kitchen,* which he coauthored with Ti Martin: "It's almost a cliché of cooking, but it's so true: Get the best ingredients money can buy and don't ruin them."[46] Shannon also created many of his own ingredients from scratch, ranging from Creole cream cheese to andouille sausage. One of his best-received dishes, still prominent on the Commander's menu today, was Shrimp and Tasso Henican: shrimp stuffed with tasso ham in a five-pepper jelly sauce.[47]

Although the James Beard Foundation did not exist for the vast majority of Commander's Palace's existence, Shannon was executive chef when Commander's received the award for Outstanding Restaurant in 1996; he later received the award for Best Chef, Southeast Region, in 1999. The restaurant also received the James Beard Award for Outstanding Service in 1993.[48]

Known to be a bit mischievous, Shannon once showed up more than an hour late to the James Beard Awards ceremony in New York at which he was to be honored because he convinced some friends from out of town it was customary to swim across Bayou St. John upon one's first visit to New Orleans for Jazz Fest, which they believed and attempted. Although Ti Martin was initially angry that he missed his flight and was tardy for such an important event, Shannon's sense of humor in explaining the situation won her over. The pair worked together well.[49]

Unfortunately, much less celebratory news would come at the end of the year 2000, when Shannon was diagnosed with cancer. Tory McPhail, who had worked for the Brennan family for years and was working at Commander's Palace in Las Vegas as Shannon's health declined, was called to return to New Orleans to serve as Shannon's sous chef during his final months in the kitchen. McPhail spoke on the emotionally trying experience in a recent interview: "My plan was just to be the best sous chef I possibly could be for [Jamie Shannon], and let him sit in the Commander's kitchen and kind of guide all of us in the right direction, and for me to be his eyes, ears, and legs, and run around and execute Jamie's vision," McPhail said. "That was always my goal. But unfortunately the big man upstairs had some different plans for my buddy and my mentor." Around a year after his diagnosis, the day after Thanksgiving 2001, Shannon passed away at the age of forty at a cancer center in Houston, Texas, where he was being treated.[50]

Jamie's family (he was survived by his wife, Jeannette, and son, Tustin) asked Ti Martin to deliver part of his eulogy at the funeral. She opened with the line, "Don't you know the food in heaven just got a whole lot better?"[51]

The following year in 2002, Tory McPhail was promoted to executive chef of Commander's Palace at twenty-eight years old. Although earning such a title would typically be cause for celebration, McPhail's experience being named head chef was more bitter than sweet, as the loss of his mentor and friend was still raw. Not only did his appointment arrive under unexpected and tragic circumstances, but taking the reins of such a culinary icon was also intimidating to begin with: "To follow in the steps of Paul Prudhomme, and Emeril, and Jamie, and what those guys did for the community, what they did for the city, the reputation of Southern cooking, and having the helm of this American icon," McPhail said. "And here's this scared twenty-eight-year-old kid, coming in to fill those shoes and put on the jacket that says 'Commander's Palace Executive Chef Tory McPhail'....I mean, I don't think I slept right for the first two years."[52]

Portrait of Executive Chef Tory McPhail. *Commander's Palace.*

That "twenty-eight-year-old kid," scared as he may have been, was prepared to continue the legacies left behind by Prudhomme, Lagasse and Shannon. By the time McPhail was named executive chef, he had already worked each one of the twelve designated stations in the Commander's kitchen (today, there are twenty). Diligently honoring the methods of his mentor and incorporating a creative streak of his own, Commander's continues to receive national recognition with McPhail as executive chef. In 2013, he was honored by the James Beard Foundation as Best Chef, South. He tries not to fixate on accolades, however: "We don't just get hung up on awards and plaques on the wall," McPhail said of himself and the entire staff at Commander's. "It's about today, it's about right now, it's about that guest in that seat, and we've gotta keep pushing."[53]

While there are certain treasured fixtures on the Commander's Palace menu that dare not be touched (the turtle soup, the Chicory Coffee Lacquered Quail stuffed with boudin and the highly coveted Bread Pudding Soufflé with whiskey sauce, to name some major players), other items on the menu are changed multiple times a day. Like his predecessors, McPhail is committed to serving fresh and local ingredients. "Our menu changes every day, twice a day, based on what we can get from our local fishermen and local farms, cattlemen, things like that," McPhail said. He knows it's important to keep the menu current and new, as many local regulars eat at the restaurant multiple times a week. "We actually had one dear friend, she came twice for Thanksgiving day. Once for lunch, and then back for dinner," McPhail remarked. "So the menu is constantly evolving."[54]

Near the end of August 2005, Ella Brennan received a call from her daughter: "I didn't want to wake you up too early, but I need you to get packed and ready to leave town by 2:00 p.m.," Ti urged her mother. "That storm, Katrina, took a turn last night and it's headed our way." After Katrina hit, they all experienced the sobering realization that they were not returning to their posts in the turquoise restaurant anytime soon. They watched the devastating news from televisions in Houston, where they stayed with Ella's son, Alex Brennan, who runs Brennan's of Houston. Despite the distractions of helping his own family, Alex was fast to work with his sister to establish the Hospitality Workers Disaster Relieve Fund, along with the Greater Houston Foundation, which raised more than $1 million to help restaurant employees return to New Orleans. Ti and Lally scrambled to contact Commander's employees, who had mostly fled to various parts of the country. In 2005, with no records of staff cellphone numbers, the work was difficult and stressful.[55]

While Katrina damaged the building and thoroughly dispersed management and staff, Ella Brennan said that it was Rita that truly "did Commander's in." While the roof was somewhat damaged after the first hurricane, Rita worsened it exponentially, and rain poured into the building by the gallon, followed by mold. "The long and short of it was that it took thirteen months and $6.5 million for us to reopen," Ella said. Despite the considerable investment of energy and finances required, the Brennans never once considered not bringing Commander's Palace back. "No way. Hell no. New Orleans is our town and she needed us as much as we needed her," Ella wrote in her autobiography. The way Ti and Lally put it is that Commander's belongs to New Orleans—they simply hold the keys.[56]

As surely as the Mississippi River curves through the city, Commander's reopened its doors for business in September 2006. Locals needed something celebratory to take their minds off of what they had just experienced, and although the staff was still scattered and ingredients were sparse, Commander's, as always, managed to provide the air of festive joy they so craved.

As time went on and employees made their way home, the day-to-day routine at Commander's Palace returned to normalcy—at least, as normal as the restaurant business ever is. Ti, Lally and Brad dealt with the majority of the minutia of running the restaurant; Ella settled into her lush retirement in her and Dottie's home right behind it. "The room service from Commander's next door is grand," Ella wrote in her autobiography. "Better still, we send the dirty dishes back."[57] In 2009, the James Beard Foundation gave Ella a Lifetime Achievement Award for her extensive contributions to the New Orleans restaurant industry and beyond.

Sadly, even the best things must one day come to an end. In late May 2018, at the age of ninety-two, Ella Brennan passed away in her home behind Commander's Palace.[58] A small consolation, according to her daughter, Ti, was that her mother went out as she lived: enjoying life to the fullest. "We were having a damn good time right up until really the very end," Ti said. "We were. We started drinking some really good wine right at the end."[59]

Ella's legacy is still strong at Commander's—the heavy weight is carried by her family, particularly Ti, Lally, Tory McPhail and the entire

Left: Portrait of co-proprietor Ti Martin at the bar at Commander's. *Commander's Palace.*

Below: Contemporary image of the Garden Room. *Commander's Palace.*

staff of her restaurant. One philosophy repeatedly echoed is: "If it ain't broke, fix it anyway." Rather than resting on their many laurels, the Commander's team honors Ella's wishes by constantly striving to improve. "And that is certainly a philosophy of mom's, and mine, and all of us there now: We are not gonna stand still; it's just not who we are," Martin said.[60]

Tory McPhail said that while he considers Ella often, after working with her in various capacities for twenty-six years, what she taught him is in many ways second nature now. "She's always in the back of my mind. Every day… certainly the ideals or fundamentals that she has instilled in us are part of our DNA. So we just keep pushing the restaurant in the right direction, and I think one of the things and values that we all adhere to is no matter what we do, no matter what decisions we make, we need to look at it through this lens: That we are ladies and gentlemen, serving ladies and gentlemen. Whatever the issue is, you do it professionally, and with pride and grace, and better things are gonna happen."[61]

Thanks to lessons from Ella and continued hard work from her heirs and employees, Commander's continues to garner praise today. *Southern Living* magazine named Commander's Palace the South's Best Restaurant of 2019; the rest of the lengthy number of awards and accolades, even just from recent years, is far too extensive to list here.

Although Ti and Lally are still going strong overseeing their culinary castle, they have given consideration to the future of Commander's when they retire. "If some of the next generation shows interest in this crazy, wonderful business (and by the look of them wandering in and out of the kitchen as comfortably as if it were their backyard, they do)," Martin wrote in *Commander's Kitchen*, "then Commander's Palace will grow and evolve with a new generation."[62]

Recipe from Commander's Palace

Turtle Soup

From Commander's Wild Side, *by Chef Tory McPhail and Ti Martin:*
"This dish is usually mentioned in the same sentence as Commander's Palace. We are famous for it, but it can easily be made at home when you want a hearty soup to warm your bones."

12 tablespoons (1 ½ sticks) butter
2½ pounds turtle meat, diced (beef or a combination of lean beef and veal stew meat may be substituted)
kosher salt and freshly ground black pepper to taste
2 medium onions, diced
6 celery stalks, diced

1 large head garlic, individual cloves peeled and minced
3 bell peppers, diced
1 tablespoon ground dried thyme
1 tablespoon ground dried oregano
4 bay leaves
2 quarts veal stock or low-sodium chicken broth
1 cup all-purpose flour
1 bottle dry sherry
1 tablespoon TABASCO, or to taste
¼ cup Worcestershire sauce
2 large lemons, juiced
3 cups peeled, seeded and diced tomatoes
10 ounces fresh spinach, coarsely chopped
6 medium eggs, hard-boiled and chopped

Melt 4 tablespoons butter in a large pot or Dutch oven over medium-high heat. Add meat, salt and pepper and cook until liquid is almost evaporated, about 18 minutes. Stir in the onions, celery, garlic, bell peppers, thyme, oregano and bay leaves and cook, stirring occasionally, for 20 to 25 minutes, until vegetables are caramelized. Add the stock and bring to a boil. Reduce heat to low and simmer, uncovered, for 30 minutes, stirring occasionally and skimming away any fat that comes to the surface.

Meanwhile, prepare the roux by melting the remaining 8 tablespoons butter in a small saucepan over medium heat. Gradually add the flour, stirring constantly with a wooden spoon, and cook for 3 minutes, until nutty and pale with the consistency of wet sand.

Vigorously whisk the roux into the soup a little at a time to prevent lumps. Simmer soup for another 25 minutes, stirring occasionally to prevent burning. Then add the sherry, TABASCO and Worcestershire and cook for 10 minutes, skimming away any fat or foam that may rise to the surface while cooking. Lastly, add the lemon juice, tomatoes, spinach and eggs and then bring back to a simmer for another 10 to 15 minutes, allowing to incorporate. Adjust seasoning with salt and pepper as needed. Soup can be made up to 3 days ahead and frozen up to 1 month.

No turtle? Substitute ground veal for "mock" turtle soup.

Recipe courtesy of Commander's Wild Side *by Chef Tory McPhail and Ti Martin, with permission from Ti Martin.*

Chapter 5

Angelo Brocato

(1905)

Then there is the ritual of visiting Brocato's, a ritual passed down through ice cream–loving families over five and six generations.
—*Adam Nossiter,* New York Times, *2006*

After expanding from its French, Spanish, African and Caribbean roots, the Creole culinary landscape enjoyed the robust addition of Italian influence with a massive influx of Italian and Sicilian immigrants to New Orleans in the nineteenth and early twentieth centuries. While it is worth noting that records indicate Italians were living in New Orleans to some extent from as early as 1718, when the French first settled the area, Italian presence in the city multiplied exponentially following the Civil War. By the year 1910, Italians and Sicilians would make up approximately 80 percent of French Quarter residents, garnering the neighborhood's nickname of the time, "Little Palermo." While some just traveled to New Orleans to work on the docks for the season before returning to Italy, others stayed and established businesses inspired by those in their home country.[1]

One of the Sicilian immigrants who chose to plant roots in New Orleans was Angelo Brocato. His parents brought him to New Orleans as a young child from his birth town of Cefalù, but when his father died in one of the yellow fever epidemics that were common in New Orleans throughout the 1800s, his mother brought him and his siblings back to Sicily, where they settled in the capital of Palermo. There, at twelve years old, Angelo began to apprentice with his brother Giuseppe at one of the most refined ice cream parlors in the city. Angelo learned not only the classic techniques for making granita (shaved ice), gelato, spumoni and cassata, but also, during Mediterranean winters, he perfected the skills of making cannoli, biscotti and other traditional Italian pastries.

Angelo worked in several ice cream and dessert shops throughout Palermo in his teenage years, joining the Italian navy, as was his obligation, at the age of eighteen. When he finished his time with the navy, he made his way back to Louisiana, cutting sugar cane on plantations in Donaldsonville to save money for his wife's passage to join him from Sicily. New Orleans must have made an impression on young Angelo, because in 1901 he returned, thereafter calling the French Quarter his home and sending for his wife and son to join him there in 1907, where his Italian dessert shop was already established. Only months after the birth of their second child in New Orleans, Angelo's wife died of yellow fever. He eventually remarried, having five more children, seven in total.[2]

In 1905, Angelo Brocato opened his ice cream and pastry shop just off Ursulines Avenue on Decatur Street, in the heart of the Italian neighborhood of the French Quarter. The first ice cream sold at Brocato's was torroncino—a cinnamon ice cream with thin slices of almond throughout, served cut in a rectangular slice long before ice cream cones or scoops were invented. Chocolate and vanilla, and a combination of the two, were also popularly sold by the slice in the early days of Brocato's. Spumoni, featuring multiple flavors of ice cream with a cream center, and cassata, which is similar to spumoni but contains a layer of fruit and cake, have been longtime staples at Brocato's, particularly for special occasions like baptisms or bridal showers. Lemon ice—served instead in a glass with a spoon, softer than the early ice creams—was always a favorite, particularly among the Italian community, both at the turn of the century and today.[3]

Making traditional Italian ice, particularly in the time before refrigeration and mechanized equipment, was a labor of love. Angelo would buy lemons from the nearby French Market on Decatur, peeling them to minimize acidity and juicing them with the back of a spoon. Sugar and water came next, which would be stirred and combined with the lemon juice and then strained. The mix would be transferred into a cylinder packed with ice, the ice being surrounded with salt. Angelo or his employees would take a large, very sharp knife to the concoction, spinning the cylinder by hand to obtain the signature product. The lemon ice would be served soft directly from the container into a glass. Not only was it enjoyed as dessert, but French Quarter Italians would also often spread lemon ice onto warm Italian bread or dip

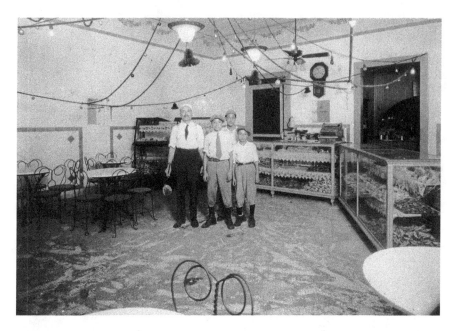

Early twentieth-century image of Angelo Sr. with his sons, Angelo Jr., Joe and Roy, in their French Quarter dessert shop. *Angelo Brocato Ice Cream & Confectionery.*

the bread into the soft ice for breakfast.[4] One Italian restaurateur in the French Quarter, known as Diamond Jim Moran for his extravagant jewelry, would send his sons for a pitcher of Brocato's Italian ice and a fresh loaf of bread each morning for such purposes.[5] Other flavors of granita—such as strawberry, peach, watermelon and cantaloupe—were cycled in depending what was in season and available at the French Market.[6]

Brocato's did not take long to outgrow its small original storefront. After opening the first store on Decatur, Angelo soon moved his business to a larger shop in the 500 block of Ursulines Avenue. In 1921, Brocato's moved again, this time to a grander location at 617 Ursulines, with classic white tiles, decorative archways and ceiling fans modeled after the parlors in Palermo where Angelo apprenticed.[7]

As automobiles became more common in the French Quarter, Angelo incorporated carhop service into the business model—now families could pull up on their evening drive for a gelato or granita, brought right to their car window. Local teenagers were employed as carhops, including the three LoCicero sisters, who lived in the neighborhood, two of whom would eventually marry Angelo's sons. Car service at Brocato's lasted until the

Ladies' entrance at the former French Quarter location of Angelo Brocato's on Ursulines, now housing Croissant D'Or Patisserie. *Creative Commons/Infrogmation.*

1940s and World War II. The business continued to thrive in the grand shop on Ursulines for sixty years, through the Great Depression and World War II sugar rationing that mandated its closure on Mondays.[8]

Angelo, a hardworking man who loved his business, died in 1946 at the age of seventy-one, never having retired. His sons Angelo Jr. and Joseph, along with their mother, continued to operate the store to their father's precise standards. But at the end of the Second World War, the Italian neighborhood where Angelo Sr. had established his dessert shop was changing rapidly. As the population of New Orleans expanded out of the French Quarter and more toward Lake Pontchartrain, Italian families who once could send their children a just a few blocks to grab lemon ice each day for breakfast would now drive into the French Quarter just to pick up Brocato's desserts for holidays or special occasions.[9]

The home freezer was rising in both mass production and popularity at the end of the 1940s, and Angelo Jr. and Joseph capitalized on the trend by shifting the business to wholesale. In addition to maintaining the Ursulines shop, they would sell their products to restaurants, grocers and specialty stores, bringing Brocato's desserts to a wider New Orleans audience than the primarily Italian French Quarter residents that made up their early customer base.[10]

The famous Palermo-inspired shop in the 600 block of Ursulines was sold to one owner in the late 1960s by Angelo Sr.'s surviving wife and later sold again to Maurice Delechelle, who moved his French patisserie from Chartres Street into the former gelato parlor. To this day, Croissant D'Or remains in the former Brocato's space.[11]

NEW HOME, SAME FAMILY

In the beginning of the 1970s, Joseph retired when trouble with his legs would not allow him to do the necessary physical labor, and Angelo Jr. brought his two sons, Arthur and Angelo III, into the business. Their mother met Angelo Jr. when she worked as a carhop at the Ursulines location as a teenager. Arthur was still studying business administration at Loyola University at the time his uncle retired, but he grew up working in the French Quarter store on afternoons and weekends. He had always taken a liking to the business and felt that it was something special, even though his parents did not particularly encourage him to pursue the family business. "It's the typical immigrant story, that you want your children to do better, and you want them to get an education and to be somebody special," Arthur said. "And the business they were doing [at Brocato's] was to make a living, you know, and so they didn't encourage it."

Certainly not the first college student to buck his parents' wishes, in 1973, while still attending Loyola, Arthur purchased his Uncle Joseph's shares of the business. Angelo Brocato's current home on Carrollton Avenue was purchased and renovated in 1978, allowing more space and easier parking and accessibility for its now more far-spread customer base. To this day, Arthur Brocato is the primary owner and operator of the business his grandfather Angelo started, although his brother, Angelo III, and other family members are co-owners and contribute as well.[12]

Arthur and his wife, Jolie, lived in an apartment in the raised upper level of the Carrollton Street shop for a while. Eventually, they converted the space into more seating for the store to meet New Orleans's ever-ravenous dessert demand. When renovations were complete in July 2005, the family held a festive celebration to commemorate the expansion of the space, as well as

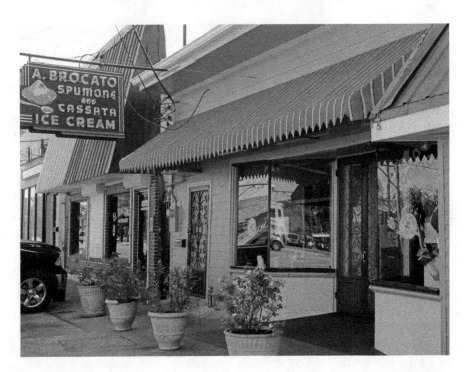

Contemporary exterior of Brocato's current location on Carrollton Avenue. *Angelo Brocato Ice Cream & Confectionery.*

the centennial of Angelo Brocato's first opening in the French Quarter. The turnout was massive, as people from all over the city and beyond were eager to celebrate their beloved gelato purveyor.[13]

In a matter of weeks, Hurricane Katrina made landfall, flooding the Mid-City neighborhood. Arthur and Jolie anxiously watched the news footage from Houston, eventually seeing their own storefront on Carrolton Avenue submerged. As the days went on, they were able to observe how high the flood had risen: six feet on their particular block, meaning five feet of water was filling Angelo Brocato's. "So everything was just completely inundated," Arthur remembered. "All our equipment, the store. We were able to salvage, thankfully, pictures. The water didn't get that high up."[14]

When Arthur and Jolie were able to return to the city to assess the damage firsthand, they hardly knew where to begin. Their first priority was cleaning everything out that had been below the five-foot water line. "The ironic part is, we didn't really have any damage to the building itself, besides the floodwater," Arthur said. But their iconic neon sign had fallen off the front of the building in the wind, consequentially knocking the electricity out for the front of the building. The gas lines in the neighborhood were not restored until the following January. The family was torn, looking at options for perhaps reopening in a smaller building. "We researched things in other places, and [sigh] it was a heart-wrenching time," Arthur recollected. "You didn't know what direction to go in. And it wasn't until probably in December or January that we made the decision: 'Well, let's give it a shot and see.'"[15]

They began renovations toward the end of January 2006. In the meantime, Arthur made arrangements with a woman who owned a bakery in the Marigny neighborhood to use her equipment a few days a week. Storm or no, St. Joseph's Day was fast approaching, and the Italian community remaining in the city could not go without Brocato's cookies for their altars. Arthur, his wife and any family members who were available to contribute baked traditional seed and fig cookies, packaging them and stocking them in the few specialty stores that were still able to open following Katrina. They could not keep up with the demand.[16]

Just over a year later, they were able to officially reopen the Carrollton Avenue shop. A band was hired for the celebration, and dessert devotees stood for hours in a line wrapping around the block for a coveted cannoli or cantaloupe ice. Brocato's reopening signified the return of a certain lighthearted normalcy that Katrina had ripped from so many. "They have a void that everyone is trying to fill," Arthur Brocato told the *New York Times*. "They want that comfort, that everything is back to normal, some sense that their lives are back in place. They're not just coming here to shop."[17]

While the reception from customers after the reopening was "phenomenal," in Arthur's words, there were still hang-ups for some time after: there were times when the gas would go out because there was still water in the lines, necessitating calls to both the plumber and electrician. Many of their staff members were also displaced, and it would be about another full year before most would return to New Orleans. Arthur said it took several years, though, for the operations to really resume something like normalcy, and even then they were not quite the same. "We wouldn't say normal—we always said, 'There's gonna be a new normal,' and it really was, and still is. [laughs dryly] Just a whole different outlook on things," Arthur said. "But we came back and have been successful. And we're really happy about that and thankful to our customers—our loyal customers who have been with us many years, and new people who have come into the area."[18]

Today in 2019, Arthur, Jolie and the other family members continue to fulfill their customers' sweet teeth and operate Angelo Brocato's Italian Ice Cream Parlor in Mid-City. While Arthur has no plans to retire anytime too

Contemporary interior of Brocato's current location on Carrollton Avenue. *Angelo Brocato Ice Cream & Confectionery.*

soon, he conceded that he would like a little less responsibility when it comes to the business. As for who will continue running Brocato's when Arthur finally does want to retire, that is still to be determined. "We'll see what the future brings. We hope that it's gonna continue; it's a family operation that is very special," Arthur said. "It just has to have the right person or people there to carry it on. And you have to love what you do."[19]

Recipe from Angelo Brocato's

Italian Cantaloupe Ice

When Angelo Brocato first opened Angelo Brocato's in 1905, he would make Italian ice by hand, without refrigeration. Since he made it sound so easy, here is a slightly more modern recipe for Brocato's Italian Cantaloupe Ice to try at home.
Yeilds: 2 quarts

2½ cups sugar
1 quart (4 cups) water
2 medium-size ripe cantaloupes
juice of 1 lemon

Dissolve sugar and water in a 2-quart saucepan over medium-high heat. Bring to a boil and cook for 2 minutes. Remove from heat and cool. Peel and seed the cantaloupes. Cut into 2-inch pieces. Puree in a food processor and strain through a medium sieve. Mix strained cantaloupe juice, sugar syrup and lemon juice with a wire whisk and pour into an ice cream machine. Add some of the cantaloupe pulp if desired. Freeze according to manufacturer's directions. Harden for a few hours in a freezer if desired.

Recipe courtesy of Angelo Brocato's Ice Cream and Confectionery.

Chapter 6

Galatoire's
(1905)

The Crescent City has no shortage of gracious gastronomical institutions, but Galatoire's stands out for maintaining standards without getting mired in the past.
—*Sadie Stein,* New York Times, *2013*

Yet another chapter in this book and in Creole fine dining begins with a French immigrant. Jean Galatoire was raised in the small village of Pardies in the foothills of the Pyrenees Mountains.[1] Unlike Antoine Alciatore and Guillaume Tujague of earlier chapters, however, Jean Galatoire made the diversion of traveling to Mexico before arriving in New Orleans. While in Vera Cruz, he opened a restaurant and then eventually boarded a ship for the United States in 1876. After settling into his low-lying new home of New Orleans, he secured work as a waiter and then as manager of the prominent Marchal's Bistro at the age of twenty-two.[2]

Although Jean Galatoire longed to become a restaurateur himself, he lacked the money to manifest his aspiration, so he continued to learn on the job and bide his time working at Marchal's until he was able to secure a partner for his own endeavor in Louis A. Trapet. The pair soon opened a saloon and oyster bar at the foot of Canal Street called the Pelican Exchange. During this period, Jean (who used the more American-sounding "John Galatoir" then) and his former employer, Marchal, developed a running antagonism that eventually ended in violence. In 1883, Marchal and Galatoire broke into a physical fight, ending in Marchal being charged with assault and battery, although he bore fairly extensive wounds from the encounter as well.

Jean Galatoire portrait. *Galatoire's Restaurant.*

Soon after the altercation, the Pelican Exchange closed, and around a year later, Jean secured another partner and opened John's Restaurant on the site that had formerly housed his boss turned rival Marchal's business.[3]

In 1886, Jean wed Gabrielle Marchal and then closed John's Restaurant and moved with his new wife to Birmingham. Jean quickly became a successful caterer in his new city, eventually opening John's Saloon and Restaurant there. After their stint in Alabama, the couple lived in Chicago for a brief time to open a restaurant during the 1893 World's Fair. By the end of that decade, however, Jean and Gabrielle had returned to New Orleans.[4] After moving back, Jean befriended the aging Victor Bero, who had operated Victor's Restaurant on Bourbon Street since the mid-ninetieth century. Jean's goal was to win Bero's good favor so that when Bero retired, it would be logical for him to sell his well-established restaurant to Jean. Sure enough, their friendship continued to grow until 1905, when Jean was offered the opportunity to purchase Victor's.[5] He bought the restaurant, changed its name to Galatoire's and began serving the type of provincial French cuisine he grew up with in the Pyrenees foothills.[6]

Although Jean was successful in luring the most established New Orleanians and travelers to dine at Galatoire's, he required help in the management and duties of running the restaurant. He looked back to his home country of France, where his three nephews were coming into adulthood and in need of work. At Jean's suggestion, Justin, Gabriel and Leon Galatoire also left the French mountainside for the port of New Orleans to work for their uncle at his new restaurant. With a family team assembled, Galatoire's quickly became regarded as one of the finest French restaurants in New Orleans. While Jules Alciatore a few blocks over was experimenting with new dishes and ingredients, regulars at Galatoire's could expect the same shrimp remoulade (which Galatoire's claims to have invented), trout meunière amandine, Brabant potatoes and other classic dishes each time they dined there.[7]

Something else established by Jean Galtoire that remains staunchly implemented today is the strict "no reservations" policy for the first-floor main dining room. An egalitarian of sorts, Jean believed that ordinary locals and celebrity VIPs deserved the same opportunity to dine at his restaurant. When lines of hopeful patrons attempting to secure a table would regularly form around the building, Jean was incredulous: "This is just a little chicken place, what's the big deal?"[8] It would seem that after all of his shorter-lived previous ventures, he finally had a restaurant that was a grand success and would be for a long time to come.

In 1916, Jean Galatoire's heart and kidneys were failing him, so he retired, leaving day-to-day operations of his restaurant to his nephews. In 1919, having no children of his own, Jean sold his restaurant to his three nephews for a total of $40,000. A few months after the transaction, he passed away at the age of sixty-four in his home on Esplanade Avenue, leaving an estate totaling $500,000.[9] Justin, Gabriel and Leon Galatoire were then responsible for their uncle's Bourbon Street establishment.[10]

Galatoire's Bourbon Street exterior, 1964. *Galatoire's Restaurant.*

Even as the second generation took hold and Galatoire's founder died, Jean's nephews kept their uncle's restaurant nearly exactly as he established it in terms of menu, décor and service. Not long after Jean Galatoire's death, his nephew Gabriel set sail back to France for a visit and to round up his own nephew, Leon Touzet Sr., who had just completed a cooking apprenticeship in Pau. When the pair returned to New Orleans, Touzet was swiftly sent to the Galatoire's kitchen to claim his post as a sauté cook, joining five other French-born chefs. And thus the third generation of Jean Galatoire's family was ushered into business at Galatoire's.[11]

Maintaining Galatoire's high standards made for long and grueling work in the kitchen. According to Touzet, his uncle Justin in particular was a hard taskmaster, mandating that kitchen employees work twelve-hour days, seven days a week. If a cook wanted time off, he had to pay another employee to take the shift. As means of coping with the long and difficult work, Touzet said it was customary for a tray of pony glasses filled with Cognac, Chartreuse or some other stiff liquor to be passed around for the cooks early in the morning and again in the evening as the dinner period was gearing up.[12] Such was life in the kitchen of a New Orleans restaurant at the time, although similar means are doubtlessly still sometimes implemented by cooks in the city today.

During World War II, when the military draft meant there were not enough men to fully staff both the first and second floors of the restaurant, the private dining rooms offered upstairs were discontinued. The majority of private parties to utilize the rooms had been couples, and it had become something of a spectator sport for employees and customers alike to postulate about what sort of illicit activity might be taking place once the waiter closed the door behind him. Shirley Ann Grau, a local writer and regular of Galatoire's, later pointed out in *Holiday* magazine in 1956 that the private dining rooms had actually been particularly helpful for young female socialites, who prior to the 1920s would have been judged as improper for being seen in a restaurant with anyone except family. Following the private rooms' closure in the 1940s, the second floor would remain office space and storage for more than fifty years.[13]

A feature of the Galatoire's menu that was removed during the Second World War was the *plats du jours*, or daily specials served in multiple courses. Federal rations on produce at the time made the elaborate rotating menus impossible to continue. Instead, Gabriel suggested the menu transition into an expansive book of à la carte offerings, which it remains today.[14]

Galatoire's, like all of its sister grande dames, had and has a particularly impressive celebrity following. Tennessee Williams was so fond of Galatoire's and the times of revelry he had there that he eventually had his own table, and he references the restaurant in his most famous play, *A Streetcar Named Desire*, when Stella takes her sister Blanche there for a "girls' night" while her husband, Stanley, plays poker.[15]

Mick Jagger and Harpo Marx have joined the Friday lunch line as well. Some say that the "no reservations" policy is so strict that even Charles de Gaulle was denied a request to have a table held.[16] In one oft-told story, U.S. Senator J. Bennett Johnston was waiting in line for a table at Galatoire's when he received a call from President Ronald Reagan. He took the call but wasted no time returning to his place in line, unwilling to sacrifice his table for Friday lunch.[17]

Right after the new year in January 1956, a fire began in a second-floor storeroom of the restaurant just after it had closed for the night, quickly spreading up a stairway to the third floor and damaging the roof of the

Vintage postcard featuring Galatoire's from Bourbon Street. *Louisiana Menu and Restaurant Collection, Louisiana Research Collection, Tulane University.*

building. A general alarm was called by the fire department, and a crowd estimated by police to be more than one thousand gathered to watch the blaze in horror. While the first floor was spared from the flames, the kitchen and downstairs dining room suffered severe water damage from the efforts to put out the inferno. The building incurred an estimated $75,000 in total damages, a devastating loss at the time for even the most successful of restaurateurs.[18]

While his brothers, Justin and Leon, married and had children, Gabriel remained a lifelong bachelor and lived in the third-floor apartment above Galatoire's, which today is relegated to business offices, before it burned. Leon's grandson David Gooch, manager of Galatoire's today, told the *Tulanian* that his Uncle Gabriel's apartment was "lavish and full of antiques."[19] Gabriel Galatoire died there in October 1944, leaving the restaurant below in the hands of his two brothers.[20]

Justin and Leon married two first cousins, both named Clarisse Houlne. Justin had four daughters named Laurence, Yvonne, Leona and Denise, while Leon had one daughter, Clarisse, and three sons named Leon, Gabriel and René. Justin and Leon continued to manage the restaurant themselves until 1961, when Leon retired. Leon's retirement left Justin the sole second-generation proprietor still taking part in management of Galatoire's.[21]

Two of Leon's sons, René and Gabriel, who went by "Gabie," also joined the Galatoire's management team when each returned from serving in World War II. Gabie, who was known to be charismatic and suave, fell naturally into greeting customers in the front of house—he was known to use football terminology to direct guests where to sit, to their amusement. René, who earned both a Purple Heart and Bronze Star for saving a fellow soldier's life in the war and being injured in the process, first went to work in the kitchen. René would later transition into the dining room to serve as general manager until Justin died and René was named president of the company in 1973. René served as president of Galatoire's until 1984, when he retired.[22]

Justin's daughter Yvonne, who would joke she was her father's "son by default," went to work at the family restaurant in 1938 when the cashier was too sick to come in. Yvonne took a liking to the business, and the customers took a liking to her, so at Galatoire's Yvonne stayed. Later she served as manager from 1964 until her retirement in 1997 and as the first female president of the business from 1984 until she passed in 2000.[23]

When the third generation to own the restaurant was mostly retired or deceased, the fourth generation, consisting of Justin and Leon's grandchildren (David Gooch, Leon Galatoire Jr., Michele Galatoire and Justin Frey), were the primary individuals responsible for operations of the business. During this period, in 1997, an unprecedented shift for the restaurant came when family members decided to hand off direct control of the restaurant and hire Melvin Rodrigue as chief operating officer of Galatoire's. Rodrigue was a Tulane graduate who spent years working for the Brennan family at Palace Café and Commander's Palace before running a Ruth's Chris Steakhouse in Seattle for a time, and he was employed as food and beverage director for the Westin Hotel when he left to step into his position at Galatoire's.[24]

A NEW AGE FOR OLD-WORLD DINING

Becoming the first non–family member to run a family legacy is surely a daunting task, but with his own extensive restaurant experience and the Galatoire family-run board backing him up, Rodrigue was up to it. He understands and appreciates that Galatoire's has a devoted following and is careful not to upset them. "We're so fortunate to have such a passionate and loyal customer base, it was one of those things: when I came in, there was not a revolt by any stretch, but make no mistake about it, they made sure to test me," Rodrigue told the author. "To make sure that they were comfortable as a customer, that I wasn't going to turn the place upside down."[25]

One of Rodrique's first tasks was renovating the aging building and reopening the upstairs dining rooms that had previously been closed since World War II. "So when we renovated, that was an opportunity for us from a competitive standpoint to remain true to the traditions of first come, first serve in the main dining room but yet have a competitive opportunity for reservations on that floor that had been closed for so long," Rodrigue said. Although there were a few grumbles from older clientele who opposed change of any variety when it comes to Galatoire's, the general response was positive. Most appreciated the ability to reserve a table, having a quieter dining option than the frequently bustling main dining room.[26]

The year 2005 was an important one for Galatoire's in many ways. Foremost, the restaurant celebrated its centennial. In May of that year, Galatoire's was recognized by the James Beard Foundation with the Outstanding Restaurant award, reserved for an American restaurant that "serves as the standard-bearer for consistence of quality and excellence in food, atmosphere and service."[27] Melvin Rodrigue also partnered with Jyl Benson to write an updated *Galatoire's Cookbook* that was published in 2005,

Galatoire's main dining room at lunch, which maintains a strict "no reservations" policy. *Galatoire's Restaurant.*

Galatoire's waiter Mark jovially taking care of the busy lunch crowd. *Galatoire's Restaurant.*

with Benson writing the majority of the history and Rodrigue organizing the recipes, since he has kitchen experience himself.[28]

Unfortunately, the remainder of the year would prove more difficult. Even having the fortune of being located on the high ground of the French Quarter, between staffing issues and building damage Galatoire's was closed for more than four months following the storm.

In 2008, the oldest member of the Galatoire family approached Rodrigue and asked if he would be open to organizing a group of investors to buy them out—"he believed that a consolidation would help ensure the legacy of their ancestors even longer," Rodrigue explained. At the Galatoire family's request, Rodrigue put together an investment group, which was then outbid by another faction of family members along with businessmen Todd Trosclair and John Georges, who owns the *New Orleans Advocate*. Although Trosclair initially controlled 75 percent of the restaurant, the day of the purchase he sold a majority of his shares to Georges. "He's the largest stockholder, but not a majority stockholder," Trosclair clarified to Boston.com. "I will be the chairman of the board."[29] The other 25 percent of the business is still controlled by the Galatoire family.[30]

While the traditions that make Galatoire's are still firmly in place, updates continue. In 2013, Galatoire's expanded by adding Galatoire's 33 and Steak in the adjacent building. In 2018, the restaurant again turned heads by hiring Philip Lopez to step in as executive chef. Lopez formerly owned and was chef of hyper-contemporary Warehouse District restaurant Root and later Square Root in the Garden District, known as the most expensive restaurant in the city and for exclusively offering a multicourse tasting menu. A feature of both Lopez's previous ventures was dishes that incorporated molecular gastronomy, so some scratched their heads when one of the most progressive-seeming chefs in the city was hired to take charge of one of New Orleans's most traditional restaurants.[31] Lopez said that his background has thoroughly helped him in the kitchen at Galatoire's, not hindered him. "It allows me to take the recipes that are currently being used and help them introduce better technique of modern gastronomy," Lopez explained. "Utilizing the freshest ingredients and helping highlight individual flavors, while not changing the experience."[32]

Although 75 percent of shares of the business are now outside of family hands, President Melvin Rodrigue said he and his team are still devoted to maintaining the Galatoire family tradition that diners have so loved for more

Above: Contemporary exterior.
Alexandra Kennon.

Left: Portrait of Chef Philip Lopez.
Galatoire's Restaurant.

than a century. On navigating upholding the classicism of Galatoire's while also evolving subtly to improve and expand the business, Rodrigue used the analogy of a tightrope:

> *It is a tightrope that we walk, because one of the things that we don't want to do is ever kind of get caught in a fad, by any stretch. Twenty-five percent of the restaurant is still owned by that portion of the Galatoire family, so we're into the fifth generation of the Galatoire family owning the restaurant. But one of the things that's really amazing is that we're multi-generational; our customers are multi-generational. So their passion for us makes it easy to buck the trend, so to speak. And they come here looking for a specific thing. There are a lot of great restaurants out there that change their menu every day. And I love some of 'em. But there's also comfort that you find in the tradition of knowing when you order the shrimp remoulade here, it evokes memories of when your grandfather brought you for the first time forty years ago. So we have that as our calling card.*[33]

Recipe from Galatoire's

Soufflé Potatoes

These soufflé potatoes are a must-have at Galatoire's and crave-able enough to be worth making at home, although the technique can admittedly be tricky.

1 gallon vegetable oil
6 Idaho potatoes, scrubbed
salt to taste
béarnaise sauce to dip

In a large, heavy-bottomed pot suitable for frying, heat the oil to 325 degrees Fahrenheit. While the oil heats, slice the potatoes lengthwise ⅛-inch thick using a mandoline or very sharp knife. Trim the square corners from either end of the strips of potato. The result will be a long oval shape.

Place the potatoes into the oil, not more than two layers at a time. Overloading the pot will cause the temperature to drop. In order to maintain a consistent temperature, move the potatoes constantly with a slotted spoon. Cook the potatoes for 4 to 5 minutes, until light brown. Some will form small air bubbles. This is an indication that the meat of the potato has cooked away.

Once the potatoes have become inflated, remove them from the hot oil and set aside to cool until just prior to serving. To prepare this dish in advance, cook the potatoes until they puff and immediately remove them from the oil and lay flat on a sheet pan. Place wax paper between the layers of potatoes.

When you are ready to serve the potatoes, increase (or reheat) the temperature of the oil to 375 degrees Fahrenheit. Place the potatoes back into the oil and they will puff instantly. Cook for an additional 30 seconds, stirring continuously until they are golden brown on both sides and crispy enough to hold their form without deflating. Remove the potatoes from the oil and drain them on paper towels. Sprinkle with a pinch of salt while hot. Repeat with remaining potatoes. Serve immediately.

Recipe courtesy of Galatoire's Restaurant.

Chapter 7
Parkway
(1911)

*Parkway tops "best po-boy" lists annually and earned a visit last year from the
Obamas. It wins our love with its fried shrimp po-boy and super-sloppy "classic"
roast beef, dressed to the nines.*
—*Steve Garbarino,* Wall Street Journal, *2011*

A POOR BOY'S BIRTH: THE ORIGINS OF THE PO-BOY

Like many facets of New Orleans history, a laissez-faire attitude toward
recordkeeping and the distractions of the rise of jazz and fall of
Prohibition make determining the po-boy's true origin a difficult task.
Lore asserts that the sandwich was invented by brothers Bennie and
Clovis Martin at their shop on the edge of the French Quarter during a
streetcar conductor strike in 1929. The story goes that Bennie and Clovis
moved to New Orleans from their hometown of Raceland, Louisiana,
to work as streetcar conductors themselves, leaving those positions to
open the Martin Brothers' Coffee Stand and Restaurant at the corner
of Ursulines Avenue and North Peters Street. When Bennie and Clovis's
former coworkers and fellow members in Division 194 of the conductor's
union went on strike in 1929, Bennie and Clovis ran the following letter
in at least one local paper that August:

Dear Friends,

We are with you heart and Soul, at any time you are around the French Market, don't forget to drop in at Martin's Coffee Stand and Restaurant, Cor(ner) Ursuline & North Peters Sts. Our meal is free to any members of Division 194.

We have thirty nine employees, all riding Jitneys to help win the strike.

We are with you until h--l freezes, and when it does, we will furnish blankets to keep you warm.

With best wishes to your cause, we are,

Your friends and former members of Division 194
Clovis J. & Bennie Martin

Customers eating po-boys outside Parkway during the Great Depression. *Parkway Bakery and Tavern.*

By providing the striking men with a free sandwich made of French bread filled with ham or roast beef (or often roast beef and potatoes, to cut costs in those early days), the brothers followed through on their promise. Because "Our meal," as referenced in the letter, does not specify its sandwich nature, some historians have come to question the Martin brothers' claim to inventing the po-boy. Some forty years later, in 1969, Bennie asserted their role in naming the creation: "We fed those men free of charge until the strike ended. Whenever we saw one of the striking men coming, one of us would say, 'Here comes another poor boy.'"[1]

Forty years, however, is certainly long enough for a story to be embellished or even invented entirely. This gap in the narrative, along with a smattering of accounts that reference the poorboy sandwich prior to 1929, have led many historians to question the accuracy of the Martin brothers' story.

Jazz musician Sidney Bechet, for example, recalled in his autobiography that he ate "poor boys" with Louis Armstrong once after a gig, which would have occurred sometime in the 1910s, long before the Martin brothers opened their coffee stand: "We went out and bought some beer with the money and got those sandwiches, Poor Boys, they're called—a half a loaf of bread split open and stuffed with ham. We really had good times."[2]

It is, of course, possible that Bechet, having later encountered similar sandwiches referred to as "poor boys," retrospectively misremembered that those he ate with a young Louis Armstrong were called the same name. It is also possible that the poor boy does, in fact, predate the Martin brothers' restaurant and the streetcar conductor strike—it is, after all, known with certainty that meat was being stuffed into French bread for more than a century before the term "poor boy" was used to describe the phenomenon. But in a city with a flare for the dramatic such as New Orleans, the narrative that makes for the most interesting story typically wins out. Thus, the Martin brothers inventing the sandwich to feed their fellow streetcar conductors has been etched with pride, if not certainty, into New Orleans's history.

PARKWAY BAKERY & TAVERN

Long before Parkway was designated "for Poor Boys," the institution at the corner of Hagan Avenue and Toulouse Streets was Parkway Bakery, opened by German baker Charles Goering in 1911. Goering owned and ran the traditional German bakery for a decade and a year, selling the business to

Henry Timothy Sr. in 1922.[3] Timothy Sr. continued to operate Parkway as a neighborhood bake shop, serving fresh breads and eventually adding doughnuts and "Seven Sisters" sweet rolls to the menu, which quickly became a neighborhood favorite.[4]

In 1929, Timothy received word that as an act of solidarity, brothers Bennie and Clovis Martin were offering free sandwiches called "poor boys" to striking streetcar union members at their restaurant in the French Quarter. Timothy followed suit and began to offer French fry "poor boys" to the strikers free of charge at Parkway as well, and thus "Tavern" was tacked onto the end of the bakery's name. Timothy also sold the French bread sandwiches to the workers at the American Can Company right across Bayou St. John for only ten cents. The factory remained open twenty-four hours a day, so after 1929, Parkway adopted these long hours as well. Throughout the 1930s, Parkway sold its economical "poor boy" sandwiches, feeding many New Orleans families during the difficult times of the Great Depression. Timothy Sr. would continue to run Parkway Bakery and Tavern until he retired in the 1960s, leaving the corner establishment to his two sons, Henry Jr. ("Bubby") and Jake, who would run Parkway via their own methods for nearly the next thirty years.[5]

According to Parkway's current owner, Jay Nix, the Timothy brothers kept a tight staff of just the two of them and, for a period, their sister; because of the associated pressures, po-boys were served with a blunt, to-the-point variety

Jake Timothy Sr. serves Sadie. *Parkway Bakery and Tavern.*

of hospitality—or lack thereof. "They didn't have time to charm the public," Nix said.[6]

Despite the abruptness of the brothers' service, their aversion to basic maintenance and their fondness for betting on horse races, they continued to successfully sell the staple sandwiches, establishing Parkway as a legendary neighborhood institution. Eventually, the inevitable for a restaurant in the Mid-City neighborhood of New Orleans occurred: in 1978, Parkway flooded, destroying the original brick ovens installed by the Goerings. No longer able to produce their own bread, the Timothy brothers opted for the next best (and arguably better) thing, a seemingly obvious choice for a New Orleans po-boy shop: they began sourcing bread from Leidenheimer Baking Company, which is still used to make sandwiches at Parkway today.

A decade later in 1988, the closing of the nearby American Can Company throttled Parkway's business, prompting the Timothy brothers to close and sell the restaurant in 1993.[7] The closure left a po-boy–shaped void on the corner of Hagan Avenue and Toulouse Street for the next decade.

ROAST BEEF RENAISSANCE

Meanwhile, in the beginning of the 1990s, New Orleans born and bred real estate developer Jay Nix purchased a raised shotgun double next door to the building that once housed Parkway from his boss. Shortly after he completed extensive renovations to convert the second floor into a large single unit he could live in, the former Parkway building next door on the corner went on the market.

"So I'm thinkin, 'Oh God, it's gonna become an all-night liquor store, or something undesirable, and I'm gonna have to move,'" Nix said. Then he had an alternate idea: if he bought Parkway, he could prevent the appearance of a disreputable store directly adjacent to his new home, as well as the resulting drop in property value. "So, long story short, I bought Parkway to save my house," Nix concluded. In 1995, with no intent of reopening the restaurant, Nix purchased the building that once housed Parkway from the Timothy brothers for $45,000, signing the paperwork on the hood of a car. For the next ten years, the former Parkway building served as little more than Nix's toolshed. "It was almost like a Sanford and Son junkyard, 'cause I used to collect old antique toilets and old claw tubs, and it was filled with old doors," Nix recalled.[8]

Throughout this decade of Parkway purgatory, Nix's nephew Justin Kennedy would occasionally drop in from his childhood home in Biloxi,

Mississippi, to help his uncle work on weekends. "I don't know if he knew what he wanted to do with it, but he knew it was something special," Kennedy remembered. "And whenever I'd go work with Jay when I was like ten, eleven years old, he'd brag that Parkway was his toolshed."[9]

It didn't take long for neighbors and other locals to begin to hound Nix to return Parkway to its former sandwich-serving glory. Anyone who had tasted a Parkway po-boy in their life wanted another, and although Nix owned the building, he had no restaurant experience or desire to operate a sandwich shop. But the urging from locals was too impassioned to ignore, and eventually, he decided to give the po-boy business a go. "So finally I succumbed to the pressure, and I had enough guts and time and money to open it," Nix said. "I went from cutting two-by-fours to French bread in six months."

The financial burdens of converting a toolshed back into a restaurant were more massive than expected. Nix had to sell all three of the rental properties he owned at the time so he could begin construction on Parkway.

Owner Jay Nix with a shrimp po-boy. *Parkway Bakery and Tavern.*

When he ran out of money again, his only remaining asset was his home—the raised shotgun double he bought Parkway to save the value of in the first place.

Despite having bought Parkway to save his house, Nix ultimately sold the shotgun to allocate those funds toward reviving Parkway. "But it was really one of the great moves I made, and guess who bought [the house]?" Nix quipped. "The veterinarian across the street."

Even after selling all his major assets to complete renovations on Parkway, the difficult part of running the po-boy shop was just beginning. Nix's experience was in construction and contracting, after all, not the restaurant business, meaning the learning curve was steep. "As it wound up, I had drank and got drunk in tons of barrooms, and had eaten and had great meals in tons of restaurants, so I thought that qualified me to open a bar and restaurant," Nix said. "But I quick learned that that wasn't the recipe for success."

Nix did succeed, however. While most new businesses experience some flux upon opening, the name Parkway Bakery and Tavern resulted in a more-than-steady stream of customers from the moment Nix reopened the doors. "I've had people in here ever since, crowds coming back to say, 'We've gotta go see Parkway, it's back open!'" Nix remarked. "It's really been magical."

Nix reopened Parkway on December 20, 2003, although no sandwiches were sold until January of the following year—instead, roast beef po-boys were given away free the remainder of that month—"for practice," in Nix's words. "Because we didn't really know what we were doin'," Nix said. "We really didn't have any big guns, and when you give away sandwiches, it's hard to get complaints. So, we didn't get any negative feedback. But it made us feel like we had made sandwiches a week, and then January 1 [2004] we opened. And we have been blessed for success. Though we have worked hard."

According to Nix, there were two things that were absolutely crucial he get right in order to succeed: the name Parkway Bakery and Tavern, which fortunately he was able to purchase with the building from the Timothy brothers, and the roast beef. When Parkway reopened, Nix naïvely asked the first customer what kind of po-boy he wanted. The reply was, "What do ya think, stupid? I want roast beef!"

"So they measured us against the roast beef, but the name got 'em here," Nix said. "And after they got here, they said, 'Gimme a roast beef, I'm gonna see if Parkway's really back or not.' And we passed." But the way Nix was able to win over returning customers was not by re-creating the previous owners' roast beef but by using his own mother's recipe from when she used to make pot roasts for the family after Sunday mass. After several "cook-offs" to sample potential recipes for Parkway's roast beef, Nix, his sisters and the rest of the family concluded that in this case, mother does know best.

Although Parkway had the bare necessities of the name and the roast beef down, Nix and his staff floundered somewhat due to lack of experience during that first year. When Parkway first reopened, Nix purchased the wrong kitchen equipment. Not only that, but he also placed it incorrectly during the installation. "So, unlike a basketball player pivoting on one foot, we were just running, useless steps," Nix remarked.

Fortunately, in this case, New Orleans sometimes provides an opportunity for a fresh start. After running Parkway for more than a year and a half with improper and misplaced equipment, at the end of August 2005 Hurricane Katrina flooded the restaurant. "Not far before the storm, I said, 'If I had my way, I'd throw all this crap on the street and buy it all over again and get it right,'" Nix said. "Well, guess what happened?"

Parkway flooded post-Katrina. *Parkway Bakery and Tavern.*

Because Nix took out loans to complete initial renovations, he was forced to buy ample insurance, providing the money to pair with his newly obtained restaurant know-how to finally outfit Parkway to perfection. A year and a half of making due with the wrong equipment installed incorrectly meant that Nix knew precisely how to get it right this time. "So, I bought all the right equipment, put it all in the right place, and we started shooting sandwiches out like machine gun bullets, like we do today. So Katrina was a big help."[10]

Another big help, in the early days of the rebooted Parkway as well as today, was Nix's nephew, Justin Kennedy. After spending countless childhood weekends helping his uncle with construction projects in his unconventional "toolshed," Kennedy was present for Parkway's opening day in December 2003, when he was eighteen years old. He has been an integral part of Parkway ever since.

Kennedy remembered the first day that Parkway reopened in 2003 vividly, but admitted that when it came to restaurant experience, at the time he knew little more than his uncle did. "I remember the first day we reopened, there's a line out the door. Of old people who wanted to see the place, wanted to revisit. And we had people cryin', right when they hit the door, before they got the first sandwich," Kennedy recalled. "And we didn't know what we were doin', you know? We did a good job, we learned you've gotta do a lot of research, and you've gotta make a lot of your own stuff, you do it from scratch, and what you can't do from scratch you get quality. And we've always stood behind that; that kept us going. But we definitely learned and are still learnin' as we go."[11]

The old adage that the best way to learn is by doing seems to ring true in the case of Parkway. Nix said that throughout the past fourteen years, he and his staff have had near constant revelations about how to maximize quality, minimize costs and streamline procedures.

Another revelation Nix had was about creating an employee culture of "kindness, trust and love," in his words. One of the ways he has helped cultivate that is by paying his employees well. When Parkway was first reopening, an outside advisor told Nix, "If you pay anybody more than $6,000, you'll be closed in ninety days." While Nix acknowledges that fifteen years ago there was perhaps more truth to that, he quickly learned that paying better wages created the employee culture he wanted to foster at Parkway. "What we wound up with was forty-nine angry employees, until we realized that we had to pay a decent living wage. And now, we're paying people...more, but we're paying less people," Nix said. "So actually now we have a culture who want to be here and are making a

Left: Manager Justin Kennedy at order counter. *Alexandra Kennon.*

Below: Longtime employee Michael Tannen at order counter. *Alexandra Kennon.*

Three-hundred-foot po-boy for the tricenntenial celebration. *Tammie Quintana Photography*.

decent wage, but the payroll hasn't really grown." For a restaurant that serves sandwiches likely born out of a workers' strike for better wages, this is felicitous.

Parkway's employee turnover is impressively low, as a result of Nix's philosophy. James Adam, who rode his bicycle to apply at Parkway when it first reopened back in 2003, still works there in 2018. Michael Tannen, whose brother introduced him to Nix after he moved to New Orleans from New York City back in 2004, has worked there for eleven years. And, of course, in addition to the workers who feel like family, there are Nix's actual blood relatives: his three sisters, particularly Eileen, who still works in the back office. Three of Eileen's children are also employed at Parkway: Justin manages the restaurant, Catherine manages the bar and Johny manages the kitchen.

In 2018, in celebration of New Orleans's tricentennial, Nix and his staff created a three-hundred-foot po-boy—an entire foot of fully dressed fried shrimp on Leidenheimer for each year since the city was founded, given away for free.[12] Although Nix never intended to go into the sandwich business, it's safe to say that he, his family and his staff have thoroughly embraced it. New Orleans, particularly the Mid-City neighborhood, has certainly embraced them in return.

Recipe from Parkway

Roast Beef

When Jay Nix first reopened Parkway in 2003, the customers judged whether the restaurant was truly back based on the roast beef. His mother's recipe for Sunday pot roasts was a hit, letting the locals know it was safe to welcome Parkway back. Originally, Justin Kennedy sent a recipe for ten pounds of chuck roast; it has been scaled down here to better fit a slow cooker at home.

A note regarding seasoning: Justin at Parkway mentioned in our interview that he recently started adding garlic to their roast beef, which had a great reception from customers. The author's test cook/ boyfriend, Dominic Rivera, is from the Southwest, so he also added a jalapeño, which adds a nice spice as well (although a true Louisianian can always just reach for the Crystal or TABASCO, alternately).

A note regarding bread: Parkway has used Leidenheimer Bakery bread since the original brick ovens installed by the Goerings flooded in 1978. Leidenheimer is sold under the name Reising's at Rouses Markets in South Louisiana.

2.5–3 pounds chuck roast
salt and pepper
½ yellow onion, chopped
4 stalks bunch celery, chopped
½ bell pepper, chopped
2 cloves garlic, minced (optional)
1 quart beef stock

Season roast liberally with salt and pepper. In a braising pot or slow cooker, add chuck roast, onion, celery, bell pepper, garlic (if desired) and beef stock. Roast may be browned and vegetables may be sautéed in skillet before slow cooking for additional flavor. Slowly cook at 250 degrees for about 4 to 6 hours, until it falls apart when handled with a fork.

Recipe adapted from Justin Kennedy at Parkway by Dominic Rivera.

Chapter 8
Pascal's Manale

(1913)

*Pascal's Manale customers always rate this establishment high in their praises of
the cuisine and the enjoyable atmosphere in which they dine.*
—Times-Picayune, *1953*

The Brocato family were far from the only Sicilians to find success in the
New Orleans culinary scene after the turn of the twentieth century.
While most Italian immigrants to the Crescent City during the 1900s hailed
from Sicilian towns such as Palermo, Cefalù or Ustica, the patriarch who
would come to open Manale's Restaurant, now Pascal's Manale, had a slightly
different background.[1] Frank Manale, along with his parents, Francesco and
Domenica (who went by Marmie), originated from Contessa Entellina, a
town founded by Albanians just outside Palermo, with a dialect and culture
distinctly different from those of most Sicilians.[2] The Manales and other
"Arbëreshë," as residents of Contessa Entellina are called, practiced a
variety of Catholicism that was more Byzantine than Roman and were
joined in New Orleans by many other Arbëreshë families—the Monteleones
among them, of one of the longest-standing continually family-run hotels in
America that sits on Royal Street housing the famed Carousel Bar.[3]

On April 22, 1892, young Frank Manale traveled with his parents and
six siblings (Francesca, Margherita, Antonia, Gioacchino, Rosalia and
Paulo) from the port of Palermo, Italy, to America. Just over a month of sea
travel later, accompanied by produce and goods from their home country,
the Manale family arrived in New Orleans on May 23. The children were

between ages two and twenty, and Frank fell right in the middle of them. Two years after moving to New Orleans, Frank's sister Francesca married another Arbëreshë immigrant named Matteo (or Martin) Joseph Radosta. Like the prior generation, Francesca and Matteo's marriage produced seven children: Pascal, Lulu, Mamie, Frank, Vitda Rose, Peter and Jake.

Meanwhile, their Uncle Frank had other plans in the works. In 1913, he opened a restaurant at the corner of Dryades and Napoleon Streets, in the building that formerly housed P. Buchler Grocery. Rather than attempting to replicate the French Creole fare popular in New Orleans then and now, Frank Manale and his family incorporated flavors and foods from their home country. Pasta, tomatoes, olives, spicy cured meats and anchovies were, and still are, peppered onto the restaurant's comforting yet refined Creole-Italian menu. The family joined in the efforts of the business, with Frank's mother and sisters working in the kitchen while his brothers and nephews ran the bar. Conveniently, an Italian butcher named Charles Ciacco next door provided meats to the Manales until 1954, when the butcher shop closed and the family bought it out and expanded the restaurant into the space.[4]

In a 2017 interview, Martin Radosta said of Frank Manale, "He was a bootlegger who owned racehorses and loved to play the stock market before the 1929 crash."[5] New Orleans was notoriously rife with mafia activity for decades after Manale's opened, with Carlos Marcello named mafia boss of the city in a backroom ceremony in a North Galvez nightclub in 1947.[6] Guns were fixtures at Manale's at the time, once kept hanging on the wall near the

Corner of Napoleon and Dryades in 1905. *DeFelice Family Collection.*

Pascal's Manale exterior, late 1930s. *DeFelice Family Collection.*

cash register, later stored more low-key in cubbies that remain today. One night in the 1930s, Frank and his wife, Alice, pulled into their driveway in Broadmoor when two armed men approached, demanding "Stick 'em up!" Frank reached for his gun as his nephew Frank Radosta, who lived nearby, pulled up from the restaurant and proceeded to chase the robbers to South Rendon Street, where he abandoned the chase after they opened fire on him. Frank Manale was taken to Baptist Hospital to treat a gunshot wound in his shoulder, although he told police he could think of no one with a motive to "get him."[7]

The bar at Manale's, now a long-revered local watering hole, earned a reputation even before the ratification of Prohibition. Frank and his family had a contract with Dixie Beer where Dixie supplied the Brunswick bar in exchange for carrying exclusively Dixie products. But it was the deals that happened off the record that are of interest. In 1917, Frank and his nephew Pascal Radosta were arrested for allowing a sixteen-year-old employee to deliver liquor. Once the Prohibition laws were passed, it is said that absinthe frappes and other boozy libations were served to patrons discreetly in coffee cups.[8]

Following the repeal of Prohibition in the 1930s, bar sales were better than ever. Manale's continued to incorporate liquor delivery into the business model, touting in a 1936 *Times-Picayune* advertisement that "a complete stock of wines, whiskeys, beer, gin, liqueurs, etc., is on hand at all times," with delivery available to "all sections of the city, day or night." Curbside service was also available then: "If you do not care to step out of the car and into the bar for your favorite cocktail or highball, or to make a purchase of packaged liquor, drive by Manale's and you will be promptly served at the curb." Pascal Radosta's skills as a bartender were lauded in particular. "Try Pascal out on a cocktail to test his knowledge and ability as a mixologist. You will agree with all Manale frequenters that he is without a peer in this department."[9]

Frank Manale married a girl named Alice Hager in 1920. The couple had no children, although Alice had a daughter named Dolores whom Frank helped raise. In 1937, Frank self-diagnosed a cold that in reality was double-pneumonia. Within forty-eight hours, he died in his home at the age of fifty-seven. Manale's fell into the hands of his nephews, the Radostas. Pascal Radosta, in particular, had been working the bar since he was nineteen, managing the bar when his uncle passed away. Pascal then stepped up to manage the business as a whole.[10] Keeping his Uncle Frank's influence strong, while adding some of his own, years later the restaurant's name was changed to what it goes by today: Pascal's Manale.[11] Other Radostas continued to contribute when Pascal took over, including

The Radostas and Manales at the bar. *DeFelice Family Collection.*

his brother Pete, who waited tables; Jake, who cooked; and Frank, who tended bar.[12]

In 1922, Pascal married Frances Sanson, a devout Catholic girl who had been heading into the convent before opting for family life instead. The couple settled into their home on Louisiana Avenue Parkway and raised four children: Frances, Virginia, Pascal Jr. and Martin John. Frances and Virginia, who enjoyed the benefits of being beautiful and young at a time when the New Orleans social scene was exploding, would become close friends of Ella and Adelaide Brennan. Isabel Monteleone, whose father owned the famed Royal Street Hotel, was also in their circle. None of Pascal's sisters married, but Lulu and Mamie frequently joined Frances at her and Pascal's home to stuff artichokes, make meatballs and prepare other staples for the restaurant.[13]

One of Pascal's Manale's most famous dishes, and arguably the restaurant's greatest contribution to the New Orleans culinary repertoire, is the Barbecue Shrimp. The elusive dish that reflects none of the mesquite sweet and smokiness of typical barbecue is said to have been invented for regular customer Vincent Sutro in 1954. The story goes that Sutro, upon

Pascal Jr., "Papa" Martin Radosta and Bruno the dog. *DeFelice Family Collection.*

returning from a trip to Chicago, asked Pascal's Manale chef, Jake Radosta, to re-create a dish he tried there containing shrimp, butter and a generous amount of pepper. Despite the vague specifications, Jake Radosta created his interpretation of the dish and served it. Vincent Sutro proclaimed that it was not the same exact dish he ate in Chicago—in fact, it was better. Barbecue Shrimp became a permanent staple on the menu at Pascal's Manale, although no one is quite certain why "Barbecue" was included in the name. A running theory is that perhaps it has to do with the dish being created around the same time the backyard barbecue craze was sweeping America in the 1950s. Regardless of where the name comes from, Barbecue Shrimp is now a long-standing New Orleans culinary staple, thanks to its origins with Jake Radosta and Mr. Sutro at Pascal's Manale. While home-cook approximations and alternate interpretations of the recipe exist, the exact recipe for the Barbecue Shrimp served at Pascal's Manale remains a closely guarded family secret.[14]

When Pascal's younger brother Peter was sent to army camp during the Second World War, a large party was thrown at the restaurant to send him off. Pascal's Manale continued strong through the war, touting in a 1944 *Times-Picayune* advertisement, "At Manale's, you see your friends, and your friends' friends, many of them in Uncle Sam's becoming uniform…and the service, it may be said, will measure up to, if not improve upon, anything the public has been accustomed to in these wartime days." The restaurant settled into its place as a family and neighborhood fixture. Times of joy and difficulty were celebrated or braced for at Pascal's Manale.[15]

Pascal eventually was known throughout New Orleans more familiarly as "Pas." Even Louisiana's longest-serving member of the United States House of Representatives, F. Edward Hebert, referred to him as such, signing the Pascal's Manale guestbook, "It all began at Manale's with Pascal." Politicians were not the only sort to frequent the Napoleon and Dryades fixture: athletes, actors and all manner of local and national celebrities have made their way through Pascal's Manale, many of whom are immortalized on the wood-paneled walls of the bar. Dickie Brennan Jr. ate his last meal with his father at Pascal's. Archie Manning remembered how crowded the bar was when he was first drafted as quarterback in 1971, but he brought Peyton, Eli and Cooper there for dinner after every Sunday game regardless. Elton John, Buzz Aldrin, Marilyn Monroe with Gregory Peck as her escort, Liberace and countless others have enjoyed meals there. Even with high-brow guests, Pascal was known to run the restaurant to his preference, allowing very few concessions. "Manale's is the only restaurant I know where the customer is always wrong," Hebert remarked. "[Pascal] ran the restaurant as he pleased."[16]

In May 1954, Pascal's friends and neighbors threw a party celebrating him at his own restaurant. Most of New Orleans's most respected businessmen were in attendance to honor Pascal and thank him for the contribution of his restaurant to their Garden District neighborhood. Four years later, on July 23, 1958, Pascal suffered a heart attack while watching a televised boxing match in his office, dying in the bar of his restaurant. Pascal's brothers Pete and Jake, along with his sons Pascal Jr. (who went by simply "Junior") and Martin John, stepped up to continue Pascal's legacy and namesake.

Pascal's two daughters, Virginia and Frances, settled down from their lives as New Orleans socialites to marry the DeFelice brothers, Stephen and Savare, from Plaquemines Parish. The brothers owned a canning plant in Myrtle Grove, where Virginia and Savare would move to raise their children. Although they opted for rural rather than restaurant life, each son Frances birthed was brought directly from Touro Hospital to Pascal's Manale before returning to the country. When the children were older, the family was returned closer to New Orleans. Martin John and Junior retired not long

Bob, Sandy, Ginny, Savare, Virginia and Mark on New Year's Eve 1988. *DeFelice Family Collection.*

after, leaving operations of the restaurant primarily to Virginia and Frances. Frances, in particular, embraced her role as the glamorous hostess, known for a sparkling diamond brooch in the shape of a shrimp.[17]

Frances's nephews, Pascal III (who went by Jay) and Scott, assisted their aunt closely with managing Pascal's Manale. When Frances's husband, Steve, died in the 1980s, Frances became overwhelmed with the demands of the business. Virginia and Savare stepped in as sole proprietors, with Savare running the front of house and Virginia managing the office. Virginia and Savare's children—Sandy, Bob, Ginny and Mark—worked in the restaurant throughout high school and while attending university.[18]

The family nature of Pascal's Manale is reflected in the warm hospitality of its staff. One waitress, Catherine Daniels, served at Manale's for fifty years. Karry Byrd has been a fixture in the Manale's kitchen for more than forty years; his twin brother, Kenny, at one point worked with him as well. Longevity is a running theme: Pascal's nephew Johny Sansone was a staple regular at the bar for more than fifty years, always equipped with a story, the theme frequently racehorses.[19]

THESE DAYS ON NAPOLEON AVENUE

"Uncle Jake" Radosta, Pascal's little brother and the longtime chef at Pascal's Manale, created the majority of the restaurant's menu during his extensive tenure in the kitchen. "Uncle Jake" passed his beloved recipes and practices on to his nephew Mark DeFelice, chef-owner of Pascal's Manale today. In 2019, Pascal's Manale is officially the second-oldest restaurant in New Orleans to be continually owned by the same family, and it is truly a family affair. Each one of Virginia and Savare DeFelice's eight grandchildren worked in the restaurant at some point growing up, typically starting out dusting the many picture frames holding celebrity photographs on the walls of the bar.[20]

DeFelice pointed out that of each of the four generations that has run Pascal's Manale, he and the rest of the fourth generation have been at it the longest at thirty-one years—more than one-third of the life of the restaurant. "We got a couple of family members who come here and their grandfather and their father ate here. So it's generational; we have second- and third-generation customers and friends who come here and eat," DeFelice explained. "So as far as the history goes, we've been around a while, and we take care of our locals and our good customers and good friends over

Chef-owner Mark DeFelice. *Alexandra Kennon.*

Pascal's Manale honors the celebrities who have enjoyed Barbecue Shrimp and other dishes at Pascal's over the years on the walls of the bar. *Alexandra Kennon.*

the years. So between the longevity in the kitchen and the longevity of our customers, I think that's a good mix in the history of Manale's."

When Hurricane Katrina struck the city, Pascal's Manale would not reopen until the Thursday after the following Mardi Gras in early February 2006. Like most businesses, the employees were scattered across the country, including longtime chef Frank Robinson, whose house in St. Rose was destroyed. Robinson had considered retiring prior to Katrina, and the storm solidified the decision. Catherine Daniels, the waitress of more than fifty years, also retired after the hurricane. Because of the lack of staff, the DeFelices stopped opening the restaurant on Sundays, exempting special occasions—an effect of the storm still evident in the restaurant's operating hours today.[21]

While Mark runs the kitchen, his sister Ginny's domain is the office. Ginny's daughter, Elizabeth, runs the restaurant's social media and coordinates private parties and events. Sandy still greets guests as a hostess, but often her daughter, Dana, can be found at the host's stand as well. Chef Mark's daughter, Rachel, also pursued a career in the culinary field, obtaining a degree from the John Folse Culinary Institute in Thibodaux. In 2018, she was employed as sous chef at Cavan on Magazine Street, but her cousin Elizabeth told the *New Orleans Advocate* that she hopes Rachel will one day return to the family restaurant.[22] If the staff is not literal family,

Contemporary bar. *Alexandra Kennon.*

Bartender Jerry Cooper serves heavy pours of drinks and sarcasm. *Alexandra Kennon.*

they're usually treated as such regardless. The same goes for customers at Pascal's Manale.

Mark DeFelice emphasized the loyalty of many regular customers, some of whose families have been dining at Pascal's for generations. "We have some of the best regular customers of anybody. They're very loyal to us, they're very successful in business in the New Orleans community and they're tried-and-true Pascal's Manale fans," DeFelice said. "And I see it every day, you know, every week."[23]

"I love it, man. What I enjoy about this is people. Working for the family, that I enjoy," said oyster shucker Thomas "Uptown T" Stewart, who has been working at Pascal's for about thirty-six years. "I mean, if I've been here for that period of time, there's something I must like about it or have in my heart. Waking up in the mornings to get here in the afternoon, put the time in, leave out of one building to another, from my home to my job. Not many people can say they do that without getting bored or tired of being in that place all the time. And it gets hectic, but you know that's what you have to do, and you can't just shake a stick at it so you just have to suck it up, muscle up and work it out."[24]

Banquet room. *Alexandra Kennon*.

Main dining room. *Alexandra Kennon*.

"World's Most Famous Oyster Shucker" Thomas "Uptown T" Stewart. *Alexandra Kennon.*

Pascal's Manale from Napoleon Avenue today. *Alexandra Kennon.*

Recipe from Pascal's Manale

Barbecue Shrimp

The name has nothing to do with barbecue but came from around the same time that backyard barbecues were becoming popular in the 1950s. Perhaps the dish adapted the name because the two sauces, though dissimilar, are similar in orangish-brown color.

Note: The exact recipe for the Barbecue Shrimp Mark DeFelice serves at Pascal's Manale is a family secret, but this home approximation works nicely. Typically Barbecue Shrimp are cooked and served with the heads on because they contribute to the flavor of the sauce. This home approximation supplements the flavor of the shrimp heads with additional seasoning but can also be made with the head-on shrimp for even more flavor.

1 pound or 21 to 25 headless shrimp (wild caught is vastly superior to farmed shrimp)
Manale Spice Mix (see following)
½ teaspoon chopped garlic
½ cup Lea & Perrins Worcestershire sauce
¼ teaspoon TABASCO sauce
¾ cup olive oil
½ cup white wine

Manale Spice Mix

4 teaspoons black pepper
¼ teaspoon cayenne pepper
1 teaspoon paprika
1 teaspoon salt
1 teaspoon thyme
1 teaspoon oregano
1 teaspoon basil

Wash and pat shrimp dry. Add Manale Spice Mix, garlic, Lea & Perrins and TABASCO. Then pour the olive oil over the shrimp, adding the white wine. Stir together. (Although it's not in Mark's recipe, I saw him put a big pat of butter in the pan.) Cook over high heat until shrimp are done, approximately 10 minutes. Do not overcook shrimp.

To Serve

Serve the shrimp in a wide soup bowl and have hard-crust French bread on hand for dipping in the buttery, peppery sauce. Peel the shrimp and eat.

Recipe courtesy of Pascal's Manale restaurant.

Chapter 9
Napoleon House

(1914)

*Lunching within the yellowed walls of Napoleon House, I watch the bartender
pour two Pimm's Cups at a time, moving precisely through steps that result in the
best version of the drink I've had.*
—M. Carrie Allen, Washington Post

While most of the buildings that serve as vessels for New Orleans's
great old restaurants have storied histories of their own, the
Napoleon House and the National Historic Landmark building it resides
in makes an all but irrefutable claim to the most captivating pre-restaurant
past. In 1914, Giuseppe (Joseph) Impastato opened a grocery and tavern in
the building that would set the stage for his family to build and sustain one
of New Orleans's most iconic restaurants and bars for more than a century.
Yet one hundred years before the Impastatos moved in, when the building
was the home of Mayor Nicholas Girod, there was an elaborate scheme
in the works on the very site that would become a mecca for Pimm's Cups
and muffulettas.

At the tail end of the eighteenth century, François Claude Girod possessed
a corner lot at Chartres and St. Louis Streets and built a two-story building
on the side closest to the Mississippi River in 1794. When Claude passed
away in 1814, he left the property to his brother (and at the time New Orleans
mayor), Nicholas Girod. That year, Nicholas set to work having the grand
three-story townhouse added. It was Nicholas's motivation for building the
striking French-style home that would become the source of oft-repeated

Vintage exterior shot of the Napoleon House. *From Thelma Hecht Coleman Memorial Collection via Tulane University Digital Library.*

legend surrounding the building.[1] Like most good New Orleans legends, it is quite possible there is truth to these stories; it is also possible they have been fabricated for the sake of entertainment. Regardless, they continue to stoke the imaginations of locals and visitors to the French Quarter as they have for close to two hundred years.

As echoed incessantly on the corner of St. Louis and Chartres from tour guides, carriage drivers and the plaque on the building's wall, the story goes that Nicholas Girod hatched a plot during his tenure as mayor to rescue the exiled Napoleon Bonaparte from his imprisonment on the island of St. Helena. Although Nicholas Girod arrived in New Orleans when it was part of a Spanish colony and presided as mayor after it became American, he himself was a Frenchman originating from Savoy in the Western Alps. A staunch devotee of Emperor Napoleon, joined by many New Orleanians in his fervency at the time, Girod and others funded the construction of a fast-moving ship named the *Seraphine* sometime around 1821. The plan was to board the ship under the cover of night for a secret journey with the goal of breaking Napoleon out of his island prison isolated in the South Atlantic. Allegedly, the expedition was to be led by Dominique You, Jean Lafitte's lieutenant from the Battle of New Orleans, although other versions of the tale cast Lafitte himself at the helm. The idea was that once Napoleon was recaptured, he would be brought back to New Orleans, where Nicholas Girod offered his newly completed home for the emperor to reside. But three days before the expedition was set to depart, word was received that their beloved Napoleon had died—the cause being either stomach cancer or arsenic poisoning, depending on whom is surveyed. Regardless, with no emperor to rescue and re-home, Girod and his co-conspirators' plot was soiled.[2]

Of course, this is history recounted by New Orleans's often loose standards when it comes to evidence, in a city where an entertaining narrative is often upheld higher than fact. What we do know definitively about Nicholas Girod is also fascinating, but it is admittedly difficult to compete with elaborate conspiracies to kidnap an emperor. We know that Nicholas Girod was mayor of New Orleans during the War of 1812 through the Battle of New Orleans's conclusion in January 1815, although the battle took place after the treaty to end the war had already been signed. During this tumultuous period for the city, Girod was a crucial leader when it came to assisting General Andrew Jackson recruit and organize local militias in addition to funding supplies. It is said that with Girod's French pride came a staunch distaste for the British that helped motivate his actions.[3]

Girod had no children of his own, but other relatives of his remained in the home he had built until close to the turn of the twentieth century, by which point most of them were deceased or elsewhere. At the start of the 1900s, the first floor of the already legendary building became Labourdette's Grocery. The Impastato family arrived in New Orleans from their native Sicily when Joe, their oldest son, was fifteen years old in 1901.[4] Due to the surge of Sicilians to the city, pasta factories were nearly as plentiful in the French Quarter as bars at that time, and thus Joe's first job in America was at Greco's Macaroni Factory. Joe worked his way up to a management position but was still only making two dollars for an entire day's work.[5]

Black-and-white exterior with palm from the Louisiana Supreme Court Building across the street. *Ralph Brennan Restaurant Group.*

An enterprising young man, Joe saved his money and, by 1914, had begun to rent the iconic corner building that formerly housed Nicholas Girod, then Labourdette's Grocery (but lamentably never Napoleon Bonaparte) for $20 per month. He and his family continued to operate a corner grocery while living in apartments above. In 1916, Joe married Rosie Giuffre, who would become his business partner and handle the accounting for the family business. In 1920, he bought the Nicholas Girod House and the grocery store and apartments within it for $14,000.[6]

From there, the Impastato's grocery would begin to evolve into the bar and eatery it remains. During Prohibition, family members later admitted that a side room was used to serve alcohol and that "Uncle Joe" even made his own libations to sell. "Wine and beer, though, [Joe Impastato] did not like whiskey at all," explained Chris Montero, executive chef of Napoleon House today. Joe Impastato's distaste for whiskey and those who imbibed in it is the reason the originally British Pimm's Cup remains Napoleon House's signature drink. "He did not like hard alcohol, he did not like whiskey drinkers. He thought they were rude and crude, you know, he's a Catholic Italian—loves drinking, but not hard whiskey. He liked wine and beer," Montero pointed out. "And so the drink that he wanted to sell as a cocktail was the Pimm's Cup, because it was low alcohol."[7]

Today, more Pimm's no. 1 liqueur is distributed to the Napoleon House than any other bar in America, and many agree with Montero in crediting Joe Impastato with the drink becoming available in the United States at all. "So the reason the Pimm's Cup tradition is here is because of the Napoleon House, and this one character. He introduced it," Montero said. "So to me, that's a really neat story. And the Pimm's people tell us that we sell more Pimm's no. 1 than anyone in America, not even close. And we're number two behind the bar in London that takes credit for originating the Pimm's Cup."[8]

At some point during the 1920s, although the specifications of when exactly are debated, the Impastatos also began to sell sandwiches from the corner business. The clientele was made up predominantly of workers from the nearby docks, therefore early iterations of the po-boy and muffuletta were sold to accommodate a laborer's schedule, as the sandwiches could easily be enjoyed on the go. The muffuletta (New Orleans's famous Italian sandwich made with cured meats, cheeses and olive salad) remains the most popular food item on the menu today, although the Napoleon House distinguishes its creation from the original at Central Grocery around the corner by toasting the sandwich rather than serving it cold.[9]

Joe would bring his Victrola down from his apartment during business hours to play opera and classical records for his customers, and a soundtrack of exclusively opera and classical music maintains that atmosphere he created today. In 1935, Joe had the tile work laid in the doorway marking his business "The Napoleon House," as well as a marble-tiled floor installed in the front bar and dining room. The craftsman who laid the tiles also created a chess table that today remains imbedded in a round table in the center of the main room.[10]

In the 1940s, Joe tired of the long hours required to operate his grocery/restaurant/bar and leased the first floor for a time to a group that used it as a dance hall where bookies also took bets on racehorses.[11] At the conclusion of World War II in 1946, Joseph's much younger brother, Peter, left Europe, where he was serving in the army, to join his family at their growing business in New Orleans. With his younger brother to step in and lead the operation, Joe remained content in his retirement, although he would live in the building until his death at the age of one hundred.[12]

Peter had been born in New Orleans and attended Spring Hill College in Alabama. Before serving in the army during the war, he married Tammie

Former owner/bar manager Peter Impastato. *Ralph Brennan Restaurant Group.*

Samaritano; the couple had four daughters and one son. Soon enough, Peter set about returning the Napoleon House to its place as a corner restaurant and bar. By the 1950s, Peter's family had moved out to Gentilly. Pete would take the bus to work and get off at the French Market, where he would purchase any necessary supplies before walking into the French Quarter.[13]

Peter Impastato's generous tendencies, in a way, continued the philanthropic traditions of the mayor who formerly resided in his building, although it is doubtful he realized it. While Pete did not drink or smoke, somewhat of a paradox for a New Orleans barkeep, he was frequently observed providing beds or meals for the homeless or offering a dollar or two to those in need of it. Customers observed that he would prefer doing charity work to working in his own bar and restaurant, but they loved him despite or because of this.[14]

Peter discouraged his own children from becoming involved in the family business, likely due to his own aversion to the vices that kept it running. Nevertheless, his son Salvatore would join his family at the Napoleon House, eventually taking the reins from his father after Peter passed in 1971.[15] Sal joining the family business at the age of twenty-four marked the second generation of Impastatos at the Napoleon House. In 1970, just before Peter's death, the building his family so diligently kept up was placed in the National Register of Historic Places.[16]

When "Uncle Joe" Impastato celebrated his one hundredth birthday, he began his day with a cup of coffee with a shot of Wild Turkey in it, as his nephew Sal told the *Times-Picayune States Item* he always did in his later years (apparently his aversion to whiskey had been abandoned by the time he reached a century of age). An estimated crowd of four hundred of Joe Impastato's closest friends came to the Napoleon House to wish him a happy birthday and partake in the cutting of three massive birthday cakes. When time came to blow out the candles after "Happy Birthday" had been sung, Joe "walked over and blew out the six candles without the slightest difficulty."[17] When asked for his secret to longevity, ever-Italian Uncle Joe answered, "I eat pasta. I lived good, I rest, I worked hard, and I am honest."[18]

Founding owner of the Napoleon House Joe Impastato. *Ralph Brennan Restaurant Group*.

Sal continued to operate the Napoleon House, accompanied by his wife, Vivian; sisters, Maria Impastato and Janie Lala; and brother-in-law, Leonard Lala, until well into the twenty-first century. Vivian did the accounting, Maria oversaw the kitchen, Janie handled banquets and Sal more or less filled in the gaps as front of house and maintenance.[19]

On busy nights, when the restaurant was open, Sal was always present in the service staff uniform of a white shirt and black bowtie to greet guests at the door and oversee service in the dining room. On Tuesday, he would arrive at the building in work clothes, checking every door hinge and every lock, flitting back and forth to his tool room filled with all manner of screws and nails and other hardware that gathers over one hundred years of owning a building. "The buck started and stopped with Sal. He made every rule, every policy, and he saw to it that everything was done. Just mind-boggling to see how many things he dealt with, and none of it organized like we do it today, with technology," marveled current executive chef Chris Montero. "All on a piece of paper or in his head. And a little rolodex of phone numbers for when he had problems that he couldn't resolve."[20]

When Hurricane Katrina blew through New Orleans, the Napoleon House emerged relatively unscathed, and within weeks, the Impastatos were back in the French Quarter working toward reopening. Although structural damage was minimal, few of their employees returned after the hurricane.[21] Another devastating effect of Katrina for the Napoleon House, as well as Central Grocery and other muffuletta vendors, was that the Union Bakery that made its muffuletta buns never reopened following the storm.[22]

In 2014, with the Impastato legacy within the Mayor Girod Building going strong for more than a century, Sal became weary of the constant

Gas lamp inside the Napoleon House. *Alexandra Kennon.*

Above: Stairwell inside the Napoleon House. *Alexandra Kennon.*

Left: The attic of the Napoleon House. *Alexandra Kennon.*

upkeep and responsibility required to run a restaurant in a more than two-hundred-year-old building. Although Sal's son Nicholas had worked in the family business for more than thirty years, he did not want to take on the responsibility of operating it.[23] Thus the difficult question arose: with whom could the Impastatos trust their legendary restaurant and building?

THE BRENNAN YEARS

Meanwhile, a block over on Royal Street, Ralph Brennan was in the process of completing renovations to reopen his own family legacy. The Impastatos made the decision that if Brennan were capable of restoring Brennan's while maintaining its tradition and soul, he could surely do the same for the Napoleon House. The Impastatos had their CPA call Brennan to run the idea by him. Throughout his life, Brennan had periodically popped into the Napoleon House for a cup of red beans and rice or a Sazerac and knew what the corner restaurant and building meant to the city. "Oh my God," he thought. "What an opportunity. What an iconic restaurant and bar."[24]

At first, the Impastatos had to meet with Brennan in secrecy to avoid the rumors that would erupt if they were seen together. They met on Sundays at the Napoleon House when the restaurant was closed and came to an agreement about the numbers fairly quickly, according to Brennan. "And then it kind of stopped, and I think what they had to deal with was the reality of selling it," Brennan postulated. "That they'd grown up there." Eventually, Sal called Brennan and said he and his family were ready to close the sale. The timing, however, was not ideal—Brennan was still in the midst of renovating Brennan's and getting everything prepared for its reopening. They agreed to hold off a few more months, and finally, on May 1 (during the week between Jazz Fest weekends is how Brennan remembered it), the sale was finalized.[25] The more-than-century-old Napoleon House and the more-than-two-centuries-old building housing it from that point onward have remained in the hands of Ralph Brennan.

Of course, New Orleanians' allegiance to tradition meant that the response to Brennan purchasing the Napoleon House was all but uproarious at first. The concern was that Brennan would make changes to their beloved

The outside of the Napoleon House today—horse-drawn carriages are commonplace on the corner. *Ralph Brennan Restaurant Group.*

institution, and to them, any change made to such a legendary restaurant would surely constitute its ruin. Ralph Brennan, being born and raised in New Orleans and having enjoyed many Sazeracs at the Napoleon House himself, knew better than to make any tangible alterations. "Sal and I had a handshake agreement that we would leave it alone," Brennan said. "And we really have."[26]

During the transition between owners, the Napoleon House did not once close for business. A month prior to when Brennan finally took ownership on May 21, 2015, Brennan's executive chef, Chris Montero, went in to work with the Impastato family, particularly Sal and Maria, who he says were the primary managers, to observe their practices. "And our goal was to, number one, honor the great legacy of the Impastato family and those great dishes and Pimm's Cups and things that were famous—if it ain't broke, you don't fix it," Montero said.

While the service, atmosphere and dishes were to remain unchanged, Montero set about finding ways to make the business more efficient. "Because what I observed from the moment I walked in the door was this forgotten, lost business model. What we would refer to as a 'mom and pop operation'

Left: Front door tiles of the Napoleon House. *Alexandra Kennon*.

Below: Main dining room and bar. *Alexandra Kennon*.

Above: Courtyard at the Napoleon House, still maintaining its historic appearance despite renovations. *Alexandra Kennon.*

Left: Executive Chef Chris Montero on the stairs. *Alexandra Kennon.*

Executive Chef Chris Montero in the cupola, which has one of the best views of the city. *Alexandra Kennon.*

inside of a multimillion-dollar business. Something you'd rarely ever see today," Montero marveled. He began to incorporate certain restaurant procedures that are typically commonplace today—things like expediting in the kitchen and food runners. The experience for diners was unaltered, but within a matter of weeks, output had been increased by 25 percent.[27] All of the original employees were offered to maintain their jobs at the Napoleon House, including Sal's son Nicholas Impastato, although he left the business after the sale.[28]

While most of Montero's changes have been modernizations behind the scenes, he admits one particular subtle improvement. Amusingly, in this area Montero implemented a *more* old-fashioned technique than the one already in place. The Impastatos had begun to utilize a large stainless steel Hobart mixer to blend the olive salad together, while Montero encouraged resorting back to a simple bowl-and-spoon method instead. "So this is diametrically opposed to what I was just telling you, about putting in some more modern techniques to make it more efficient, where in this case, the best method was the old method: hand-making olive salad with a big bowl and spoon, because you want to fold together these ingredients, for the preservation and for the integrity. It just makes for a way better product," Montero said. "And

Mario Suazo, who has been a bartender at Napoleon House for nineteen years, fifteen for the Impastatos and four for Brennan, and has doubtless made more Pimm's Cups than any other human. *Alexandra Kennon.*

Uncle Joe wouldn't have done it sixty years ago in a big mixer, that's how he would have done it. Sometimes the old techniques are the best."[29]

While Sal had diligently worked to upkeep the building, any structure dating back to 1814 inevitably needs restorative work sooner or later. Brennan's team set about restoring the building slowly, piece by piece, always with the goal of not making it apparent that work had been done. The second-floor rooms, which previously housed the Impastatos, were remodeled but kept as close to the original as possible. While the paint colors were matched, Brennan admitted that they could not find the precise fabric for the draperies, so a very similar Napoleonic-themed fabric was chosen instead. After the building was re-stuccoed, the walls were sprayed with buttermilk so the mold would return the aged look of the building. "And we're working with a wonderful architect, someone I grew up with," Brennan said. "He does a lot of historical renovations. Because what we're trying to do is do the work that needs to be done to preserve the buildings for another two hundred years and not let people know. Do it in a way that it's not apparent that we're taking the building apart and putting it back together."[30]

One change that Brennan and Montero admit has been fairly substantial is with banquet and private event business on the second floor of the building. While the downstairs portion of the restaurant slings essentially the same muffulettas and po-boys as ever, banquet dinners with menus ranging from hundred-year-old traditional Creole recipes to vegan gastronomy have been hosted upstairs where Napoleon was once intended to live. Parties seek out the Napoleon House not solely for the cuisine but also for the rich history of the building, which Montero is frequently asked to talk about before the meal is served. One client told Montero, "This wasn't just a meal, it was a total experience: a destination history tour and some really great food."[31]

When it came to hiring Chris Montero as executive chef, it was a clear choice because of his passion for history and background working for Brennan since 1999. While some of Montero's friends thought it might be a difficult transition for him to go from elevated fine dining to the more casual cuisine offered at the Napoleon House, Montero said that could not be further from the truth between the two portions of the business he runs on the first and second floors of the building. "It offered everything inside of what the restaurant is: an iconic, authentic, not like any restaurant in a lot of ways, it's as much of a museum as it is a restaurant," Montero mused. He also appreciated the opportunity to offer popular, authentic New Orleans cuisine. "What we really eat here. Shrimp po-boys and

Pete Impastato, Sal Impastato and Napoleon on the wall of the bar. *Alexandra Kennon.*

The Napoleon House today from the corner of Chartres and St. Louis Streets. *Alexandra Kennon*.

gumbo, you know. And it's not a stretch at all to say that's why locals love it," Montero said pridefully. "Because we don't go the route of institutions in the high tourist areas that don't necessarily do it authentically. We do it as good as you're going to get it at any neighborhood popular dining destination. So I love that, that's a no-brainer, doing that well, that's something I have a passion for."[32]

While the Napoleon House's upstairs banquet business has grown, Sal has remained an advisor to Brennan and his team for five years, ensuring that the downstairs restaurant and bar remain more or less unchanged from when his Uncle Joe established it. Although Sal's contract as advisor ends in 2020, portraits of him; his father, Peter; his uncle, Joe; and, of course, Napoleon will continue to knowingly watch diners enjoying their Pimm's Cups from their place among New Orleans legends for a long time to come.

Recipe from the Napoleon House

Muffuletta
Yields: 2–4 servings

1 (9-inch-round) seeded muffuletta bun or Italian seeded bread, halved
extra virgin olive oil
4 slices ham
5 slices Genoa salami
2 slices pastrami
3 slices provolone cheese
3 slices Swiss cheese
⅔ cup Napoleon House Olive Salad (recipe follows)

Preheat oven to 350 degrees Fahrenheit. Brush bottom and top half of bun lightly with oil. Layer ham, salami, pastrami and cheeses on bottom half of bun. Top with Napoleon House Olive Salad and cover with top half of bun. Wrap in foil. Bake until thoroughly heated, about 20 minutes. Unwrap and cut in half or quarters.

Olive Salad
Yields: 3 cups

1 cup pimiento-stuffed Spanish queen olives, chopped
½ cup canned chickpeas, drained and coarsely chopped
½ cup pickled vegetables*, drained and coarsely chopped
⅓ cup canned artichoke hearts, drained and coarsely chopped
¼ cup cocktail onions, drained and coarsely chopped
¼ cup finely chopped green bell pepper
1 tablespoon capers, drained and chopped
½ teaspoon minced garlic
¼ cup extra-virgin olive oil
2 tablespoons red wine vinegar
1 teaspoon dried oregano
½ teaspoon ground black pepper

In a large bowl, combine olives, chickpeas, pickled vegetables, artichoke hearts, onions, bell pepper, capers and garlic. Add oil, vinegar, oregano and pepper, stirring to combine. Cover and refrigerate for at least 8 hours. Will keep refrigerated for up to 1 week.

*Note: Napoleon House uses giardiniera, a mixture of pickled carrot, cauliflower, celery and green pepper.

Recipe courtesy of Chris Montero at the Napoleon House, as adapted from the Impastatos' recipe.

Chapter 10

Arnaud's

(1918)

*It might properly be said also that Arnaud's "is" the heart of the Vieux Carré,
for, in this commodious eating place, under the urbane, Old-worldly direction of
The Count (Arnaud Cazenave, proprietor) himself, the patron is sure to feel that
he is enjoying the best New Orleans has to offer in the way of food and service
and in an atmosphere that is Vieux Carré down to the last little detail.*
—Times-Picayune, *1947*

Arnaud Cazenave was born in France in the year 1877 and traveled to
America at the young age of sixteen, just before the twentieth century
turned, easily making a home in perpetually French-obsessed New Orleans.[1]
"Count" Arnaud Cazenave's title does not come so much from his position
of nobility as it does his eccentrically hospitable personality. As far as New
Orleans was concerned, Count Arnaud might as well have been the highest-
ranking nobleman in the city—he and his restaurant were beloved by enough
New Orleans royalty to merit the title.

Cazenave began his career as a wine salesman, and like his friend and rival
Owen Brennan, his first business venture in New Orleans was a small bar and
eatery in what would later be known, and still is, as the Old Absinthe House.
Cazenave's Bourbon Street tavern was a success almost immediately upon
opening in 1918, largely because Count Arnaud embodied New Orleans's
lust for life and good food to the fullest. According to the *Arnaud's Restaurant
Cookbook*, "For him, a simple, less-than-festive meal was a shamefully wasted
opportunity for making the better." Thus, at the Count's restaurant, an

opportunity to serve or enjoy an extravagant meal was never missed. He regarded New Orleans as the "Paris of America" and took great pride in contributing to what he believed was without contest "and without boasting" the superior food city in the New World.[2]

In under two years, Cazenave's business had outgrown its limited quarters on Bourbon Street. When a former warehouse nearby on Bienville Street became available, Count Arnaud was quick to purchase it and have the space transformed into his restaurant. The 1920 Room, an intimate dining room for two to twelve guests that today is decorated with lavish red-and-gold wallpaper, was named for the occasion of Arnaud's moving into the current main building. In the following years, as business continued to grow and prosper, the Count purchased other adjacent properties and continued to expand, eventually encompassing thirteen total buildings, in the process claiming the title of the largest restaurant in New Orleans, which Arnaud's maintains today. Call buttons are used for guests to summon waiters through the labyrinth-like passageways to a particular dining room.[3]

When Cazenave opened his restaurant in the smaller first location on Bourbon Street in 1918, Madame Pierre was hired as his initial chef. Of French descent and training but also skilled in the more Spanish style of cooking, her proficiency preparing Creole cuisine helped ensure the success of Count Arnaud's venture. Louis Lamothe was then hired to run the kitchen after Arnaud's was moved into its larger permanent location. In his home country of France, Lamothe apprenticed under the Gardere brothers, who served as chefs to Napoleon III. When his culinary training was complete, Lamothe decided to make use of it in New Orleans, quickly striking up a friendship with the also-French Count. Lamothe trained other chefs at Arnaud's, and his influence in the grand kitchen there would continue to be touted by the restaurant for decades.[4]

One could say that Arnaud's rose to popularity in its first decade despite the misfortune of opening just before Prohibition began. One could more accurately make a case that Arnaud's early popularity was due in large part to the fact that Cazenave was so deft at avoiding the Prohibition laws. Right at the end of the Prohibition era in 1932, undercover agents charged the restaurant with serving them whiskey highballs on multiple occasions. The agents, one of whom admitted to posing as Nicaraguan to win the waiters' loyalty, also said they bought a pint of liquor from one of the waiters during the stint. Cazenave's attorney sought to quash the indictment, partially on the grounds that his client, the Count, was cited as a "habitual liquor law violator" when he allegedly had only one prior case against him.[5] Although

od job of playing coy, with less need for subtlety
s, "Throughout the Twenties, liquor and classic
naud's but always under cover of hard-to-find
k bars and coffee cups." In time, federal liquor
t, and he was imprisoned for a brief period as
hile, his restaurant was padlocked. Knowing
...ves an exciting story, particularly over a meal, Cazenave
parlayed his newfound infamy into more press for Arnaud's.[6]

By the 1930s, Arnaud's was regarded as one of the finest and most successful restaurants in the city. Not only did well-to-do locals and businessmen working on Canal Street make meals at Arnaud's a regular occurrence, but the restaurant was also a favorite with tourists, especially of the celebrity variety. Count Arnaud and his socialite/actress daughter, Germaine Cazenave Wells, attracted many VIPs of the era, ranging from Arthur Godfrey to Loretta Young and Errol Flynn. One of the most oft-repeated stories has New Orleans mayor Robert Maestri turning to Franklin

Historic exterior of Arnaud's with vintage cars. *Arnaud's Restaurant.*

Roosevelt as they dined on Oysters Rockefeller at Arnaud's and ᵪ president, "How ya like dem ersters?"[7]

In 1939, when the original restaurant was consistently reaching caₚ and mandating that Arnaud's devotees wait on the sidewalk often exteᵣ periods of time for a table, Cazenave decided it was time for an expansₐ Never one to do things halfway, he doubled the original space of ᵢ restaurant, erecting an entirely new building and a massive undergrouᵣ cellar. "In the past, Arnaud's dining rooms and kitchens have been taxeᵣ far beyond their capacity at certain seasons, particularly Carnival, and it was to relieve this situation that Arnaud's has doubled its space," Count Cazenave told the *Times-Picayune* when the expansions were completed. Even in 1939, attention was paid to the integrity of the historic structure, and a new building was erected behind the first rather than disturbing the architecture of the original.[8]

The new building included a massive kitchen that boasted being the largest in the French Quarter, complete with a huge refrigerator and other modern equipment such as steam tables and dishwashing machines that had only recently become available. Beneath the new building, Cazenave took advantage of the French Quarter's high ground compared with the rest of the city and had a cellar built to store "fine wines and rare liquors."[9] Plentiful dining space was also added, and the expansion raised the seating capacity of the restaurant to eight hundred. "Its popularity, therefore, does not mean that anyone need perish for want of sustenance; it means only that at the hour of peak patronage, there might be a brief period of waiting," the *Picayune* reassured readers in 1947 as Arnaud's continued to enjoy the height of its popularity in the years that followed World War II.[10]

The *Times-Picayune* kept some excessively well-fed and social cats in the 1940s, among them Prettypuss, who reportedly attended a grand party at Tujaque's to visit Madame Castet's cat, Baby. In the summer of 1946, one of Prettypuss's relatives, a feline named William, escaped his columnist owners and had a temporary stay down the street at Count Arnaud's residence, where Cazenave's dogs chased and trapped him under the house. According to the update published in the *Times-Picayune*, once or twice a day "Miss Marie," who worked for Cazenave as a maid, would call off the dogs to feed William some delicacy left over from Arnaud's: "Mr. William been eatin' restaurant food. He say he sho' like the board but he ain't like the room," Marie told the *Picayune*. "We have not been able to check whether William was served 'Shrimp Arnaud,' or merely filet mignon," the paper concluded.

After ten days of enjoying fine cuisine under stressful circumstances, William the cat was returned to his home with the paper.[11]

In late May 1948, one month before he would have made seventy-two years, Count Arnaud Cazenave died at Baptist Hospital. Funeral services for the beloved Count were held in St. Louis Cathedral before he was interred in his family tomb at Metairie Cemetery.[12] Today, the Count's stately portrait still watches guests from its position in the main dining room, flanked by paintings of his wife, Irma, and her sister, Marie. New Orleans never neglecting potential gossip, it is alleged that the Count never could definitively choose one sister over the other. "The slightly roguish twinkle in the Count's eyes might fill in the rest of that story for you," the Arnaud's website teases today, well aware that a good story never fails to liven up a meal.[13]

Prior to his death, Cazenave's daughter, Germaine Cazenave Wells, had been called from where she was performing on the vaudeville circuit to return home to New Orleans and care for her father and his business. The Count made it clear that rather than his mild-mannered wife, his dramatic and strong-willed daughter was to take on his French-Creole fine dining legacy. A true product of New Orleans, Germaine reveled in excessive liquor and men, especially by the standards of her time, but certainly maintained the incessant rumors surrounding Arnaud's that she and her father both knew generated business.[14] Although her passion was not the minutia of running a restaurant, Germaine was a natural when it came to the elaborate pageantry required for fine service and easily fell into the crowd of New Orleans aristocracy that most loved Arnaud's. She would come to regard the restaurant industry as like "a play in two acts," referring to the lunch and dinner services and the performative nature of front of house versus the veiled chaos often taking place "behind the scenes" in the kitchen. "There's the theatrics and the show that you put on for the customers, and then there's what takes place in the back, which could be organized chaos, it could be smooth sailing, it could be disorganized chaos," current proprietor Katy Casbarian chuckled as she explained her predecessor Germaine's philosophy. "And you're out there making sure the customers don't know what's going on, that it's just a seamless well-executed show."[15]

Germaine continued to perpetuate her father's saying that "New Orleans was the Paris of the South" and garnered global praise for Arnaud's partially on that basis. She ensured that Arnaud's was included in a Paris newspaper's list of "Top 5 Restaurants in the World" and again on a similar list published in New York. As she was a rabid socialite, media attention followed Germain wherever she went, and she seldom stayed home.[16]

Perhaps rooted in her passion for performance, Germaine easily fell in love with the theatrics and costumes of New Orleans's Mardi Gras celebrations. During her lifetime, she ruled as Queen or on the court of twenty-two different Carnival balls. Her first in 1937 was with the Krewe of Iris, although her professed favorite was in 1938, when she was named Queen of Prometheus while her father reigned as King. Because it is considered bad luck to wear a Carnival Queen's gown on more than one occasion, Germaine had a replica of her gold gown made so she could wear it as she pleased.[17] Germaine even founded a parade of drawn carriages on Easter Sunday with the primary purpose of displaying her newest hats, a pastel-colored tradition that continues strong today.[18]

One of Germaine's very favorite dining rooms, particularly for her excessive Carnival festivities, was the Gold Room. Aptly named, the Gold Room is adorned floor to ceiling with gold wallpaper and paint, and a display showcases Mardi Gras memorabilia from years past.[19] Always one for grandeur and theatrics, Germaine instituted "Dress-Up Night"

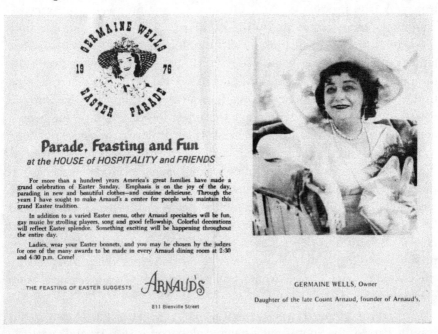

Parade, Feasting and Fun
at the HOUSE of HOSPITALITY and FRIENDS

For more than a hundred years America's great families have made a grand celebration of Easter Sunday. Emphasis is on the joy of the day, parading in new and beautiful clothes—and cuisine delicieuse. Through the years I have sought to make Arnaud's a center for people who maintain this grand Easter tradition.

In addition to a varied Easter menu, other Arnaud specialties will be fun, gay music by strolling players, song and good fellowship. Colorful decorations will reflect Easter splendor. Something exciting will be happening throughout the entire day.

Ladies, wear your Easter bonnets, and you may be chosen by the judges for one of the many awards to be made in every Arnaud dining room at 2:30 and 4:30 p.m. Come!

THE FEASTING OF EASTER SUGGESTS ARNAUD'S

811 Bienville Street

GERMAINE WELLS, Owner
Daughter of the late Count Arnaud, founder of Arnaud's.

Easter with Germaine Wells, 1976. *Louisiana Menu and Restaurant Collection, Louisiana Research Collection, Tulane University.*

at Arnaud's every Saturday. On these occasions, men were required to sport formal black or in summer "formal white," while ladies were to wear formal or cocktail attire. The idea was taken from the famous Maxime's in Paris, of which Germaine was a fan, and received with great enthusiasm in New Orleans. Funny to think that in the early '60s, Arnaud's owner was instituting strict formal dress codes as a marketing tactic, while current ownership has had to continually loosen the dress code to accommodate more casual modern crowds.[20]

To honor Germaine Wells and the plethora of beautiful Carnival regalia she amassed over the course of her life, the Casbarian family, who currently owns Arnaud's, established the "Queen's Collection," a Mardi Gras museum on the second floor of the restaurant. The exhibit, which remains on display year-round, includes thirteen of Germaine's gowns and accompanying accessories, along with pieces worn by her mother and daughter, four of her father Count Arnaud's King's costumes and six children's costumes. Three months after the gallery displaying her treasures was opened to the public in 1983, Germaine Wells passed away. She was buried in her favorite golden gown with her father in the family tomb at Metairie Cemetery, but not before the funeral procession took her past Arnaud's Restaurant one final time.[21]

KEEPING UP WITH THE CASBARIANS: ARNAUD'S SECOND FAMILY

In the mid-1970s, Archie Casbarian, who had been involved in the hotel and hospitality industry for decades and was regarded as one of America's most prominent hoteliers, was employed as general manager at the Royal Sonesta Hotel across Bienville Street from Arnaud's Restaurant. He developed a friendship with the amicable Germaine, taking an interest in her family establishment. Archie always had a particular fondness for the restaurant side of the hotel world and saw a potential opportunity to make a go of being a restaurateur across the street. Archie and others made Germaine offers to buy Arnaud's on multiple occasions, but as the restaurant's website puts it, "She saw the transaction not as selling a business but as abdicating a throne." Only when Germaine was on the cusp of financial devastation was she forced to choose a suitor to purchase the restaurant her father founded.[22]

Germaine always had a style of operating Arnaud's that was arguably more performative than practical, and she implemented similar measures when it came to choosing to whom the restaurant would be sold. Fortunately for Archie Casbarian, he reminded Germaine a great deal of her own father the Count: both were similar in height; both enjoyed the fine material things in life such as nice suits, Cognac and cigars; and both were fluent in French and born outside the United States (although Casbarian was born in Egypt, rather than France). Archie Casbarian even shared his initials with Arnaud Cazenave, which perhaps is what solidified Germaine's decision to begin leasing the property and business of Arnaud's Restaurant to Casbarian and his wife/business partner, Jane, in 1978.[23]

Of course, any shift in ownership of a long-standing New Orleans restaurant garners rumors at best and outright outrage at worst. In a calculated attempt to avoid the latter, one way that Archie Casbarian retained Germaine and the Count's regular customers through their renovations in the late 1970s and early '80s was by offering "skeleton keys" to the Richelieu Bar to the most loyal patrons. The esteemed guests could use the key to enter the bar from Bienville Street and thereby walk through other parts of the restaurant to observe the work being done. The keys were also imprinted with the patron's account number, allowing them to be used to charge food and beverages. But, as Archie Casbarian's daughter, Katy, laughingly put it, "accounts are tricky in terms are getting repaid," so eventually the skeleton keys fell out of use. Katy said that occasionally, a skeleton key will still be seen at Arnaud's. "I find now customers of a younger generation will bring in the keys that they found from their parents when they cleaned out a closet or a home, God forbid, to turn back in to us. But it's always kind of interesting to see one that pops through the door sometimes still. A lot of people say 'Can I still use it?' and I say 'No you cannot, account is closed,'" Katy laughed.[24] Following renovations in 2003, the name of the Richelieu Bar would be converted back to its original name, the French 75 Bar, named for the Champagne cocktail invented by American soldiers stationed in France during World War I that is the bar's signature drink.[25]

While Archie had ample experience managing massive and complex properties in the hotel industry, restoring Arnaud's restaurant to its former glory utilized all of the management skills he could muster. The restaurant's website put it least delicately and best: "The place was a wreck." The majority of the now eleven total buildings and seventeen dining rooms had been closed under Germaine's ownership years ago, and most of the buildings were in dire need of work. One friend later told the *Times-Picayune* that there were pigeons living on the second floor and holes in the roofs in some places. Committed to maintaining Arnaud's original old-world charm,

Contemporary French 75 Bar. *Arnaud's Restaurant.*

Casbarian set about carefully restoring his newly leased restaurant. Floor-to-ceiling pebbled-glass windows facing Bienville were replaced by beveled glass, while original chandeliers, cypress panels, ceiling fans and iron columns remained.[26] The now-iconic beveled windows facing Bienville were recently blown out using computer-generated imagery for the television show *NCIS: New Orleans,* and patrons the following day called the restaurant concerned about whether their reservations were still valid.[27]

Casbarian also renovated Arnaud's massive kitchen, rendering it better equipped and more modern than ever before. By the time the Casbarians completed restorations, about $2.5 million had been invested into returning Arnaud's to grandeur.[28] On the night of the restaurant's reopening in 1979, the following message from Archie was printed on every menu: "Tonight marks the rebirth of a grand and noble restaurant and heralds a new era in the history of a world-famous establishment."[29]

According to Katy Casbarian, Archie's daughter and current vice-president of Arnaud's, the restaurant was not far from closing when her parents first leased it. "Well honestly, I'm not certain Arnaud's would still be here but for my parents," Katy reasoned. "You know, it was a tough go. Literally the restaurant was on the brink of closure. There's eleven buildings, [and] they were all in pretty bad shape. So it wasn't just, 'Okay, how do we restore the reputation of a restaurant?' But it's, 'How do we restore all these

Retro main dining room. *Arnaud's Restaurant.*

Contemporary main dining room. *Alexandra Kennon.*

Owner Katy Casbarian in the main dining room. *Alexandra Kennon.*

buildings so that they're operable?' I mean, it was a big undertaking, and I don't know that just any restaurateur could have done it. I think it fell in the right hands, and I think that's their legacy."[30]

In building that legacy, the first meal served at Arnaud's under Casbarian's ownership was not to be soon forgotten. Internationally acclaimed wine connoisseur and collector Lloyd Flatt provided a magnum of 1929 Chateau d'Yquem, while Casbarian supplied the meal and service. Like his predecessor, Casbarian understood the importance of an excellent meal, particularly when paired with one of the rarest and most coveted wines in existence. The meal was a grand success, setting the tone for the remainder of Archie Casbarian's tenure as owner of Arnaud's. Flatt would contribute the décor for a former linen pantry turned private dining room whose walls were lined with his personal collection of impressive vintages of wine, as well as a "Methuselah" (which equates to six bottles) of 1796 Napoleon Brandy. When Flatt moved away from New Orleans in the 1990s, he sadly took his cellar with him, and Jane Casbarian hired local artist George Dureau to complete a painting of the Greek wine god Dionysus to fill the space on the wall once taken by the Napoleon Brandy.[31]

The largest dining room is the Count's Ballroom on the second floor, which is frequently utilized for weddings and debutante galas and can seat up to two hundred guests. The Count and his staff were using the space for storage when Casbarian bought the restaurant and later restored it to a grand banquet room as was intended.[32]

Jane Casbarian, who took the lead in planning and executing special events at Arnaud's for some time after her husband bought the restaurant, has certain unique ways of hosting to keep guests entertained. One trick is to set place cards at the beginning of the meal but have ladies move two places to their left after each course is finished. The tactic ensures that conversation is never dull and that diners are afforded the ability to charm a maximum number of fellow guests. Special occasions are thoroughly celebrated at Arnaud's, particularly Halloween and Carnival, where in the tradition of Germaine Wells costumes are "de rigueur."[33]

Count Arnaud and Germaine Cazenave had a flare for entertaining, and Archie and Jane Casbarian followed their lead when it came to amusing and impressing even the best-connected diners. According to author of *Arnaud's Restaurant Cookbook*, Kit Wohl, Adelaide Brennan once had a "beau" who approached Archie for help planning a special gift for her for Thanksgiving. Ever over-the-top, Casbarian had a live turkey brought to Adelaide—naturally, the bird was delivered wearing a diamond necklace.[34]

While diamond-drenched game birds and impeccable service are necessary parts of the experience, the food served at Arnaud's must also remain top-notch. Archie Casbarian initially had one chef, while local-born Tommy DiGiovanni worked his way up the ranks of the giant kitchen to earn the title of sous. After four years at Arnaud's, DiGiovanni left to gain outside experience at hotels throughout New Orleans.[35] Three years later, Archie approached Tommy and asked if he wanted to return, but this time with a coat bearing the title "Executive Chef." Upon his return, a banner stretched across the giant kitchen proclaiming, "Welcome home, Tommy."[36] Between the familial relationships of many staff members and the long hours they spend at the restaurant, Arnaud's certainly feels like home for many.

While the Count's original menu was extensive, featuring nine different preparations of oysters and fifty-six seafood entrées, to give one an idea, the French-Creole menu at Arnaud's remains one of the more elaborate in town. One of the more popular appetizers is a sampling called Oysters Arnaud, which features five distinct recipes for baked toppings on oysters on the half-shell: Oysters Bienville, Oysters Rockefeller, Oysters Kathryn, Oysters Ohan and Oysters Suzette. Oysters Bienville are an

Arnaud's executive chef, Tommy DiGiovanni, in the main dining room. *Alexandra Kennon*.

Arnaud's original, named for the founder of New Orleans and the street the restaurant adorns, proudly and imposingly encompassing most of the 800th block. The dish features oysters on the half-shell baked with shrimp and oyster dressing atop, garnished with lemon and various Italian cheeses, and was purportedly invented in direct response to the praise the Count's competitors were receiving for Oysters Rockefeller at Antoine's nearby. Oysters Kathryn, Archie's daughter and current proprietor Katy's signature recipe, feature brighter toppings of artichoke hearts, parmesan cheese and other ingredients.[37] Shrimp Arnaud, Arnaud's preparation of shrimp in remoulade sauce, has been on the menu since the Count owned the restaurant, and to this day the recipe for the sauce remains a family secret, although it is bottled and sold. In keeping up with the fact that not every visitor to the city has time or means for an elaborate meal, the Casbarians also have Remoulade, a café on Bourbon Street catered toward more casual family dining.[38]

Following Katrina's unwelcome appearance in New Orleans, Arnaud's was impressively reopened less than three months later in November 2005. Fortunately, many of Casbarian's employees were available and ready to work, so before the year was out the full menu was being served to celebratory guests, as usual. Something about a formally attired waiter serving decadent Oysters Bienville seems to say, "It's going to be all right," and locals in town in the months following the storm appreciated having somewhere to go for the best kind of therapy New Orleanians know: a fine meal in good company.

After successfully restoring and running Arnaud's for thirty-one years, Archie Casbarian died of esophageal cancer at the age of seventy-two. His children, Katy and Archie Jr., along with their mother, Jane, continue to operate Arnaud's Restaurant today.[39]

Although with Arnaud's eleven buildings, seventeen dining rooms and built-in museum it could very easily be run as a corporation, the Casbarian family opts to maintain a more family-oriented approach. "We still very much are a family-run business, and I think that's what makes us attractive as employers, I think that's what makes us attractive as a destination for our customers," Katy posited. Although she does not have her own children, her brother and co-proprietor/vice-president of Arnaud's, Archie Jr., has three young sons, including another Archie. Although her nephews are encouraged to pursue whatever career they choose, she said that if one or all of them end up at the restaurant, it would be fantastic for the longevity of keeping Arnaud's in the Casbarian family. "So, yeah, I think that we

Senior maître d'
Augie Spicuzza in the
main dining room.
Alexandra Kennon.

would like that to continue," Katy said. "But hopefully we have a long time to figure that out."[40]

Keeping Arnaud's family-run is important to the Casbarians not only because of their own legacy but also because Arnaud's was first established as a family institution by Count Arnaud and his daughter, Germaine. As for how Germaine and the Count would feel about what Archie and his family have done with the place today, Katy believes they would be happy that Arnaud's is in capable hands. "I think Germaine was, and would still be, thrilled that she found the right suitor for the restaurant," Katy said. "I'm sure she was at some point disappointed that she didn't have a family member to take it on, as I would be, but I think she would be happy that the restaurant's continued and is thriving and is still very much a tribute to her father and her family as much as it is to mine."[41]

Arnaud's stately entryway today. *Alexandra Kennon.*

Arnaud's exterior today. *Alexandra Kennon.*

Recipe from Arnaud's

Strawberries Arnaud

From Arnaud's website: "Louisiana-grown strawberries are sweet, plump and succulent. When they are in season it is a shame to order anything else. Strawberries Arnaud celebrates them in a simple and refreshing recipe designed to crown any meal."

1 cup ruby port
1 cup red burgundy-style wine
½ orange, sliced
1 lime, sliced
1 cinnamon stick
½ cup granulated sugar
3 cups vanilla ice cream
3 cups sliced fresh strawberries
lightly sweetened whipped cream
6 whole, perfect strawberries with their stems
sprigs of mint

In a medium saucepan, combine the port and wine and place over medium-high heat. Bring to a boil and then add the orange and lime slices, the cinnamon and the sugar. Return to a boil and then remove from the heat and cool for at least 30 minutes. Strain the sauce, cover and refrigerate until serving (the sauce will keep for up to two weeks).

To serve, place one scoop of ice cream in six champagne glasses. Cover the ice cream with sliced strawberries and drizzle generously with the port sauce. Add a dollop of whipped cream, a whole strawberry and a sprig of fresh mint for show. Serve at once.

Recipe courtesy of Arnaud's Restaurant.

Chapter 11
Broussard's

(1920)

One of the great old Creole dining institutions in the French Quarter, Broussard's
serves polished, imaginative versions of the traditional Creole dishes.
—*Tom Fitzmorris, New Orleans City Business, 2010*

Joseph Cezaire Broussard was born in the bayou town of Loreauville, situated in Evangeline Parish, Louisiana, in 1889. Descended from French colonists who settled the area in the seventeenth century, perhaps a French predisposition for cuisine ran in his blood. There is little else that could explain why a boy growing up in the swamps of Acadiana in the 1800s would dream of one day becoming a chef, but that was Joseph Broussard's aspiration.

By the time Joseph was a teenager, it had become clear to him that New Orleans was the logical setting to pursue his ambitions of culinary greatness. Restaurants like Antoine's, Tujague's and Commander's Palace were already going strong there, and Antoine's in particular was garnering attention nationally. As soon as he was old enough, Joseph and his brother, Robert, moved to New Orleans to see if there was a place for them in the burgeoning restaurant scene.[1]

Antoine's was the grandest and best-established restaurant in the city, so Joseph aimed high and sought employment there first. Sure enough, young Joseph Broussard was quickly hired by Jules Alciatore, the second-generation owner of Antoine's. As is often the trajectory of the restaurant business, Joseph bussed tables and filled water glasses as an assistant waiter, and before long, Jules had promoted him to waiter, although it took years for most employees to earn the title. After two years serving all of Antoine's most esteemed regular customers and proving his deftness in the realm of hospitality in the dining rooms, Joseph tentatively approached his employer and informed him of his aspirations in the kitchen. While Jules was hesitant to transfer such a shrewd and personable server away from the guests, he understood that young Joseph had a dream, and to the kitchen Joseph went. He had grown up becoming intimately familiar with Louisiana cuisine and now had the opportunity to fuse it with its mother French influence under the supervision of some of New Orleans's finest chefs.[2]

This employment was serendipitous for Joseph, because Jules Alciatore had when he was younger done just what Joseph also longed to do: traveled to France to train in the culinary arts. Seeing promise in the young man, Jules Alciatore not only provided his charge with a letter of recommendation but also personally escorted him to Paris in 1910. While Alciatore was undoubtedly sad to lose such a competent employee, he more than anyone understood that Joseph had aspirations to start a restaurant bearing his own family name.[3]

In Paris, Joseph was taken under the wing of Chef Mornay Voiron, who reportedly invented the classic mother sauce with which he shared a name. Joseph grew up speaking French in Evangeline Parish, allowing him to speak fluently and confidently when interviewed by the great chef. Joseph served as an understudy for Chef Voiron at his renowned Restaurant Durand until he had perfected the skills of refined French cuisine as well as its popular provincial counterpart. While in France, Joseph became obsessed with all things related to the late emperor Napoleon Bonaparte, particularly the iconic honeybee symbol. It was customary at the time in France, and often still is today, for culinary apprentices to be paid very little or nothing for their work because it was considered training. When Joseph reached the last of the funds he had so frugally saved before the journey, that seemed like an appropriate time to return to New Orleans to make another go of the exploding restaurant industry there.[4]

Meanwhile, back in 1874, prominent Sicilian couple Anthony and Mary Ann Borrello had a beautiful mansion built for themselves at 819 Conti Street, mere blocks from Antoine's restaurant. Upon returning to New Orleans in 1914, Joseph served as chef for multiple restaurants, all the while planning to one day make a restaurant of his own a reality. While not part of the plan, Joseph met Anthony and Mary Ann Borrello's pretty daughter and fell madly in love. He asked for Rosalie Borrello's hand, and in 1917, the couple was wed.[5] Although Joseph was not from New Orleans, nor was he

Italian, Rosalie's parents appreciated his ambition and thoroughly approved of the union. They approved to such a degree that they gifted the young couple their Conti Street mansion where Rosalie was born and raised. It was in that building at 819 Conti that Rosalie and Joseph lived and, in 1920, finally opened a restaurant of their own.[6]

In the following years, Joseph and Rosalie established broad-reaching acclaim for Broussard's restaurant, garnering an impressive cast of fans including William Faulkner, Humphrey Bogart and Tennessee Williams. The food Joseph prepared reflected his traditional French training, along with the more varied Creole influences of New Orleans and those of his Sicilian wife. Joseph incorporated his beloved Napoleon into the business thoroughly, naming the grand courtyard after him and serving the legendary Napoleon Cognac. When the Cognac was ordered, waiters would ring an imposing bell and belt "La Marseillaise" as they marched the drink ceremoniously to the patron's table. The Napoleonic honeybee was associated with the restaurant from the time when Joseph and Rosalie established the venture and is still used thoroughly in Broussard's décor and marketing today.[7]

Directly following Christmas on December 27, 1965, Rosalie Broussard passed away. Not much more than a month later, on February 5, 1966, Joseph Broussard joined her in death after a prolonged illness. A Requiem High Mass was held at St. Louis Cathedral, to which locals flocked to mourn the loss of a great New Orleans chef of their time.[8] Although Joseph's children ran the business for a period, their hearts were not in the restaurant industry like their father's was, and in 1974, they left to pursue other ventures. They sold Broussard's to Italian restaurateur Joseph Marcello and longtime steward of Broussard's Joseph Segretto, who completed a major renovation on the restaurant and reopened in 1975.[9]

The new design of the restaurant was masterminded by an impressive team, including architect Samuel Wilson Jr., who restored the Ursuline Convent and Pontalba Buildings among countless others, and designer Charles Gresham, whose previous projects included Brennan's and Commander's Palace.[10] Local food writer Tom Fitzmorris pointed out retrospectively that of all the French Quarter grande dame restaurants, Broussard's was the first to make such a considerable change, at the risk of alienating loyal customers. Instead, the new Broussard's attracted more guests than ever, proving that even an elegant grande dame can benefit from a makeover every so often.[11]

Joseph Segretto had formerly been tour manager for Louis Prima and Kelly Smith at the height of their careers, and his connections garnered

Above: Historic exterior of Broussard's Restaurant. *Louisiana Menu and Restaurant Collection, Louisiana Research Collection, Tulane University.*

Left: Historic interior of the Josephine Room. *Broussard's Restaurant.*

Left: Historic patio. *Library of Congress*.

Below: Louisiana's Dairy Princess, Sandra Girouard, at Dairy Month Luncheon, 1960. *Broussard's Restaurant/F.H. Methe.*

Broussard's an impressive celebrity following that included Elizabeth Taylor, Tony Bennett, Sammy Davis Jr. and many others. Knowing that even a beautifully restored restaurant needed even better food to be sustained in the French Quarter, famed Creole chef Nathaniel Burton was poached from his former position as executive chef of the Caribbean Room in the Hotel Pontchartrain. Despite their success, just a few years after the restorations were complete Marcello and Segretto sold Broussard's to a group of new owners, among them Gunter and Evelyn Preuss.[12]

One influence on Creole cuisine that is much less evident than its French roots, but nonetheless still present, is German. It is therefore perhaps fitting that Chef Gunter Preuss of Broussard's originated from Breslau, Germany. When he was in Berlin in 1958, he met the beautiful Evelyn, who had grown up there. Two years later, in 1960, they were married, and by the end of the year they had immigrated to the United States. Eventually, they made their way to New Orleans, and in 1972, when the Versailles restaurant Uptown went up for sale, the couple bought it.[13] In 1984, a friend approached them with another potential venture: becoming partners in the purchase of Broussard's Restaurant. They jumped at the offer but remained relatively silent partners, helping improve the décor and food behind the scenes but never publicly. In 1993, Gunter and Evelyn Preuss bought their partners out and became the sole owners of Broussard's.[14]

When the Preusses stepped in to handle the operations of their newly obtained French Quarter restaurant, that is when the work truly began. Evelyn restored the courtyard and redecorated the dining rooms and then deftly ran front of house, while her husband revamped the restaurant's menu and held domain in the kitchen. Praise from restaurant critics began to pour in. The Preusses had restored Broussard's to its position as one of New Orleans's best restaurants, an honor it formerly received under the care of its founding chef, Joseph Broussard. Eventually, Evelyn and Gunter's son, Marc, joined his parents in managing the business as well.[15]

When Pope John Paul II visited New Orleans in September 1987, he dined at several restaurants, including Antoine's. What was less publicized was his in-residence meal, which was prepared for His Holiness and His Papal Entourage by Gunter Preuss.[16]

When Hurricane Katrina struck the French Quarter in 2005, Broussard's was relatively fortunate to receive minimal damage to its building, but it still had to close for two months to clean up and replace the ruined food, and because their employees were no longer available. Even when the restaurant reopened, it was still incredibly short-staffed. "That's how Marc [Preuss] found out I could wait tables," laughed Rita, a longtime bartender at the restaurant. "Because we couldn't get good help. Everybody was spoiled with that FEMA money and didn't wanna work, but we didn't stop workin'. But it was a mess. They lost bottles of wine that...unbelievable."[17]

By 2013, the Preusses' business had declined, and they began to give consideration to selling Broussard's. Meanwhile, the Ammari brothers, who had the company Creole Cuisine Restaurant Concepts, were considering launching a more upscale venture than their other restaurants, which include Pierre Maspero's and Royal House Oyster Bar. In 2013, the Ammari family purchased Broussard's restaurant, completed yet another extensive renovation totaling around $1 million and continue to operate the French Quarter grande dame today. "We are honored to carry on the traditions of excellence that Joe and Rosalie Broussard passionately shared with diners," Zeid Ammari, chief operating officer of Creole Cuisine Restaurant Concepts, told the *NOLA Defender* after restoring the restaurant in 2013. "As we look to the future we remain resolute in our commitment of returning Broussard's Restaurant to the glamour and refinement of the past, while providing an elegant sense of modernity."[18]

Contemporary main Napoleon Dining Room. *Alexandra Kennon.*

The Magnolia Room today. *Alexandra Kennon*.

The Josephine Room today. *Alexandra Kennon*.

The Courtyard today in daytime. *Alexandra Kennon.*

The Courtyard today at dusk. *Broussard's Restaurant.*

The French Quarter's oldest wisteria vine in Broussard's Courtyard, planted in 1887. *Alexandra Kennon.*

RECENT DEVELOPMENTS

Continuing the trend of Broussard's chefs being trained in Europe, the first executive chef hired by the Ammari brothers, Guy Reinbolt, was both born and trained in France. After obtaining several culinary degrees from a prominent *lycée*, Reinbolt worked in multiple Michelin-starred restaurants in France and Germany, all the while longing to one day journey to the United States—he was a big John Wayne fan. Eventually, Reinbolt followed his idol to America, where he landed in New Orleans and, eventually, at Broussard's. Reinbolt headed the kitchen at Broussard's until 2018.[19]

After Reinbolt left the position, Jimi Setchim stepped into the executive chef role right around St. Patrick's Day of that year. Originally from Connecticut, Setchim graduated from the University of the South in Sewanee, Tennessee, with a degree in economics and philosophy—admittedly a divergence from the classically trained Europeans of Broussard's past, but he worked in restaurants throughout his entire time in college. After graduating and completing a few interviews, Setchim realized that he would not be happy working in the world of finance. He had always felt at home in the kitchen, and so he decided to take the plunge and move to New Orleans to pursue a career in the restaurant scene.

Unfortunately, his timing could not have been worse: his flight to New Orleans was scheduled for the day Hurricane Katrina made landfall in Florida, where he was staying with a friend before he planned to make his final move to the Crescent City. At first, he attempted to wait the storm out from his friend's place in Miami, but eventually it became clear that there would not be work for him in the fine kitchens of New Orleans any time in the immediate future. He moved back up to Connecticut until January 2006, when he finally made it to New Orleans and was almost immediately hired at the Palace Café on Canal Street. Setchim worked for the Brennan family for nearly the next twelve years. "It was interesting to see the difference between trying to get into the culinary field down here pre- and post-Katrina," Setchim observed. "So pre-Katrina, I was interviewing everywhere, and it was tough. After Katrina, there was nobody here. So for me it was good, I was able to get my foot in the door."[20]

One of Setchim's primary goals, he said, has been to revive many of the French-Creole dishes that were previously on the menu when Gunter Preuss was chef-owner of Broussard's. "We're going through some of [Gunter's] ideas, and finding those classic French-Creole dishes, but making them fun. We found a menu upstairs in a cabinet from the '30s that had chicken livers

Executive Chef Jimi Setchim in the Courtyard. *Alexandra Kennon*.

sautéed in mushrooms and onions. Simple. So we brought that back, but livers aren't everybody's go-to, right? It's tough to get people into. So: fried chicken livers, grilled baguette, wild mushroom butter, red onion jam. It's bright, it's vibrant," Setchim boasted. "And we've gotten a lot of feedback from guests that [say] 'I don't normally eat livers, but I love this.' So trying to bring back some of those dishes that everybody might not be into, or that have kind of been lost over the years, and get people back into them."

Many of Setchim's most popular menu items have been cultivated in this method, by pulling vintage menus and adapting the dishes for a contemporary audience. Instead of a traditional Oysters Rockefeller on the half-shell, as is served at Antoine's, Setchim serves lightly battered and fried oysters atop Herbsaint-creamed spinach with chunks of smoky bacon and Crystal hot sauce aioli. Traditional it is not, but the inspiration and flavors are there, and diners seem to be pleased with the contemporary flair.

The food is not the only aspect of Broussard's that Setchim and management are attempting to make more accessible to modern diners. About two years ago, the strict coat-and-tie policy was lifted. "And the influx of people we're getting is amazing now. It's making people feel comfortable, feel welcome," Setchim said. "We want you to feel like you're at your house, but you've got all these people taking care of you."[21]

Brunch is offered seven days a week now to provide more brunch opportunities not only for tourists who often fly out on Sundays but also for the service industry professionals whom, Setchim pointed out, often work brunch shifts themselves but seldom have an opportunity to enjoy the luxury of enjoying the service that they so often provide others.

Rita, the longtime bartender who worked for the Preuss family, left Broussard's for a few years after the Ammaris purchased it to work at Mittendorf's. When she heard that Setchim had been hired as chef and that he was earning praise for his cooking, she returned. "With Chef Jimi here, people are starting to learn that he's here, and the food's good. Because he cooks a lot like Gunter [Preuss], and he's got that same feeling with his food," Rita remarked. "And Joe Broussard, if he didn't like the food that was presented to go out, he would throw it on Conti Street. He would throw it on Conti Street, yes he would. He was something else. He was fierce."[22]

Not only does she appreciate the work Setchim does in the kitchen, but she also said that the Ammari brothers are fair and personable employers. "I gotta be honest, these people are good. Really good to me," Rita said. "They really are good people. They think about family. They come in and say, 'Thank you for working so hard for me.'" Backing her up is the *Times-Picayune* "Top Workplaces" survey for 2016, which ranked Creole Cuisine

Chef Jimi Setchim and bartender/server Rita Pastrano. *Alexandra Kennon.*

Restaurant Concepts best large company to work for in New Orleans that year. "As you evolve, you realize the only way to move forward, and the only way to grow, and not only grow but to do things the right way, is with a team," Zeid Ammari told the *Times-Picayune* of his and his brothers' philosophy. "The word 'family' in our vocabulary isn't really our last name. As family, we mean all of our employees."[23]

Broussard's restaurant, with the help of that team, has undeniably evolved in many ways while still maintaining certain traditions from Joseph and Rosalie Broussard, Gunter and Evelyn Preuss and even Napoleon Bonaparte. The year 2020 will be the grande dame's centennial, and staff and regulars alike look forward to the one hundredth birthday celebration. "And we'd like to be open another hundred years after that," Chef Setchim beamed.[24]

Recipe from Broussard's

Raspberry and Mascarpone Stuffed Pain Perdu

From Broussard's Restaurant: "'Pain Perdu,' also known as 'Lost Bread,' is a French-Louisiana breakfast staple. The use of left-over, or 'lost,' bread from dinners throughout the week was an inexpensive way to feed a family. At Broussard's we dress up ours with fresh raspberries and stuff it with mascarpone cheese. This makes for a sweet, creamy brunch treat with a little tartness from the berries. The addition of almonds and bacon adds texture, salt and smoke, creating delicious layers of flavor. At Broussard's, we use Brioche, a rich and buttery bread, for our Pain Perdu. It is made locally by Leidenheimer Bakery and adds a lovely decadence to the dish."
Yields: 4 each

½ loaf brioche, cut into 8 individual ½-inch slices
1 cup raspberry mascarpone
1 quart French toast custard
½ pound unsalted butter
8 bacon strips, cooked
½ pint raspberries
½ cup raspberry coulis
¼ cup sliced almonds, toasted

1. Lay four of the pieces of brioche on a pan.
2. Using a spoon or spatula, evenly spread the raspberry mascarpone to cover the pieces of brioche.
3. Top each mascarpone toast with a second piece of brioche.
4. Pour custard into a mixing bowl or baking dish and soak the stuffed brioche for several minutes.
5. Over medium heat, melt 2 tablespoons of butter.
6. Remove stuffed brioche from custard and shake off any excess.
7. Pan-fry stuffed brioche in butter for 3 minutes until golden brown.
8. Flip brioche and add more 2 tablespoons of butter.
9. Fry brioche for 2 more minutes until golden brown.
10. Remove from heat and repeat with all three remaining pieces of stuffed brioche.
11. Cut each piece of stuffed pain perdu on a diagonal.
12. Overlap two pieces of pain perdu on a plate and top with two pieces of bacon and 4 or 5 raspberries; repeat with remaining pain perdu.
13. Drizzle each plate with 2 tablespoons of raspberry coulis and garnish with toasted almonds and powdered sugar.

Raspberry Mascarpone
Yields: 1 pint

2½ ounces mascarpone cheese, room temperature
2½ ounces cream cheese, room temperature
½ ounce powdered sugar
¼ each lemon, zested
1½ ounces raspberries

1. In a stand mixer with the paddle attachment, cream together mascarpone and cream cheese until soft and combined.
2. Add sugar, lemon zest and mix until incorporated.
3. Fold in raspberries.
4. Chill and reserve.

Raspberry Coulis
Yields: 1 cup

1 cup raspberries
2 tablespoons water
3 tablespoons granulated sugar
¼ lemon, juiced

1. Over medium heat, combine raspberries, water and sugar and bring to a simmer for 5 minutes.
2. Remove from heat and add lemon juice.
3. Puree coulis and strain through a mesh strainer.
4. Chill and reserve.

French Toast Custard
Yields: 1 quart

6 eggs
3 tablespoons granulated sugar
½ teaspoon ground cinnamon
¾ cup heavy cream
2 cups half and half

1. Whisk together eggs, sugar and cinnamon.
2. Add heavy cream and half and half.
3. Whisk until combined well.
4. Chill and reserve.

Recipe created and provided by Executive Chef Jimi Setchim at Broussard's Restaurant.

Chapter 12

Dooky Chase

(1941)

Some restaurants are merely restaurants. One goes, sits, orders, eats, enjoys, pays the bill, and returns home. Through the years, Leah Chase has cooked for clients and she has cooked for movements. Her restaurant is more than a restaurant; it's an institution.
—*Carol Allen,* Leah Chase: Listen, I Say Like This

It is crucial to note that while restaurants such as Antoine's were enjoyed by white clientele as early as the 1840s, a full century later African Americans in segregated New Orleans still had few options for dining out beyond perhaps picking up a sandwich or plate lunch from an enterprising woman in their neighborhood. The origins of Dooky Chase's Restaurant are comparable, beginning with Edgar "Dooky" Chase Sr. moving his door-to-door lottery ticket sales to a fixed location in 1939 and opening a small sandwich shop in conjunction in 1941.[1]

In the early days, the offerings at Dooky Chase were simple: lottery tickets, soft drinks, beers and chaurices (sausages) on French bread. Dooky suffered from ulcers, making walking door to door selling lottery tickets no longer possible. With the storefront, he could continue the lottery business despite his declining health and offer a social respite for the neighborhood as well. Dooky's charisma, and his wife Emily's good cooking, were hits with the community—eventually, they outgrew their first location and moved into another. Even after the lottery was removed, the business still went strong as the only one of its kind in New Orleans where black and white customers

Dooky Chase's Restaurant today. *Alexandra Kennon.*

were welcome despite the "separate but equal" law that remained in place in Louisiana since *Plessy v. Ferguson.* When there were no black-owned banks, African Americans working freight jobs on the Mississippi River could have their checks cashed at Dooky's while they waited for their po-boys to go.[2] Dooky's thrived as a necessary meeting place for the black community, for everyone from high schoolers seeking a place to go after prom to civil rights activists and politicians utilizing the upstairs dining room as a pivotal meeting place.[3]

Soon after the move, Dooky and Emily expanded the growing enterprise into the neighboring living quarters. Emily's skills were not exclusive to the kitchen. Shrewd with money management, she arranged for a $600 loan from a local brewery to fund the expansion.[4] Emily learned to cook from her father, Emile Tennette, the chef and owner of the first black Creole restaurant in New Orleans, Tennette & Montegut, open from 1933 to 1935 on North Claiborne Avenue.[5] Dooky and Emily's collective business instincts, personality and culinary skills served them well. They enjoyed what Dooky referred to as the "Good Life," reflecting that spirit in the restaurant's ambiance. Dooky Sr. was, after all, credited with helping invent the second-line umbrella,[6] and he was one of the first black men in New Orleans to own a Model T Ford in the 1930s. His success only multiplied after establishing the sandwich and lottery ticket shop in his name.[7]

While Dooky Chase Sr. was making a name for himself as an entrepreneur, his son, Edgar "Dooky" Chase II, was garnering attention on the music scene. In 1945, at the age of sixteen, Dooky Jr. was known throughout the city for his sixteen-piece big band called the Dooky Chase Orchestra, which he led featuring himself on trumpet and his sister Doris Chase's vocals.[8] His father's entrepreneurial tendencies were not lost on Dooky Jr. either. When he was just nineteen, Dooky Jr. co-promoted the first racially integrated concert at the Municipal Auditorium, featuring Duke Ellington with his entire orchestra among the lineup.[9]

In 1945, when Dooky Jr. was taking a break from touring his band on the road, he met Leah Lange at a Mardi Gras ball held at a local labor union hall.[10] Leah "hated musicians" because they "are always in their own little world." She conceded, however, that at that point in her life she was likely in her own "little world" too, and in 1946, just three months after they met, she and Dooky Jr. married.[11] In the hands of Leah Lange Chase, known today as the "Queen of Creole Cuisine," Dooky Chase would transition from a sandwich shop and bar into one of the first fine dining restaurants for African Americans in the United States.

Although her legacy is inextricably linked to New Orleans, and that was in fact where she was born, Leah Lange grew up on the north shore of Lake Pontchartrain in the small town of Madisonville, Louisiana. She was the youngest of nine girls among her mother Hortensia's eleven surviving children. Despite her segregated, rural and poor upbringing, Leah showed great promise at a young age. She started school a year early, was cast as the lead in every school play and even memorized the entire Latin Mass.[12]

"People say, 'Oh, did you have a hard time in segregation?'" Leah said in an interview with the author conducted in April 2019. "I didn't have a hard time because for one thing, I was so poor. I didn't have the money to go anywhere, so I didn't try to get in places where I didn't have no money to go, so I didn't suffer what people who had the money…I didn't feel that because I didn't have the money anyway."[13]

When it was time for Leah to go to high school, the only option available close to home was a public school in nearby Covington, which Leah's father, Charles, forbade his children attending for fear of them encountering too many "non-Catholics." Instead, at the age of thirteen, Leah moved across the lake to live with her aunt and attend St. Mary's Academy, an all-girls school in New Orleans.[14]

When Leah graduated high school at sixteen years old, she returned home to Madisonville and was disappointed that her only job opportunities there were in housekeeping. Instead of settling, she begged her parents for permission to move in with her cousin Mary in the Seventh Ward of New Orleans, where she could find work in the city. Although Charles and Hortensia Lange were hesitant to let their youngest daughter leave the safety of small-town life, Leah was successful in convincing them, and the determined young woman returned to the city that would eventually come to embrace her as a culinary queen.[15]

Most Creole girls of Leah's time and upbringing who lived in New Orleans were expected to work in the Haspel Brother's Factory sewing pants. Although Leah was a skilled seamstress, she saw the factory work as boring and repetitive. Eventually, Leah sought work in the French Quarter, despite the negative associations with girls who worked in that part of town at the time. She found a job at the Oriental Laundry and kept it for two days before a coworker there chided her for working too fast. Realizing that she had no time to waste, particularly on laundry, Leah left in search of more fulfilling work.[16]

Leah's first foray into the restaurant business was working as a waitress at the Colonial Restaurant on Chartres Street for Bessie Sauveur. When Leah first applied and began working there, it was her first time setting foot in a restaurant. "There were no restaurants for black people to go back then," Leah said in *The Dooky Chase Cookbook*, published in 1990.[17]

When Bessie Sauveur closed the Colonial and instead opened the Coffee Pot Restaurant on Royal Street, Leah followed as one of three teenage girls who ran the restaurant serving short-order breakfast and lunch items. Leah and the girls wanted to offer hot plate specials, which the restaurant implemented at their suggestion. The first was Creole wieners and spaghetti for just sixty cents per plate. While working at the Coffee Pot, Leah often wished she owned it. After three men came into the restaurant and proclaimed they were buying it, and wanting Leah to work for them, she took her cue to leave—she was wary of allowing strangers to do something perceived as a favor to her, knowing they would have expectations in return, and she had bigger plans.[18] Ever beyond the norm for her age and time, and wanting to experience new things, as young people do, she then became the manager for two amateur boxers and was the first woman to work for a local bookie marking the racehorse board.[19]

Not long after, Leah met and married Dooky Chase II, a restaurant heir in his own right. Her parents were not informed of the marriage until it had already taken place. Although Dooky was Creole and Catholic, two points decidedly in his favor, he was also a musician from the city and five years younger than Leah—her parents would have been skeptical of his ability to provide for their daughter. After their marriage in 1946, when he was eighteen and she was twenty-three, it was still some time before Leah Lange, now Leah Chase, went to work at the family restaurant.[20]

The Korean War put an end to Dooky II's big band, and the couple started their family. For years thereafter, Leah was too busy raising her own children, whom she said came "one right behind the other" in the early years of their marriage, to have any hand in the family business. First was Emily in 1946, followed by Stella in 1947 and her only boy, Edgar Chase III, in 1949. In 1953, she delivered her fourth and final child, a little girl named Leah. The first Leah was an excellent mother, sewing elaborate costumes for the entire family each year for Mardi Gras and setting out huge piles of candy on the neutral ground for Halloween.[21]

Although she spurned sewing jobs when she first moved to the city, Leah began to take seamstress work, eventually establishing a successful business and later creating drapes for Dooky Chase's dining rooms when it was remodeled. Then, when her children were in school, Leah went to work at Dooky Chase three days a week, steadily making moves toward updating and elevating the restaurant to her and her husband's vision.[22]

When Leah first went to work at her husband's family's sandwich shop, she expected that she might be a hostess or perhaps set tables, which was not yet a standard practice in black-owned restaurants. Her mother-in-law, Miss Emily, known to maintain a pristinely styled and manicured appearance, would greet guests in the dining room and manage finances, while Dookys I and II ran the bar.[23] Eventually, Leah found her place in the kitchen: "When I started talking about cooking and no one in the kitchen knew where I was coming from, I had to get back in the kitchen and start creating dishes," Leah said in *The Dooky Chase Cookbook*. "And that's where I stayed."[24]

Once in the kitchen, Leah began to push the limits of what she could get away with. Sometimes she tried to create specials and add menu items that would appeal to the customer base, and other times she would change things drastically to see what she could get away with. Oftentimes it was a game of trial and error. The clientele did not know what to make of the elaborate fine dining dishes Leah had picked up on in the French Quarter, calling Leah's mother-in-law, Emily, and proclaiming, "That girl is gonna ruin your business. Nobody wants Lobster Thermidor."[25]

"So I had to back off and start doing the things that I know black people like," Leah reflected in a recent interview with the author. "They

Edgar "Dooky" Chase II and Leah Chase at Dooky Chase's Restaurant in 1985. *Photo by Harold F. Baquet; Gift of Harold F. Baquet and Cheron Brylski via the Historic New Orleans Collection.*

like stuffing, so we used the oyster dressing, the chicken stews, so I had to make that up. We started stuffing chicken breasts with oyster dressing, and that went over. And making Shrimp Creole, and making gumbo. Those houses in the Quarter did not have gumbo at those times. They didn't, they had cream soups; they didn't have gumbo. That was black food. I started doing that, and it worked. But that wasn't easy to do. It was hard. And you learn to introduce people to different kinds of food. That was the worst thing about segregation: It kept black people from learning. It kept you from learning."[26]

When Leah compromised by serving broiled lobster tails with the heads stuffed with shrimp dressing, however, customers approved. While most of the guests embraced her alterations, others preferred for Dooky Chase to remain as it was. "There was talk among the older ones that I was going to ruin everything with my attitude, whatever my attitude was," Leah said.[27]

What Leah wanted to create was a restaurant where black people could sit down and be served a nice meal—a privilege white people had been enjoying for more than a century in the French Quarter but was still hard to come by for African Americans. "I want my people to have the finest things they can have. And if I can give it to 'em, and make them feel like a queen or a king, I'm gonna do that," Leah told the author. "They appreciate that. I like good things, I like nice things. I think people coming out to eat deserve nice things. You know, if you chide and worry, and you come in the restaurant, you want people to treat you kindly. You feel better when you leave! You could serve anything, just serve it and present it nicely. You'll have them on their knees. So if you can make people happy, that's a wonderful thing. And people appreciate that. They say, 'We can go to Dooky Chase because she can do everything. They can serve us on fine plates, like we deserve.'"[28]

Despite the constant effort Leah put into the restaurant and her husband, she often felt excluded by the Chase family. While the voting members of the family corporation that owned Dooky Chase met upstairs, Leah remained in the kitchen cooking. She was typically paid after other family members when money was tight, frequently in IOUs.[29] Despite this, when her father-in-law, Dooky Sr., was in the hospital near the end of his life, she cared for him until he passed. Leah had been raised to believe that "one's rent on Earth is paid by services rendered to others," which explains why she found her calling in the restaurant business. "Working in the restaurant industry has now become my way of serving others....It is the guest who

Main dining room with buffet. *Alexandra Kennon.*

Main dining room. *Alexandra Kennon.*

enjoys the meal and services given that makes me happy. It is truly the best feeling to see happy people and to know that, in some way, you have contributed to their happiness."[30]

One of the only restaurants to seat blacks and whites even before integration was acknowledged in Louisiana, Dooky Chase's Restaurant housed many important civil rights meetings in the 1950s and '60s. Important players regularly seen at Dooky Chase during this time were local attorneys A.P. Tureaud, Lionel Collins and Ernest "Dutch" Morial (who later became New Orleans's first African American mayor in 1978; Dooky II wrote the first major campaign check); Revius O. Ortique Jr., the first African American individual elected to the Louisiana Supreme Court; Counsel to the NAACP Defense Fund Thurgood Marshall; and the national leader of the Congress on Racial Equality (CORE), James Farmer—all dined and discussed in the Upstairs Room. Local white integrationists, including Moon Landrieu and Rosa Keller, frequented the restaurant to meet with their black allies. In the 1960s, Freedom Riders including Reverend A.L. Davis, Reverend Avery Alexander, Oretha Castle Haley, Rudy Lombard, Virginia Durr and Jerome Smith were all welcomed to Dooky Chase. "The Freedom Riders, when those left from New Orleans to meet them in Birmingham and other places, they came here first," Leah remembered. "I fed them, and they would really always have their meetings over a bowl of gumbo and some fried chicken."[31]

If the Freedom Riders arrived unbathed and dirty, straight from jail, Leah would send them around the corner to Vergie Castle, Oretha Castle's mother and the assistant chef, who would let them bathe and clean up at her house before they returned to the restaurant to eat and plan their next move. Even Reverend Martin Luther King Jr. traveled to New Orleans to start the Southern Christian Leadership Conference, and he too discussed ideas and strategy over Miss Leah's cooking.[32] While integration came to some southern cities with a violent uproar, the transition in New Orleans was somewhat more peaceful, if still far from easy. Many would credit Dooky Chase use as an integrated meeting place as a major factor.

"We just did what we thought we had to do," Leah said of the time in a recent interview with the author. "We had a place that the people could meet, so we let them use the space. Sometimes they would have money to buy a sandwich, sometimes they didn't. But we let 'em use the space. And nothin', the strange thing is, nothin' ever went down at this place. Once you entered this place, not one policeman came in. You felt safe. So the black people called this their 'safe haven.' They felt safe comin' here.

Because they knew that once they sat, no one was gonna bother them. Not one policeman would come in here and try and take 'em to jail. Now that was amazing."[33]

For the most part, the subversiveness required to unite blacks and whites to overturn institutional racism was overlooked by the New Orleans Police Department when it came to Dooky Chase. The politics occurring therein seemed less incendiary under the cover of the smell of filé gumbo, and every well-respected member of the African American community in New Orleans was a frequenter of Dooky Chase at that time. To take action against the restaurant would put the New Orleans Police Department at risk of antagonizing not only the black community but also the community at large, and the all-white police force in the department during this tenuous time seemed to know better, for the most part.[34]

Freedom Rider Jerome Smith commented on the restaurant's unique relationship with local police at this time: "This was no ordinary place. They [the police] had to be careful how they handled it. You have to remember that everyone in the world in the black community who was somebody had come through those doors. It wasn't just the ragtag activist like myself. I think in some way the powers that be had to be careful."[35]

"And I think it's because my mother-in-law was like she was. She would like to give things. You know, we had no black policemen in those days. All we had was white policemen. But they were all right. They would come by, and she would say to them, 'I'm gonna fix you a little sandwich.' Fix them a shrimp sandwich, give 'em a root beer. They went on their way. But they never ever bothered us about anything that went on here," Leah told the author. "I'll never forget when Jesse Jackson ran for president, oh we had security all over the roof. I said, 'My God, Jesse been comin' here for years, nobody can hurt Jesse in here. So you don't need all that. Nobody gonna attempt to get to Jesse Jackson in here.' We were fortunate that way."[36]

That said, NOPD did storm the restaurant in 1961, at the height of the Freedom Riders' movement. The officers demanded to know "What's going on in there?" doubtlessly referring to the Jim Crow ordinances still in place that were being broken inside. Dooky Jr. responded calmly, "This is a restaurant. We're just feeding our clients." The officers went on their way.[37]

While the local police usually left the restaurant alone, some whites who opposed integration in New Orleans were more aggressive. On one occasion, someone threw a pipe bomb from a passing car at the restaurant, which fortunately only partially exploded and rolled under the vehicle of a dining guest. The attack resulted in no injuries and minimal damage, but it was evident that not everyone in the city approved of the efforts toward equality being fueled within Dooky Chase's Restaurant.[38]

Despite the occasional threat, Leah and Dooky never shied away from using the business to make a political statement. When the black community in New Orleans boycotted Mardi Gras celebrations in 1961 in support of activists protesting and marching for equal rights in Montgomery, Dooky Chase followed suit and shuttered its doors. Although the loss of Carnival business was a massive financial hit, the Chases were the most respected black restaurateurs in town and knew that if they closed, other businesses would follow suit. Their participation made the boycott a success, and instead of funding the annual parades and balls, African American organizations in New Orleans donated to the NAACP legal defense fund to provide for those protesting segregation on the front lines.[39] Dooky Jr. was an active member of the NAACP himself and would speak out on the radio encouraging all people to vote and personally canvass black neighborhoods registering eligible family members.[40]

In 1957, Dooky Sr. passed away. Much beloved by his community in the Tremé neighborhood and beyond, his funeral procession is reported to have been one of the largest anyone had seen at the time. Then came the first redecorating of the restaurant, which would become another point of contention for Leah and her mother-in-law, Emily. While the two strong-willed ladies were usually able to come to an agreement about Leah's choices in the kitchen, their tastes differed wildly when it came to décor. When Leah first started working at Dooky Chase, the dining room wallpaper was black with pink elephants. Leah replaced it with red velour on one wall, mirrors on another and gold drapes she sewed herself to coordinate. She was able to talk Emily into the look because they were both fond of the color red, but Leah had more difficulty when it came to buying the chairs she wanted. The ones she had seen and liked at Vieux Carré Restaurant in the French Quarter were deemed too expensive; Leah managed to order them regardless. In exchange, her mother-in-law decided that she would take the lead on redecorating the upstairs dining room. Leah, having no fight left in her after the chair battle, conceded, and the Upstairs Room was painted pink.[41]

When Emily was bedridden near the end of her life, Leah cared for her until her death as she had for Dooky I. Years earlier, when the live-in security guard for the restaurant died, Leah's husband, Dooky II, had taken up living in the apartment above the business where the guard had resided. Fearful of leaving the restaurant unattended, Dooky continued to live in the upstairs apartment even after his children moved away. With the children now grown, rather than reconnecting with her husband, Leah would return after long days in the kitchen to an empty house. Eventually, she decided that returning home late and alone and leaving early alone the next day were not worth the effort, especially considering she never bothered to get a driver's license, and she too stayed at the restaurant for a time.[42]

Although her commitment to Dooky and his family restaurant was far from easy or glamorous, Leah's mantra through difficult times was consistently "You do what you have to do." The emotional toll the business took on her relationship was only part of it; the work was physically grueling as well. On one occasion, Leah was steeping tea and spilled three gallons of scalding liquid down her torso. Despite the burns exacerbating her ulcers, she continued to work in the kitchen bandaged "like a mummy," regardless of the pain. "I've just damaged myself all to pieces in this restaurant," she remarked in her biography. Another time, no one could clean the grill to her standards so she did it herself, burning her arms extensively. "But you keep going. You put a little powder on your face and you keep going."[43]

Leah's perseverance has been known to withstand Gulf storms as well. When Hurricane Betsy struck New Orleans in September 1965, more than 250,000 people were forced to evacuate their homes, and those who were able to remain lost power. The freezers at Dooky Chase were filled with gumbo, oysters, catfish, softshell crabs and other delicacies, threatening to spoil in the heat. Ever quick on her feet and eager to lend a hand, Leah contacted the New Orleans Police Department and offered to cook and serve the food to the city's residents who were trapped with no power. She and an assistant used gas equipment to cook and then would meet a police escort to walk along the Mississippi River levee to bring the hot food to those in low-lying areas. It did not require a natural disaster for Leah to help her fellow man though—she once made her daughter stop the car upon seeing a man digging in a trash can and offered for him to come get something to eat at the restaurant instead. She was notorious for acts of service like this, the ideals her parents taught her never forgotten.[44]

Of course, this translated into the restaurant business as well. Leah typically preferred to take reservations herself, so she could keep track of customer preferences from the kitchen. Many regulars, often members of New Orleans society such as politicians and the like, boasted to their dining partners that Miss Chase knew exactly how they like their meals. VIP service was never reserved strictly for the restaurant's many celebrity clients, but rather for anyone lucky enough to have Leah cook for them, particularly local regulars. Leah wholeheartedly embraced tourism too, knowing that so much of New Orleans's economy depends on it. She was intimately aware not only because of the travelers from all over the world who flocked to the restaurant but also because her husband, Dooky, served as the vice-president of the New Orleans Tourist Commission from 1978 to 1983. Leah once spoke to a group of senior citizens touring from Boston before returning to the kitchen: "New Orleans has no industry. *You* are our industry. We love you. We want you to enjoy yourself. We'll roll out the red carpet for you. We want you to have a good time. And we don't want you to go home with a penny in your pocket."[45]

During the first forty years, there was only one dining room at Dooky Chase that opened out onto the street. It was fairly small, with the upstairs room being used exclusively for private parties. In 1984, Leah and Dooky expanded the space, adding a main entrance, a grander main dining room and another midsize dining room called the Victorian Room. The small original dining space became known as the Gold Room, and the Upstairs Room, once a civil rights epicenter, was converted into office space.[46]

When the renovations were completed, a proper grand opening was naturally held. It coincided perfectly with the 1984 Louisiana World Exposition, held in New Orleans. Ever invested in the success of their city and its people, Dooky Jr. sat on the committee for the fair,[47] and Leah utilized the restaurant's opening celebration as a means of raising money for a pavilion at the exposition that was struggling financially. Mayor Ernest "Dutch" Morial cut the ribbon, and $50 per person was charged for an elaborate buffet and live music. Leah and Dooky took none of the proceeds, donating more than $8,000 to the pavilion. Leah also sat on the committee to plan the fair's art exhibition and fought to ensure that African American artists were adequately represented.[48]

Leah Chase's passion for the arts extended far beyond the work she did in the kitchen or even the music her husband played when they met. Under her cultivation, the dining rooms at Dooky Chase became some of the first African American art galleries in New Orleans. Works by prominent African American artists John Scott, Elizabeth Catlett, John Biggers and others adorn the otherwise boldly painted walls of the restaurant. Leah was also a lifelong member of the New Orleans Museum of Art Board of Trustees.[49] She even championed the arts on a national level, having testified before a subcommittee of the Appropriations Committee of the United States House of Representatives in 1995 to speak out against budget cuts to the National Endowment for the Arts.

Leah and Dooky's connection to New Orleans's first black mayor, Dutch Morial, continued strong well into and beyond his tenure as mayor. At the end of the 1970s, right after Mayor Morial's election, his wife, Sybil, was exasperated with all of the ducks her husband shot piling up in her freezer. Dutch brought the game to Leah, asking her to cook them and some sides so they could host a large dinner for his friends and supporters. This was the first of what would be known throughout New Orleans as the "Duck Dinners," always referred to by that name even if another meat was served. By the time the last dinner was held in 1986, the attendance had long outgrown Dooky Chase at six hundred attendees, and Leah still prepared each meal. Leah Chase and Dutch Morial, a team that took New Orleans by storm, remained friends until Dutch Morial died in 1989 at the age of sixty.[50]

Friends of Leah's, always well intentioned, often suggested she move the restaurant out of a "bad neighborhood." Leah was always the first to jump to the defense of her neighbors' morality. Once, in the 1980s, the Chases were selling tickets to a Rolling Stones concert at the Superdome out of the restaurant for $30 apiece, cash only. Hordes of exclusively white Stones fans lined up beginning before sunrise at four or five o'clock in the morning, and despite the neighborhood being well aware of the more than $40,000 cash collectively in their pockets, not one robbery or attempt occurred. Instead, members of the neighborhood brought them newspapers, coffee and doughnuts in exchange for small tips while they waited.[51]

That said, any neighborhood in New Orleans is bound to experience some excitement, good and bad, eventually. One bizarre and tragic night in May 1998, a man carrying a baby entered Dooky Chase's Restaurant with the baby's mother to grab two oyster po-boys to go. Another woman, the man's scorned lover, charged into the restaurant screaming and wielding a knife, attacking the man. Leaping from behind the counter, Dooky was able to grab the baby as the woman chased the man out of the restaurant. Despite Dooky's quick efforts to save the infant and call 911, the man was stabbed to death. Some accused Dooky of forcing the man outside, and the man's family claimed that Dooky might have saved his life had he acted differently. While the neighborhood sided with Dooky, knowing that he needed to protect his restaurant and his customers first and did all he could, the impact of the man's death was still devastating to him.[52]

In 1990, Leah's oldest daughter, Emily, died delivering her eighth child at the age of forty-two, with the new baby, Nathan, passing days later. Leah never closed the restaurant, despite Dooky's urging. Ever a woman of strong faith, she and her daughter Stella cited prayer as the driving force that carried them through the excruciating loss. Plus, there was still food to be cooked and media appearances scheduled.[53]

Although the Chases were no strangers to hurricanes, another massive hit for the family as well as the business came when the Tremé flooded following Hurricane Katrina in 2005. One year later, when a writer from the *New York Times* visited in August 2006, the restaurant remained closed. Leah and Dooky were living across the street in a FEMA trailer keeping tabs on the slow, ongoing repairs. Leah told the reporter, "I know people say, 'My God, a year later and you're not any further than this?' They just don't understand. We're all taking a whipping down here." Despite the assistance of insurance checks, Leah also attributed the slow progress after the storm to her husband Dooky's stinginess: "He wouldn't give a crippled crab a crutch to get to a gumbo party," Leah told the *New York Times*. The work was grueling and slow but sure, and two years after the storm, Dooky Chase reopened for business.[54]

KEEPING ON IN THE TREMÉ

Leah embraced all of the influences of Creole cuisine in her cooking for Dooky Chase and occasionally some less expected traditions as well. A corned beef and cabbage special is common for St. Patrick's Day at the restaurant, as is pasta for St. Joseph's Day. Leah even traced Chinese culinary influences in New Orleans to when the Chinese were brought to the city to build railroads and eventually mingled with slaves. Leah paid homage to these roots by offering Wok and Soul Day, when she served "Yakimi," often referred to in New Orleans as "Yakamein," a sort of soulful Asian beef and green onion noodle soup.[55]

"That's how you learn about people: through their food," Leah told the author. "That introduces you to their culture: Tell me what you eat, and I'll tell you who you are."[56]

One of the most popular annual events at Dooky Chase is Holy Thursday, when Leah prepared a traditional Creole Gumbo des Herbes—a variation on gumbo that incorporates different varieties of greens (an odd number, adhering to custom, which Leah said indicates how many rich friends will be made the following year).[57]

"Right now I'm getting ready to get somebody to help me grind my greens for Holy Thursday," Leah told the author as she prepared for Holy Thursday

Left: Leah's workspace enshrined by crucifixes, but also note the "Don't Make Me Flip My Witch Switch" sign. *Alexandra Kennon.*

Below: Leah Chase at her desk, where she ran the kitchen every day at Dooky Chase. *Alexandra Kennon.*

2019. "Now on Holy Thursday I do the Gumbo Z'Herbes. Now every Creole, white and black, on Holy Thursday was the last day that you could eat a full meal. 'Cause on Good Friday, if you're a Catholic, they didn't want you to eat a piece of bread. You didn't eat anything," Leah remarked. "So they cooked this big meal: greens, with a lot of meat in it. That's what you had. And had a big meal. Just like the Jewish people at Passover dinner."[58]

Leah used to buy pepper grass, one of the staple ingredients, from an elderly woman who sold it on the neutral ground. These days, pepper grass is harder to come by, but watercress and arugula offer a similar bite.[59]

The staples of the menu at Dooky's, and most of Leah's cooking, are what she referred to as "Creole de Couleur": Creole but emboldened with the addition of a bit more spice—"an African touch," with some Caribbean flavors incorporated as well.[60] "Here the food is unique," she noted in *The Dooky Chase Cookbook*. "I don't think you are going to get food anywhere else like in New Orleans. It's a mixture of everything: black, Spanish and French. Our cooking at Dooky Chase's reflects those traditional influences."[61]

Another aspect of Creole cuisine Leah insisted was crucial is the quality of ingredients—something that perhaps was imparted when she grew up on the rural Northshore, always hyper-aware of where her food was coming from. "I always say it's good coming up in a small, rural town because you learn about animals," Chase told *County Roads* magazine in 2012. "Kids today don't know the food they eat. If you come up in a country town, where there's some farming, some cattle raising, some chicken raising, you know about those things."[62]

Although Leah grew up poor during the Depression, with her father making only fifty cents a day, she credited her parents with teaching her how to live well off of the land—lessons she utilized at Dooky's. "But we had *food* to eat. Then if you're hunting, pull down a rabbit, that was your dinner on Sunday. Your mother knew how to cook that rabbit, you know, to make it your dinner. You could fish in the bayou, that was your fish for dinner," Leah told the author. "You knew how to get the food you needed. And fresh food that you needed. So I came up on fresh food, good food. You had no preserves, no freezers to freeze things."[63]

Of course, when it comes to the kind of cooking that feeds major political movements, a great deal of passion is required as well. "You have to love that pot and love what you are doing," Leah said in her first cookbook. "Talk to any black Creole person about their food and you will hear all the love in the world as they speak….I guess it's like Dooky says, you have to love food and love to eat. I go to sleep thinking about food."[64]

Leah Chase avoided calling herself a chef because of her lack of formal culinary education, which other chefs in the industry have vehemently disputed. John Folse remarked on the subject, "What is a chef? A chef is a leader in the kitchen. A chef is a manager of food and culinary technique and philosophy. A cook is a technician, the person with the skills to make something happen in a pot. And a chef and a cook come together to wow the palates of the guests in the dining room. Is Leah a chef or a cook? She's both, and a whole lot more."[65]

In addition to the wide range of civil rights heroes, Leah Chase fed politicians ranging from Barack Obama (whom she famously chastised for putting hot sauce in her gumbo without tasting it first) to George W. Bush and entertainers ranging from Duke Ellington to Beyoncé Knowles. Ray Charles even paid homage to Dooky Chase in song: "I went to Dooky Chase/to get me something to eat/The waitress looked at me and said/Ray, you sure look beat/Now it's early in the morning/And I ain't got nothing but the blues." Not a year has gone by since 1985 that some individual or organization has not honored Leah Chase. They are far too many to list here, but they include an honorary doctorate from Johnson & Wales, a James Beard Lifetime Achievement Award and having the first African American Disney princess drawn and animated in her image, to name a few.[66]

In her 2011 cookbook *And Still I Cook*, Leah reflected on the many changes she observed throughout her lifetime: "Since the 1950s, I've seen a lot of changes take place in the world. I've seen people—especially black people—come into their own, into their rightful places in society. I've seen changes in the way people do business. I've implemented more than a few changes in the way we do business at Dooky's. It's a necessity if your goal is to stay in business."[67]

When Edgar "Dooky" Lawrence Chase II passed away in 2016, his obituary ran in the *New York Times* as well as local papers.[68] Leah Chase, his wife of seventy years, continued to reign over the kitchen at Dooky Chase nearly every day until her recent death at the age of ninety-six on June 1, 2019. "I put my heart and soul and my life in here. It's just hard for me to say, 'I quit,'" Leah told the author from her desk in the kitchen less than two months before she passed. She is mourned by her family, the city of New Orleans and the international culinary community as a whole. Her life was celebrated with multiple second-line jazz parades, featuring local musicians including Trombone Shorty and attended by thousands.

A painting of Leah Chase and Princess Tiana given to Leah by the animators of the Disney film *Princess and the Frog* to thank her for inspiring Tiana's character. *Dooky Chase's Restaurant.*

Between sixteen grandchildren and twenty-eight great-grandchildren, there is no question that Leah and Dooky's legacy will continue strong at Dooky Chase. "I would *like* it to continue on. I would like it to grow," Leah said in an interview with the author on April 10, 2019. "And I'm grateful because I have children who want to make it grow, who want to do things to make it grow."[69] Sure enough, Leah's family told a local news outlet that they kept the restaurant open in the wake of her death because she would not have wanted anyone to miss the opportunity to eat at Dooky Chase. The Chase family is also in the process of reopening the upstairs dining room that once provided the setting for countless conversations among civil rights leaders and dedicating it to the movement that Leah championed with courage and gumbo. It is undeniable that Leah Chase's contributions have made a profound and lasting impact far beyond Dooky Chase's Restaurant.

Recipe from Dooky Chase

Gumbo Z'herbes

1 bunch mustard greens
1 bunch collard greens
1 bunch turnip greens
1 bunch watercress
1 bunch beet tops
1 bunch carrot tops
1 bunch spinach
1 bunch lettuce
1 head cabbage
2 medium onions, chopped
4 cloves garlic, chopped
water, as needed
1 pound smoked sausage
1 pound smoked ham
1 pound brisket stew meat
1 pound boneless brisket
1 pound hot chaurice sausage
5 tablespoons flour
1 teaspoon thyme leaves
1 tablespoon salt
1 teaspoon cayenne pepper
1 tablespoon filé powder
steamed rice

Clean all vegetables, making sure to remove bad leaves and rinse away all grit. In a large pot, place all greens, onions and garlic. Cover with water and boil for 30 minutes. While the greens are boiling, cut all the meats and sausages into bite-sized pieces and set aside. Strain the vegetables after boiling and reserve the liquid.

In a 12-quart stockpot place smoked sausage, ham and brisket meats, adding 2 cups of the reserved liquid. Steam for 15 minutes. While steaming the meats, place the chaurice in a skillet and steam until the fat is rendered (grease is cooked out). Set the chaurice aside, reserving the grease. Purée all vegetables in a food processor or meat grinder.

Heat the skillet of chaurice grease and then add the flour, stirring constantly, for about 5 minutes, or until a light-colored roux is achieved. (The roux does not have to be brown.) Pour the roux over the steamed meats, stirring well. Add the vegetables and 2 quarts of the reserved liquid. Simmer for about 20 minutes. Add the chaurice, thyme, salt and cayenne pepper. Stir well. Simmer for 40 minutes. Add filé powder, stir well and remove from heat. Serve over steamed rice.

Recipe courtesy of Leah Chase. When asked if the author could publish it, she replied generously, "Who cares?!"

AN INTERVIEW WITH LEAH CHASE

We were in the kitchen at Dooky Chase's Restaurant, at the desk where Leah Chase held court, gave orders and welcomed visitors and admirers daily. Mrs. Chase was enshrined in crucifixes, the hustle and bustle of the kitchen loud around her. The conversation took place on April 10, 2019, less than two months before she passed.

Alexandra Kennon: When you first came on at Dooky Chase, it was essentially just a bar and sandwich shop. I know you and your mother-in-law, Miss Emily, butted heads a bit when you started to remodel it. Could you tell me what your ultimate vision was for the restaurant?

Leah Chase: Well, she didn't know that. In 1941, I came here to go to work. Now, all the Creoles of color, the women worked in sewing factories. They worked in sewing factories. All my relatives worked for [clothing factories in New Orleans in '40s]. They sewed a lot. So I did the worst thing in the world: when I came to work in New Orleans, I got a job in the French Quarter. That was a no-no. And the job paid me seven dollars a week. Now the sewing factories were paying eleven dollars a week in those days. I could sew all right, but I didn't want to sit down making pants pockets all day long. You had to do what they call "piecework": This group made the pants pockets, this group made the flies, this group made the back pockets. I couldn't do that…it was boring to me. So I got that job in the French Quarter. That's the best thing I coulda done in my life. 'Cause I liked what I saw. I liked people being served nice. I had never been in the inside of a restaurant in my life. Wasn't nothin' for us to go to, with segregation, there was nothing for you to go to. You had to just wing it and do what you had to do. So I liked it.

AK: So that was the Colonial you worked in when you first started in the Quarter?

LC: The Colonial, the Colonial. It was just a straight little restaurant—she served breakfast, lunch and dinner. So I learned to wait tables. I knew nothing about waiting tables, and they put me on the floor by myself one morning. I didn't know what to do. Here comes a lady ordering her breakfast, she orders hotcakes. My first question is "Do you want toast with 'em?" She says, "Ya dumb—what in the world I'm gonna do with toast and hotcakes?" What I knew about hotcakes and toast, or whatever? I knew nothin'. But you learn as you go. And people come and teach you a whole lot of things. You meet people, there's nothing like people to show you the way. If you just *listen.* You gotta listen to everybody. And you can learn from everybody, if you just listen. I think that's a problem today: people don't listen. They don't listen. If they just listen, they can understand what it's all about.

Now being a waitress, we didn't work with tabs like you see today where you can write the order down. We had to remember it. Go back to the kitchen, put our order in, be able to pick it up and put it in the right place. Today, they couldn't do that. They don't even know how to take the order where they took it from. But you had to learn all of that. And you had to do those kinds of things. I remember there was an old man, they had a lot of tearooms in the Quarter in those days. They had a lot of tea houses. And it was a man who had a tea house right across the street from us, and he used to come every day and he ate the same thing every day: a vegetable plate. Every day, he ate a vegetable plate. They would divide the plate with potatoes; in this corner they put maybe some string beans, different vegetables in each corner.

AK: And how amazing you still remember just how he liked his vegetable plate.

LC: That's how he liked that plate. And he taught me one thing: he said you have to learn to remember. And I never forgot that...

AK: So, when you did start working at Dooky Chase in 1941 and eventually making changes, what was your goal?

LC: Well, to be like the restaurants I served in in the French Quarter. To be a fine dining restaurant. Nobody in the black community had that. Not a soul. We had one called "Hazy's Chicken Shack," or "Hazy's Place." He tried, it didn't work. But he didn't stick with the right things. I wanted all the right things. I wanted a cocktail bowl, for shrimp cocktail. The people did not know what a shrimp cocktail was. We did not have one, so we didn't know better. We didn't know what anything was. So I had to bring that here. I said, "If they can have it, why can't we? Why can't we do the same things?" So I had to start teaching 'em how to set the table. They said, "Oh, you can't put that silver on the table, that's not gonna be clean." I said, "I see them do it, they put it on the table, so why can't we do the same thing?" So that was hard, to make people understand that. But my mother-in-law, with time, she just let me go with it. And I did. I ran into a lot of trouble [laughs] with that, I'll never forget.

AK: Anytime you want to change things, that seems to happen.

LC: Yeah, I really brought different things. Now in the black community, we didn't know what Shrimp Newburg was, we didn't know what Lobster Thermidor was. We didn't know cream sauce. Because we didn't *have* it. They had it, they were doing French cooking. So they had the French and the Spanish mixture. We didn't have that, all we had was collard greens, fried fish, fried this. I wanted to change that. And I attempted to. I tried, the first thing, was so French: Lobster Thermidor....Well, they didn't understand lobster to begin with, and then the cream sauce, they didn't understand that. So oh, my goodness, they told my mother-in-law, "She's gonna ruin your business. She's gonna ruin everything." So I had to back off and start doing the things that I know black people like....That was the worst thing about segregation: it kept black people from learning. It kept you from learning. Now if you have a lot of people in your country or your state that are ignorant, that's bad news. You have to educate them, you have to show them what to do. So it wasn't until after integration that those of us who worked in those places who knew what to do, who knew how they ate, who knew how they lived, could do it, but the average person did not know that. Because they didn't have the opportunity to do that. So it was hard for them.

...My job all my life was fighting poverty, trying to get out of that poverty fight. I was born in 1923, so I was six years old when the Great Depression came in 1929, so I know what it is to have nothin'. My father worked for the WPA for fifty cents *a day*. Fifty cents a day. I'm tellin' ya. When I came to

New Orleans, that was a big thing. I went to work as a waitress, and I was makin' one dollar a day. And of course whatever little tips they gave ya. You might go home with ten dollars a day, that was big money. You could buy a good pair of shoes for $5.99. You could buy a cheap pair for $2.99. So, you see, things are totally different. But it was still: you had to have the money. And I didn't.

…When we were so poor comin' up, as I said, my daddy makin' fifty cents a day—he planted onion bulbs, he planted all of the vegetables we ate. We had to water them every day, we had to pull the weeds out of 'em and do work. But we had *food* to eat. Then if you're hunting, pull down a rabbit, that was your dinner on Sunday. Your mother knew how to cook that rabbit, you know, to make it your dinner. You could fish in the bayou, that was your fish for dinner. You knew how to get the food you needed. And fresh food that you needed. So I came up on fresh food, good food. You had no preserves, no freezers to freeze things, so what you did was in the okra season, you would cut 'em off, then you'd slice 'em. And then in the country we bought our groceries by the sacks because we had to buy 'em when we had the money. When you got your money once a month, you bought a sack of flour that would last you 'til the next month. And when you finished with that flour, you wash that sack, and you got all the numbers out it, and it was beautiful. You dried it out, you starch it and iron it, it can make you *anything*. It can make you a table cloth, it can make you all the things you needed to have. So you would have that flour sack and spread those okra out. In the country the sun is *blasting*, broiling hot, you got the wide-open sky, so we'd put the okra out there in the sun every day, so when it got to be out of okra season, you soak 'em in water, and you had the okra…like "sun-dried tomatoes" are the big thing. So we knew how to sun-dry tomatoes. [Laughs] It wasn't a big thing in our day. Slice that tomato, sit it in that broiling hot sun for a couple days; when they dry out, you put 'em in a jar.

…

AK: Well, Mrs. Chase, I know that you've seen so much of the civil rights movement firsthand, with the restaurant being integrated before it was even legal here. I wanted to ask if you could tell me what that was like. Did you realize what you were doing was so important and so political at the time?

LC: Nope. You know then, we didn't really do anything to get any name recognition. We just did what we thought we had to do. We had a place that the people could meet, so we let them use the space. Sometimes they would have money to buy a sandwich, sometimes they didn't. But we let 'em use the space. And nothin', the strange thing is, nothin' ever went down at this place. Once you entered this place, not one policeman came in. You felt safe. So the black people called this their "safe haven." They felt safe comin' here. Because they knew that once they sat, no one was gonna bother them. Not one policeman would come in here and try and take 'em to jail. Now that was amazing....

My mother-in-law just did what she had to do. She used to like to sit on the corner, sometimes she'd stand out there with a big bag of oranges or apples, to give it to the neighbors. She was like that, she always liked to give things. Liked to do things for other people. And I did the same thing that she did—I learned that you have to give to other people sometimes, you have to think about other people. That's the most important thing for today: people don't think about one another. They *don't* think about one another. They don't think about how they hurt people's feelings, they don't think about how they came up....

As a Catholic, we were taught that man is made in the image and likeness of God. And you look at the winos in the streets and say, "He don't look like God to me." But look again. You gonna find *somethin'* good in that man if you just stop and help. Just stop and think about him as a human being....I have this man's picture on the wall in the bar—he was the worst man in the world. A rapper named Tupac Shakur. He came up with the worst family you can ever have. But I went to an art show one time, and I saw a beautiful poem. And I looked at the bottom of that poem; it was written by Tupac Shakur. And then I start looking into this man's life—he was *brilliant*. But we didn't pay any attention to him. So sometimes you gotta stop, take a second to look at people. He was a brilliant man, he could write beautifully, but we lost him to the street. If somebody would have tried to lift him up and tell him the good work he could do, to get through the struggle that he was havin', it would have been better. But we have to stop and do that sometimes. Stop and look at somebody. Don't just get a first look at 'em, look a second time, and you'll see something totally different. You'll see something totally different.

AK: Very true, thank you, Mrs. Chase. I wanted to ask, of course, so many of these restaurants in New Orleans are run by men. Do you think your style of running a restaurant is different because you're a woman?

LC: [Laughs] No. Because let me tell you: black women started all their restaurants. Black women were hairdressers, they would fix hair in their houses. At that time you had to use a hot comb to straighten the hair out, hold the heat on, that kind of stuff. And they did that in their *kitchens*! They fixed the hair, waved it different, in their kitchens. So what they would do, they would cook. When you came to get your hair fixed, they would have a meal for you. So they knew if they could cook a meal, they could start selling 'em. So that's what they did. That's how Willie Mae's started! Willie Mae was a hairdresser, and then she was cooking for her customers, so she said, "Well, I can open a restaurant, I can cook." So she did. So you learn. And if you're interested, you keep learning.

In my position, I have to keep learning. I'm a big one for trying to know what's going on, and what's new going on and how to do things. And you learn as you go. And it's a wonderful thing, to learn. It's just a wonderful thing to learn and to bring whatever you learn to somebody else. Now when you open up, and they say, "We don't have to go there to eat shrimp cocktail, we can go to Dooky's. And no one is gonna disturb us there. It's not like a bar. We can sit at a table, and they can serve us." They needed a place to do that, a place to come and be served and appreciated....

And it's just makin' people sit together, eat together. I don't have to be your best friend, but as long as we work together to make our city, to make our state, a better place. Because that's what we try to do. That's all I try to do, is try to make our state a better place to live in. We have a good state, I'm tellin' you. You grew up in the South. There's nothin' like the South, nothin' like the South. I'm gonna take this family for instance: the Kennedys and Lyndon Johnson. Now, the Kennedys, they did all they could for black people, but it was a political thing. They learned that it was the right thing to do politically. But Lyndon Johnson comes up, he had been raised around black people. He had people working for him that were black. So he understood them, and he knew them, so it was a little different for Lyndon Johnson. You had people in the South, even though some of them are working on the farms, sharecroppers—they at least *knew* you. And because they knew you, they learned to love you and appreciate you....So you see, Lyndon Johnson knew the black people. He knew the black people and knew what to do for them and how to do it. That's the difference in the South: we not so backwards as they *think* we are. Oh, people comin' from the North or the East think that we are the dumbest, but then they come here and they find that different. We know how to dress, we know how to eat, we know everything....We might talk a little different, we might walk a little slower, but we know a *lot*. *A lot*. And we know how to get along, that's for sure. We know how to get along.

AK: That's for sure. Well, Mrs. Chase, I know you're still in this kitchen back here. How often would you say that you're in the kitchen at Dooky Chase?

LC: Every day. Right now I'm getting ready to get somebody to help me grind my greens for Holy Thursday. Now on Holy Thursday I do the Gumbo Z'herbes. Now every Creole, white and black, on Holy Thursday was the last day that you could eat a full meal. 'Cause on Good Friday, if you're a Catholic, they didn't want you to eat a piece of bread. You didn't eat anything. So they cooked this big meal: greens, with a lot of meat in it. That's what you had. And had a big meal. Just like the Jewish people at Passover dinner. I tell them, "Listen: You will acquire a rich friend for every green I had in the pot." Now, the superstition says you don't do even numbers of greens, you do uneven numbers. Five, seven, nine, whatever. They believe that. So everybody comes and gets a good lunch on Holy Thursday. You could be Jewish....It's so much fun. So we booked so solid, and then besides all the takeout we had, people ship it. If your daughter's out of town, they'll say, "I gotta ship her Gumbo Z'herbes, she's gotta have her Gumbo Z'herbes." I have two male friends in California that I have to ship their Gumbo Z'herbes to....They gotta get their good luck charm. It's fun just to do that. So all we serve on Holy Thursday is Gumbo Z'herbes and fried chicken. *It*, we don't serve nothin' else: Gumbo Z'herbes and fried chicken.

AK: I know it's hard to get ahold of pepper grass these days, you said.

LC: It's hard to get ahold of pepper grass. You used to see the old ladies in the neutral ground, lookin' for the pepper grass....It's a lemony grass, it's a distinct lemony flavor. My daddy used to pick it, wash it, you could make a salad with it. Just put some vinegar and oil on it, make a salad. But it's hard to find, so I use watercress. It works. But I'm gonna try to get me some peppergrass for next week.

AK: Absolutely. I wonder if it's like lemongrass they use in Vietnamese cuisine.

LC: I don't know, I never tried it. But that's a good idea. It's worth a shot, and that's where you bring another culture in with ya. That's how you learn about people: through their food. You learn all about people through their food. I worked with a Korean chef, and I said to her, "You know you got a dish that I hate: kimchi." I said I hate it. But honey, she made a kimchi that was perfect. So I enjoyed that kimchi. So you have to try things. And chefs are going and they're learning new ways to prepare things, so that's a good thing. That introduces you to their culture: tell me what you eat, and I'll tell you who you are.

AK: Very true, you can learn so much through food. I wanted to ask: What do you hope is the future of Dooky Chase?

LC: I would *like* it to continue on. I would like it to grow. And I'm grateful because I have children who want to make it grow, who want to do things to make it grow. Now, we have that old upstairs room, now we don't use it. Because now people don't wanna go up the steps, and so we have think about an elevator there to use that room again. So I have people learning. Like my grandson who's a chef, and he's also a big art collector too; he collects a lot of art. So he's learnin', and he went to the Cordon Bleu in Paris, so he's doing a lot of things, he's running my place and his place in the airport. But he's trying to make those businesses grow. So my children all worked here, they retired. Of course you educate your children, and usually you educate 'em right out of your business. [Laughs] But now they all retired, like Stella—she's out on the floor, but she served some years in the public school system. She was working in the public school system for years and years. And then Tracy, who's out there is a registered nurse, and she has five children, so she comes here and helps out here because she can't take a regular job and take care of five children. Because they're in *everything*; when you have children, they're in *everything*. But you have to let 'em go. Then I have one, he's been comin' here, but I'm going tonight to see him get an award at Harrah's Casino. He's big on poker games, and he does well with that, he really does well. I have one that's an engineer, one that builds houses. Then I have two that live in Atlanta, so they're doing well. And those seven children—my oldest daughter died—but of those seven children, we didn't lose a one. They all got all through college, they all grew up and are doing well. So God is with me…but we made it through that. And they're all doin' well. That's all you can ask for. I say she raised her children from heaven. She did. She raised 'em from heaven. So they all did well, she'd be proud of *all* of 'em. Even the one that's in the gambling business: he hated school, he *hated* it. And she kept sayin', "Oh, mother, if I could just get him going." But she'd be proud of him today. I said, "Now if you can count that money, *bam bam bam*, like that, you can do anything."

AK: Maybe he gets it from his great-grandfather a bit. Didn't Dooky I sell lottery tickets?

LC: Yep, yeah. [Laughs] He got that from him. Runs in the family.

AK: So how many grandkids do you have, total?

LC: I have sixteen grandkids and twenty-eight great-grandkids. Now the great-grands are something else. They age from about nine months up to twentysomething years old, but the ones that are six years old, two years old, you gotta watch: they know *everything*. I don't trust a one of 'em. I say, "I don't trust y'all!" They are somethin' else.

...Thank you so much, my dear....Because what you're doing for the South is important. People have to know how important we are in the South. They look at southerners as if we're dumb, we don't know anything. But look at us a second time. We moving. We moving. Because we have a great love for people, we learn to live with one another, we learn to work together—that is important. And there's no such thing as "my food," "your food"; we all eat the *same food*. Little white boy came in here, "What's this about soul food? I been eatin' that my whole life!" I said, "I know you have, they just prepared a little bit different." But it's always good. Thank you so much for your work.

Chapter 13
Brennan's

(1946)

Your out-of-town guests will always remember the thrill of "Breakfast at Brennan's." Leisurely and luxurious, the traditional long breakfast of the courtly Creoles is served just as you have seen it described in many magazine articles about "Breakfast at Brennan's."
—Times-Picayune, *1955*

THE ORIGINAL BRENNAN RESTAURANT: BRENNAN'S VIEUX CARRÉ

Among the plethora of French and Italian restaurateurs to make their way to New Orleans from Europe in the nineteenth century is an unlikely Irish family, who collectively have rendered an intense and lasting impression on the Creole culinary scene. Owen Brennan I traveled from his home Isles to New Orleans sometime in the 1840s, less than a decade after Antoine Alciatore came from Marseille to establish Antoine's Restaurant. Naturally, Owen found his new home in the growing Irish Channel neighborhood. His son, Owen Patrick, was to study engineering at college but became sidetracked when he met Ella Valentine, nicknamed "Nell," at a local dance. The pair soon married and moved their new family into a small rented shotgun house. Nell was naturally skilled in managing the home, and thanks to plentiful advice from other Irish Channel housewives over laundry on washday, she became an incredible cook as well.

On April 5, 1910, Owen Patrick and Nellie Brennan's first son, Owen Edward, was born. His father did not learn that the birth had taken place until he returned from his nightshift at the foundry where he worked the next morning—upon seeing his newborn son, he vowed to seek more respectable work. While Owen Patrick earned promotion after promotion thanks to his predisposition for engineering, Nell was giving birth to baby after baby. After Owen E. came baby Adelaide, followed by John, Ella, Dick and then Dottie. The expanding family was able to move into more spacious living quarters. When Owen Edward was a teenager, his father wanted him to go to college, but Owen E., like his dad, became distracted by a girl instead. He met seventeen-year-old Maude Siener, also at a dance, and two years later the pair was wed. Although Owen E. never made it to college, he managed to study accounting and other business classes and kept books for a candy store at the time he was married. Owen and Maude set up their life in the three-room half of a double shotgun house.

The era, however, was not in the young couple's favor. It was the beginning of the 1930s, with the Great Depression just getting started. Owen was cut from the candy business's payroll and set out seeking work elsewhere. But as was the nature of the Depression, work was scarce, and when it was available, it was temporary. The stakes rose when Maude discovered she was pregnant. Owen managed to secure enough work, although often grueling or degrading, to cover the hospital bills when his son was born. Owen Edward Jr. was a healthy baby but so small at birth the nurses called him "Peewee." "Peewee" became "Pip," who would later be a major player at Brennan's restaurant.

Meanwhile, Owen's younger siblings were growing up too. Adelaide had graduated from high school, taken a business class and found work, and John was a student and in ROTC at LSU. Ella, Dick and Dottie were still completing their schooling, but the siblings all remained close. The Brennans were later described by James A. Maxwell in the *Saturday Evening Post* as having "a tribal bond that would have abashed the Medicis."[1] Retrospectively, there is perhaps some irony in this statement.

Not long after his son Pip was born, the elder Owen Brennan was offered a well-paying position as a salesman for a local distillery. Not only did he secure that work, but when a friend of his converted the Court of Two Sisters into a popular nightclub during World War II, Owen also began to work there nights and observed the profits soar. He eventually had the thought, "If I can make a fortune for someone else at this, why can't I make one for the Brennans?" He turned responsibility for the Court of Two Sisters back

Owen Brennan outside the Old Absinthe House. *Ralph Brennan Restaurant Group.*

over to the absentee owner's wife and hired another manager to help her with the nightclub, and then he set out to start a business of his own.

Eventually, Owen found an offer that suited him. He bought the business operating inside the Old Absinthe House. Although Maude was initially skeptical, fearing having to pay the note in the event her husband was drafted, eventually she came around to the idea of being a saloon owner and joined Owen the next day in closing the transaction. They had made their transition into business owners but still had some work to do before becoming restaurateurs.

There are multiple and varied accounts of how Owen came to purchase the first Brennan restaurant, Vieux Carré. The restaurant had been opened some time in the 1920s, and by 1944, the business was struggling. One story says that Owen ate a disappointing lunch at the establishment, after which he heckled the owner for not providing a better meal. The owner snapped back, "If you think you can run the place better than I do, why don't you buy it?" What he did not expect was Owen to reply in earnest, asking for a quote. Another great iteration is that Owen was dining with his dear friend Count Arnaud at his restaurant when the Count asserted that "no Irishman could ever possess or display greater skill in matters of the cuisine than might be required to boil potatoes," and Owen stubbornly set out to prove him wrong. Although it is unclear what actually prompted the eldest Brennan son to pursue the restaurant business, Owen never bothered to contradict any of these narratives and perhaps even encouraged a few.[2]

Regardless of his motivation, Owen signed a lease for Vieux Carré restaurant on Bourbon Street. Not altering the original sign, another sign was hung above it, proudly declaring that Irishmen could serve Creole cuisine too. The restaurant became Brennan's Vieux Carré.

Initially, there was another shareholder, but not more than a year after the lease signing, Owen E. and his son Pip became the sole proprietors. Meanwhile John, Ella and Adelaide were all employed across Bourbon Street at the Old Absinthe House and would regularly hop across the street to Brennan's Vieux Carré for lunch. Owen's siblings were known to be tough critics of the food and service, despite their family owning the restaurant. When a cashier quit unexpectedly, eighteen-year-old Ella was called over to fill the position. From her post at a vantage point from which she could observe the entire restaurant, her untrained but shrewd eye caught all of the goings-on, and she reported them back to her elder brother. One of her observations was something along the lines of, "All you're doing is to give the people Trout Amandine, Oysters Rockefeller and things like that, every one of which is identified with some other restaurant. Why not figure out something that stands for Brennan's and make it better than any other restaurant in the whole world could make it?" Owen fired back that if she and John did not like the way he ran the place, they could come do it themselves. So they did.[3]

With Ella fresh out of high school and John fresh out of the military, neither knew much of anything about operating a restaurant. They were sharp and eager learners, however, and quickly picked up on tricks of the trade. John did the purchasing, Ella helped coach the waiters in displaying pride in their association with the restaurant. Their sister Adelaide handled the accounting for both Brennan's Vieux Carré and the Old Absinthe House. John eventually left with a desire to start his own dynasty, with his brother Owen agreeing: "There's enough of us Brennans to go 'round." Dick was finishing college, Pip was growing up and Maude and Owen had two more sons (Jimmy and Ted) on the way.

When John left, Owen handed full control of the kitchen over to Ella. Her first move was to hire a new chef. The previous chef was focused more on providing quantity of food rather than quality and had paid no mind to the eighteen-year-old girl who insisted that was not the ideal Brennan's approach. Ella wasted no time in going into the kitchen to fire him, and Paulus Blange, a soft-spoken cook from Holland, was promoted to chef de cuisine. Blange had been the sole cook to take Ella's demand for an original Brennan's dish seriously. He created a made-to-order speckled trout dish that immediately took off in popularity and remained a favorite on the menu at Brennan's Vieux Carré and later Brennan's on Royal Street, as "Troute Blange."

Owen, impressed by the success of his little sister's idea, was quick to help Ella in developing as many distinctly delicious Brennan-branded dishes as possible. Owen came up with "Les Troix Deux," or "Three Deuces," a serving of a half-dozen oysters on the half-shell: two Rockefeller, two Roffignac and two Bienville. Eventually, Owen tracked down several very old cookbooks, and Ella challenged Blange and his team in the kitchen to attempt a new meat dish, a fish dish and a poultry dish each day. In this method, Poulet Pontalba, another favorite from Brennan's Vieux Carré, was born.

Another waiter who was employed at Vieux Carré when Owen bought the restaurant began to experiment with variations on Crêpes Suzette, until a preparation was settled on that has since been described as "the finest crêpes ever confected." The extravagant dish of flambéed strawberries in crêpes is still served at Brennan's on Royal Street today. Brennan's most famous flaming dish, its original Bananas Foster, was created by Ella Brennan when her uncle requested she concoct a special dessert for his friend Richard Foster in honor of him being named chairman of the New Orleans Crime Commission. Frustrated that her uncle only gave her a few hours for the task, and recalling a breakfast dish involving bananas that her mother used to prepare, Ella grabbed a bunch of bananas, some butter, some brown sugar, some banana liqueur and some rum and got to work. She was inspired by the Baked Alaska famous at Antoine's to flambé the dish; it was served over ice cream. The Bananas Foster, too, remains an original staple at Brennan's today.

Owen, pursuing the trend established by other restaurateurs in his city at the time, always regaled VIP guests with the best of service. Elia Kazan once stopped in Brennan's Vieux Carré with Vivien Leigh while in town shooting *A Streetcar Named Desire* just to let her try their gumbo—a Creole dish with heavy African influence, served by an Irish family. So was, and is today, the nature of dining in a city as diverse as New Orleans.

It is perhaps unsurprising that those involved in a business centered on decadence and revelry are also very often involved in Mardi Gras festivities. Owen E. Brennan is credited with conceiving Bacchus, today one of New Orleans's largest Mardi Gras krewes and the first krewe to ordain celebrity monarchs for its parades. Owen observed that many of his out-of-town clients were frustrated with Carnival celebrations because non-locals were typically excluded. His solution was to create his own krewe in 1949, in which tourists were welcome, and to use personal funds to throw his own ball.

Although Brennan's Vieux Carré Restaurant did well enough through the majority of its first decade, the business's success did not truly take off until the mid-1950s. That is when restaurant critic Lucius Beebe made one of his regular trips to New Orleans and was met at the train station by Owen Brennan. Frances Parkinson Keyes's murder-mystery novel *Dinner at Antoine's* had become a bestseller, and Owen lamented to his friend that he certainly could not follow suit with anything along the lines of "Dinner at Brennan's." Beebe replied, "Why couldn't it be breakfast? What's wrong with Breakfast at Brennan's?" In fact, nothing was wrong with it—it would be embraced as the mantra associated with Brennan's Vieux Carré, and later Brennan's, for nearly a century to come.[4]

THE ROOST ON ROYAL STREET: BRENNAN'S

Just as Brennan's Vieux Carré restaurant on Bourbon Street was taking off, the landlord demanded half of the proceeds from the restaurant as part of the lease.[5] As a result of this unfortunate hang-up, and his desire to expand, Owen set his sights on another French Quarter property for the family restaurant. When he pitched his proposed location to the rest of the family, he was met with reactions ranging from skepticism to outright mockery. The building Owen considered was 417 Royal, which formerly housed international chess champion Paul Morphy. Some believe it was designed by architect of the White House and the U.S. Capitol Building Benjamin Latrobe, who drew the plans for the stately Louisiana Supreme Court building that sits across Royal Street. The location had a reputation as being cursed, or at the very least having terrible luck: businesses and homeowners who took up in the building throughout the years had been fraught with misfortunes ranging from failed financial endeavors to suicide. Despite the protests from his younger siblings, Owen decided to transfer his restaurant to 417 Royal Street.[6]

Historic Brennan's exterior. *Ralph Brennan Restaurant Group.*

In November 1955, with everything in place to move the business to its new home, Owen enjoyed a grand banquet with an organization he was involved in at Antoine's Restaurant. The next morning, when his wife, Maude, went to wake him around 10:00 a.m., she discovered that he had died peacefully in his sleep. Physicians ruled the cause of death a heart attack; he was only forty-five years old.[7] "It seemed everybody was at his wake, including everybody from the French Quarter in his or her strange attire," his sister Ella wrote in her autobiography.[8] Everyone had come out to honor the beloved "Happy Irishman of the French Quarter."[9]

While Owen's death came as a devastating shock to the rest of his family, they did not hesitate in continuing progress toward relocating the restaurant to its new building—they insisted the opening should still take place on the day Owen planned. According to Ella, Owen died on Friday, and she and his other siblings were back at work by Monday. "We had to," she said. "We had a restaurant to run and another in the pipeline."[10] Just prior to the Brennans' move to 417 Royal Street, the building had served as a public house known as Patio Royal, with a dining room right in front against the street and the kitchen tucked in the back. The Brennans instead moved the kitchen to the front of the building, with a large dining room adjacent. The courtyard, an important fixture to this day, was allocated for guests to sip drinks while waiting for their tables inside.[11]

May 31 was the day the family decided they would finally transfer operations from the Bourbon Street location to Royal Street. Although pouring rain all day seemed to be a bad omen, the plan was to serve breakfast at the old restaurant as usual and then move into the new building by lunch. Everything not explicitly necessary for the breakfast service had already been moved, so when hordes of esteemed local regulars began to arrive at Brennan's Vieux Carré just as breakfast was ending, Ella panicked. "I thought everyone understood lunch was to be at the new place," she told the growing crowd. They understood completely—everyone from bankers to reporters, advertising agents and business people, all fans and friends of the Brennans, had come to help them move. As the loyal patrons began to collect tablecloths and chairs, shoving silverware in their pockets, Ella announced that everyone would get one last drink before making the walk. She made a toast, and just as the drinks were finished, a full jazz band came parading down Bourbon Street, rain be damned. To the tune of "When the Saints Go Marching In," the Brennans and their guests marched and danced behind the musicians, their arms full of plates, utensils, tables and other wares. Arriving at the pink building that was Brennan's new home,

Servers in the courtyard. *Ralph Brennan Restaurant Group.*

Brennan's courtyard today. *Alexandra Kennon.*

the enthusiastic volunteer movers set down their loads and enjoyed the first lunch service at what would from that moment onward be considered a New Orleans icon.[12]

Once the remaining Brennans settled into the new building, Brennan's truly came into its own. The "Breakfast at Brennan's" concept was taking off: Chef Blange and Ella together concocted an egg-stravagant menu, featuring classics like Eggs Benedict and Antoine's original Eggs Sardou, along with more varied offerings such as Eggs à la Turk (or eggs with chicken livers) and corned duck hash. The decadent breakfast menu was accompanied by a list of "Eye Opener" cocktails designed to be enjoyed early in the day, such as Brennan's own creation, the Brandy Milk Punch, or a seasonal Champagne cocktail. Ever aiming to be festive and over the top, one of a series of desserts flambéed table side was to complete the meal: Ella's coveted Banana's Foster, among their top contenders. "Our breakfast was over the top and loads of fun," Ella remarked. "Just like New Orleans."[13]

In 1968, there was much discussion in the city over how to revitalize Carnival festivities, which in almost one hundred years' time had somewhat dulled. Owen E.'s son Pip Brennan, embracing his late father's idea, called for a meeting of influential people at Brennan's to work out a solution. The result was the reemergence of the Krewe of Bacchus, now with a grand parade the Sunday before Fat Tuesday and a celebrity monarch. By completely deviating from older Carnival traditions, Bacchus brought national attention to Mardi Gras celebrations, helping expand the party (or at least awareness of it) beyond just those living in New Orleans. Pip Brennan was the first captain of Bacchus that year.[14]

According to her daughter Ti Martin, Ella Brennan arranged the first celebrity king for the burgeoning Krewe of Bacchus: comedian Danny Kaye. Here is a story about Danny Kaye riding as monarch in the first annual Bacchus parade in February 1969, as Ti Martin remembered it:

> *My uncles had started the Bacchus parade, and my mom got the first celebrity king. Because they decided to bring in celebrities, rather than having us, their children, or themselves do it. They were really the first ones to do that, because they really wanted to bring Mardi Gras back to the people. And that's something I'm really proud that our family did. Well, anyway, the first king was Danny Kaye, who was a good friend of my mom. He told Ella, he goes, "I don't even know what you're talking about that you want me to come do, but I'll come do it. All I want you to know is, it's February, and I don't wanna be cold. And it's Mardi Gras, I*

Bananas Foster eagerly awaiting flambéing. *Alexandra Kennon.*

Vintage image of couples dining in the Red Room. *Ralph Brennan Restaurant Group.*

Vintage image of a bartender in a red jacket. *Ralph Brennan Restaurant Group.*

don't wanna be in a costume that's a dress." So fast-forward to that day, he's King of Bacchus, it's freezing cold and of course the Bacchus outfit is basically a dress. So, he comes by on the float, and the parades used to go through the French Quarter, so we're standing on the balcony at Brennan's, and you could practically reach out and touch him on the float, and he's standing there, and of course I've been seeing him drink the whole time, and he's got the microphone, and he said, "Ella, remember what I told ya? And I'm wearing a damn dress and I'm freezing my balls off!" And they're like "Turn off the microphone!" [15]

By the 1970s, the Brennan restaurant empire was growing quickly and exponentially. The family had just purchased Commander's Palace in 1969, and Brennan's of Houston and Brennan's of Dallas were brought to fruition. With plans in the works to open another Brennan's in Atlanta in addition to a national steakhouse chain, the Brennan family sat down for a meeting to discuss the restaurants and their ownership. Owen's surviving wife and sons said they were concerned that the rapid expansion would compromise the quality of both food and service in the family's existing restaurants, despite the fact that the original Brennan's was still filling its dining room night after night to great acclaim.

What most of the family did not expect was that when they gathered on November 5, 1973, to work through these questions of growth and responsibility, Owen's three sons—Pip, Ted and Jimmy—announced that they were claiming sole proprietorship of Brennan's, thereby firing their relatives from their positions.[16] "I was relieved of my management duties at Brennan's by Maudie's family. Fired and shown the door," Ella remembered of the meeting much later. "I couldn't believe it. My siblings joined me in walking out, and I didn't set foot in our beautiful creation for another forty years." The once Medici-tight Brennan clan was suddenly starkly divided.

Attorneys from both sides met to divide assets. It was determined that Maude and her and Owen's three sons would receive Brennan's, while the other five restaurants would be divided among Owen's siblings. "That shows you how phenomenally successful Brennan's was at the time: its value approximately equaled the value of our five other restaurants," Ella marveled in retrospect. Her services no longer wanted at the restaurant on Royal Street she had cultivated and managed since it first opened, Ella Brennan (along with her siblings Dick, Adelaide and John) went to work in the Garden District transforming Commander's Palace.[17]

One of Pip, Jimmy and Ted's first moves upon removing their family members and assuming full ownership was to appoint Gerard Thabuis from Houston as the new chef. Paulus Blange was pushed to retire but continued to occasionally supervise the dining room.[18] In the spring of 1975, a five-alarm fire tore through Brennan's, halting business for the next six months until the building could be restored. Brennan's later incurred four lawsuits as a result of the fire and following renovations. A neighboring business called Creole Specialties claimed that the Brennans should not have allowed the "ultra hazardous" activity of flaming desserts in the restaurant and asserted that they faced a loss of income because the front of their business was roped off and the construction equipment during restorations was disruptively loud.[19] This would not be the last time Brennan's was the subject of a lawsuit.

In the years after Owen Sr.'s children took over, they ran an extensive series of advertisements in the *Times-Picayune* passively slighting their father's siblings, boasting, "Unless you've had dinner at Brennan's recently you haven't dined at Brennan's at all. You see Pip, Jimmy and Ted have all come home to make sure that their late father's dream became an absolute reality." Another advertisement proclaimed that the slogan for Brennan's was no longer "A great restaurant" but rather, under the new ownership of just Owen's sons and widow, "A greater restaurant."[20]

In the 2000s, another rift within the Brennan family members who still owned the restaurant threatened the future of Brennan's yet again. This time, the dispute was among Owen's children, again over who would control their father's namesake. Blake and Clark, Pip's sons, had managed Brennan's from 1995 until 2005, when Hurricane Katrina left the restaurant badly damaged.[21] In 2006, when the restaurant was able to reopen, a shareholder vote ousted Blake, Clark and Pip, leaving Ted Brennan and his daughter, Bridget, in charge of running the restaurant.[22]

In 2010, Jimmy Brennan died, leaving his shares of the business to his two daughters. That same year, Pip retired, selling back his shares to the business. By the fall of 2012, Pip had filed a lawsuit claiming that he had not been reimbursed for his shares of Brennan's. Pip's suit asserted that his family members owed him $3.8 million, which he believed the court should force them to pay before "Brennan's Inc. completely wastes, squanders or loses all of its remaining assets."

By 2013, tensions had risen, and on April 26, 2013, Pip organized a rogue board meeting with plans of overthrowing his brother and niece and allowing his sons to reassume control of the debt-ridden restaurant. The meeting ended with the police being called and Pip's party being escorted from the property in handcuffs. Three days after the meeting, Ted and Bridget countered by filing a suit of their own claiming that Pip had no authority to call a shareholders meeting, since he had previously sold his stock in Brennan's. Pip's argument was that as he had never been paid for his shares, he was still entitled to a say in the business; furthermore, he said Ted should not be allowed input since creditors had already seized his shares.[23] The case went to the federal court, where it was decided that Pip and his sons would be awarded control of Brennan's for the time—it would be short-lived.

This contentious climax of decades of bitterness, complete with a full cast of lawyers and police officers, came to a head right on the eve of the restaurant's foreclosure: Brennan's was scheduled to go up for sheriff's auction just a month later. On May 23, 2013, the centrally located pink building with the green awning, having been foreclosed on, went up for auction. Ralph Brennan, John's son and Owen's nephew, had worked at Brennan's as a prep cook in high school before being told there would be no work available for him there after college because Owen's children had claimed sole ownership. Instead, he went to work as a public accountant in Houston before his Aunt Ella asked him to return to the family business around Christmas 1980. Ralph moved home to work at Commander's Palace and then Mr. B's Bistro. "I came back, and I went to work at Commander's, and that lasted two weeks—typical Ella, changed her mind on a dime. She said, 'I need you to go to Mr. B's. I'm short management down there, and I need your help.' So that was it. I really didn't have a choice. So I went down to Mr. B's, worked down there, and the rest is history. I've been in the French Quarter ever since," Ralph told the author. He was eager to please his aunt and happy to have the opportunity to learn from her along the way.[24]

Having fond memories of growing up playing in Brennan's restaurant when his aunts Ella and Adelaide would bring him there while they worked before the initial schism, Ralph wanted to keep Brennan's in the family. In fact, he had attempted to make Pip and his sons offers to inject capital into the failing restaurant on two separate occasions, but both were refused. "My three cousins who operated here for about forty years, they were fighting among themselves, which caused a lot of their financial problems. And I tried to work with them prior to the bankruptcy, and honestly, twice I thought we had a deal," Ralph recalled in a recent interview with the author. "And it fell through both times. And then they wound up going into bankruptcy." Ralph and his creditor turned business partner, Terry White, bought the building at the sheriff's sale for $6.85 million in the lobby of the Louisiana Supreme Court building that sits directly across Royal Street from Brennan's.[25]

NEW BRENNAN'S, SAME FAMILY

With newly obtained ownership of the building, but still not the business it housed, Ralph's party reached out to his cousins requesting a proposal regarding a lease on the property. Having still received no proposal more than a month later, and having had his own proposal outright rejected, Ralph realized that his attempts to negotiate were again fruitless. In an unfortunate but fitting turn of events, management was evicted from the restaurant on June 27, 2013. The following day—Friday, typically busy for Brennan's—staff had still not been informed by management of the eviction that had been pending more than a month, and a sheriff ordered everyone to leave the premises. That afternoon, oblivious employees were still arriving for their shifts in full uniform; guests who had made reservations showed up expecting their table and Crêpes Suzette as usual, only to be met with disappointment.[26]

Regarding the previous management's staff members who were left without work with no notice, Ralph offered the following statement:

> *Brennan's was given proper notice, knew the deadline, and made no effort to contest the proceedings. Therefore, it should have come as no surprise yesterday when Brennan's was evicted from the building. It is regrettable that they chose not to inform their employees that closure was imminent but I am committed to working with interested employees to find employment where possible.*[27]

Having obtained ownership of the building, Ralph's work was just beginning. According to him, when his restaurant group first obtained Brennan's, it had not been renovated in about sixty years. "It needed a lot of work," Ralph said, "more than I had anticipated." Because he was part of the family who had been booted out of the business by his cousins in the 1970s, he had not set foot in the building for more than forty years. Haley Bitterman, corporate executive chef for the Ralph Brennan Restaurant Group, arrived at the property before Ralph did following the eviction and immediately called him and told him not to come. The building was worse off than they had feared, and she wanted to get some of the glaring problems taken care of before he even set foot in it. "Well, that only got me here faster," Ralph said.

Within forty-eight hours, Ralph and his team had evaluated the situation and decided to begin renovations rather than trying to reopen the restaurant in its current condition. During the next sixteen months, Brennan's was closed as the building underwent extensive renovations. The physical structure was in dire need of restoration; almost nothing was up to code. It seemed as if everything Ralph's staff attempted to repair revealed "ten more things" that desperately needed fixing. Although Ralph told his accounting team he "didn't want to know" the final number of renovation costs because they were so high, he estimates that he spent about $20 million to restore his family restaurant. "But it needed it," Ralph conceded. "And the building is now in shape to last another hundred to two hundred years, with proper maintenance."[28]

In early July 2014, just over a year after Ralph acquired the building at 417 Royal and when it was already well under construction, the assets

Right: Ralph Brennan outside Brennan's on Royal Street. *Chris Granger*.

Below: The Garden Room at Brennan's today. *Alexandra Kennon*.

The front dining room at Brennan's today. *Alexandra Kennon*.

Upstairs at Brennan's today. *Alexandra Kennon*.

Another upstairs dining room at Brennan's. *Alexandra Kennon.*

of Brennans Inc. (Pip and his sons' company that formerly controlled the Royal Street restaurant) were placed up for auction. Assets included were the name, the menu, the iconic rooster logo, memorabilia, the website and the wine collection. Ralph was the sole bidder to qualify, offering $3 million in cash and various assets. Now he not only possessed the building but also the name and branding necessary to restore Brennan's to its former glory.[29] That Thanksgiving 2014, Brennan's reopened under new ownership, although it remains in the family of its namesake. For the first time in more than forty years, Ella Brennan returned to the restaurant she once built and managed to have lunch with her nephew Ralph, a story that landed above the fold in the *Times-Picayune*'s "Lifestyle" section. New Orleans loves a good legal food fight, especially one that has a happy ending for one of the city's favorite ladies.[30]

Ten things that remained of the former Brennan's were the turtles that resided in the fountain in the courtyard. During the renovations, Bitterman relocated the turtles into two kiddie pools in her backyard, where she and her young son could care for them. They named the ten turtles after classic French sauces ("Meurniére," "Bordelaise," "Hollandaise" and so on), with some New Orleans sauces thrown in for additional flavor as well—the only male turtle in the bunch is named "Cocktail." They call them "The Mothas and the Othas." When it had warmed up in March 2015, the turtles were welcomed back to their home in the Brennan's fountain in the same manner Brennan's had been relocated to its current location from Bourbon Street back in 1955: via second-line parade.

Even without the weight of restaurant equipment to burden the paraders this time, it was billed as "the slowest second-line," although wagons for the turtles did help expedite things somewhat. "This could be the slowest second-line in New Orleans' history," Ralph Brennan remarked to local news station WGNO. "We're definitely celebrating the return of the turtles back to Brennan's. They will not become turtle soup because they are part of our family," Ralph said. To solidify the turtles' safety at a restaurant otherwise known for its turtle soup, Ralph went so far as to have the turtles officially pardoned by Judge Lauren Lemmon, much like the president's turkey each Thanksgiving. Monsignor Christopher H. Nalty also blessed the turtles for good measure.[31]

While the nearly $20 million investment into renovations was certainly a leap in the right direction to restore Brennan's, Ralph knew that hiring the perfect executive chef to update the menu and lead the kitchen was equally important. When renovations and legal proceedings regarding the name of the restaurant were still underway, Slade Rushing was hired to lead the newly refurbished kitchen as Brennan's executive chef. Although Rushing grew up more than eighty miles east of New Orleans in rural Mississippi, he has memories of his family traveling to dine in the French Quarter—particularly at Brennan's, which had been his late mother's favorite of the old Creole establishments. Following his graduation from Johnson & Wales culinary school in Rhode Island, Rushing worked for Ralph Brennan at Mr. B's Bistro just down Royal Street from Brennan's. Afterward, he did stints in highly regarded restaurants in San Francisco and New York, all the while talking with wife, Allison Vines-Rushing, about how much they loved the dishes and ingredients of New Orleans's cuisine. Eventually, they followed their instincts south to Abita Springs and then back to New Orleans, where they opened the restaurant MiLa together in 2007.[32]

In early 2014, when Rushing heard that Ralph Brennan was restoring and reopening Brennan's, he knew that he wanted to apply. Each chef considered for the position, Rushing included, was tasked with creating an interpretation of Eggs Benedict. Rushing prepared a classic presentation of the dish but made his English muffins from scratch and cured his own

Brennan's former executive chef Slade Rushing. *Alexandra Kennon.*

Canadian bacon. After the tasting, Ralph Brennan and business partner Terry White said, "He's the guy."[33]

Rushing tasked himself with updating the menu to make it lighter and fresher, without losing the more decadent traditional elements that have always defined Brennan's cuisine. "The food generally has been so heavy and in the French Quarter a lot of these restaurants wanted to hit you over the head with decadence, and here we do that, but it's decadence and lightness all together," Rushing emphasized. "Instead of decadence it's more freshness, with the same flavor profiles. We still use Creole spices, we still use jumbo lump crabmeat and use a lot of Gulf seafood. It's just that our food is a little bit more, you could say, 'millennial-focused,' but we also keep focus on the old traditional stuff too. We have a little bit of both on the menu."

As for the more traditional menu items, like the Eggs Benedict that got him hired, Rushing has fun creating his own contemporary versions of those dishes. "I actually try to understand why these dishes were famous. I'm not too proud. I like a challenge, so to speak. I like elevating these old dishes and building things as a foundation off of them," Rushing said. "I enjoy it. Some people might think it's a dead end, but I see it as an open window."[34]

If award nominations are any indication of how Rushing's new menu was received, the public certainly appreciated his efforts. Every single year he served as executive chef of Brennan's between 2015 and 2019, Rushing has been nominated for the James Beard Award for Best Chef: South. Rushing departed from his post at Brennan's in May 2019, grateful for his experience at the restaurant but wishing to pursue other opportunities. With a strong team in place in the Brennan's kitchen continuing the methods Rushing set in motion, Brennan and his team plan to take their time in hiring the restaurant's next executive chef.

Ralph Brennan and his team are committed to maintaining certain traditions at Brennan's, while staying contemporary and relevant. While the breakfast menu remains fairly classic, the dinner menu gives the kitchen staff more freedom to experiment and play. According to Ralph, dinner was a slow meal during the previous ownership's tenure, and one of his goals has been to change that. "So we took a little more aggressive approach to the food at dinner. Not traditional," Ralph noted. "It has a contemporary edge to it, where with breakfast we've maintained and stayed loyal to the roots of the breakfast that was done here and has been done here for seventy years."[35]

Ralph Brennan credited his Aunt Ella with teaching him to never rest on his laurels by looking at the restaurant business as a bell curve—her thinking was that one did not want to reach the top of the curve and slide down the other side, rather than continuing upward. Ralph has adapted his aunt's

Brennan's exterior today. *Alexandra Kennon.*

concept slightly, so that it is a staircase rather than a curve. "And my fear is that there's a landing, and the stairs go down on the other side. Same principle, I just visually look at it a little bit differently," Ralph mused. "But if you're not continually trying to improve, you stagnate and eventually decline. And we don't want that. If my children were here, they would tell you exactly that. I've told 'em that for a long time, since they were kids. That you always have to keep trying to get better and better and better. And it can be in so many different ways: it can be new menu items, new staff, new wine offerings, redecorating a dining room."

Now that Brennan's has made it through the premature death of its founder, a family schism, a bankruptcy, another family schism and back into a different Brennan's hands to be newly renovated and restored, it seems that under Ralph Brennan and Terry White's ownership, Brennan's might finally be able to catch a break. Although Brennan's history has been tumultuous, the pink building's colorful past contributes a certain spice to the hollandaise today.

Charming, contentious or a combination of both, history is part of what makes New Orleans unique. "My mother and my grandmother used to have a phrase: 'If the walls could talk,'" Ralph said. "The stories that are in these walls! To me, that's what makes New Orleans really unique. In addition to everything else: the music, and the architecture and the history, but the *food* is so important in what we do."[36]

Recipe from Brennan's

Bananas Foster

1 ounce butter
½ cup light brown sugar
¼ teaspoon cinnamon
1 ½ ounces banana liqueur
½ banana per person
1 ½ ounces aged rum

Combine butter, sugar and cinnamon in a flambé pan. As the butter melts under medium heat, add the banana liqueur and stir to combine. As the sauce starts to cook, peel and add the bananas to the pan. Cook the bananas until they begin to soften (about 1 to

2 minutes). Tilt back the pan to slightly heat the far edge. Once hot, carefully add the rum and tilt the pan toward the flame to ignite the rum. Stir the sauce to ensure that all of the alcohol cooks out. Serve cooked bananas over ice cream and top with the sauce in the pan. Note: Please be mindful not to burn your home or person in the process of making this delicious dessert.

Recipe courtesy of Brennan's restaurant.

IN MEMORY OF LEAH CHASE
1923–2019

Author Notes

ON IMPARTIALITY

One major perk of writing about restaurants that have lasted for more than seventy years is that New Orleanians would have likely run them out of business a long time ago if they weren't any good. While I chose the thirteen restaurants included primarily for their fascinating family histories, I think I can say without being accused of bias (though now I certainly will be) that each of the restaurants in this book maintains an incredibly high standard and helps set the bar for the rest of the city. That said, there are dozens of other historic restaurants in the city that are equally worthy of being featured in this book—I wish I could include all of them. I also feel that it is important I point out that if it seems any one restaurant is covered in more detail than another, it is no indication of me favoring one, but rather a reflection on the amount of material that was available to me.

ON RESTAURANTS PAST

While these are the restaurants that have the fortune of remaining open (or rather, New Orleans has the fortune they have remained), it is worth honoring the other great restaurants from New Orleans's history to whom time and circumstance have been less kind. Without a doubt aspects of each of these institutions live on in the New Orleans restaurant scene of today.

ON FRIENDLY COMPETITION

Ella Brennan recalled in her autobiography that Owen Brennan once told her, "You have to meet everybody in the restaurant business. You have to make friends with them because they are in the same business as you. We're all in this together, and New Orleans is a great city, so let's get going." Owen E. Brennan enjoyed a grand last meal at Antoine's (which decades later would become an admittedly dark source of humor between the Brennans and the Alciatore family, according to Ella Brennan's autobiography). Dickie Brennan Jr. dined with his father, Dick, for the last time at Pascal's Manale, according to Poppy Tooker's Manales cookbook. This sentiment remains strong among New Orleans restaurateurs today as well. Even just during the course of the interviews I conducted for this book, Ralph Brennan mentioned that he was returning a call from Katy Casbarian, who owns Arnaud's, to confirm a reservation for her at Brennan's. Manager of Parkway Justin Kennedy ran out of our interview to greet his friend and executive chef at Napoleon House Chris Montero as he drove by. New Orleans is a small town, and while the restaurant scene here is grand for its size, those involved in it share a strong bond, even if they are competitors. I was utterly charmed by these restaurant owners' friendliness toward not just me but also their entire community.

ON DICHOTOMIES AND GHOSTS

As a tour guide in New Orleans, I frequently find myself volleying almost comedically back and forth between incredibly appetizing culinary history and much darker and more macabre information. A great deal of New Orleans's history and culture is evident in our food, but what isn't covered there often lies within the walls of our many aboveground cemeteries. It is fitting, in a way, that Commander's is directly across from Lafayette Cemetery Number One. In fact, the Garden District tours I give with New Orleans Secrets Tours begin in the cemetery and end at Commander's Palace. Locals typically take the opposite trajectory in their lives, but the importance of both is evident. It was therefore completely unsurprising to me that, without any solicitation, I heard many ghost stories throughout the course of conducting interviews and researching for this book. I have been informed that most if not all of the restaurants included have a resident ghost, all of which have been experienced firsthand. Joe and Rosalie Broussard are believed to haunt the upstairs portion of their restaurant where they died—Executive Chef Jimi Setchim swears that he heard a door slam, knocking the knob off late at night when not another soul was in the building. Multiple employees of the Napoleon House have told of late-night encounters with someone they believe is surely Joe Impastato. An air conditioning repair man at Arnaud's once swore that he gave directions to a woman in vintage attire leaving the banquet hall, only to realize that it was three o'clock in the morning and no one else was in the building. Tujague's perhaps takes the cake, as it claims to be haunted by the ghost of famed nineteenth-century drag queen Julian Eltinge, and she apparently has been known to photobomb selfies taken in the back dining room. Wedged between the Mississippi River and Lake Pontchartrain, New Orleans is full of dichotomies: the revelry of Carnival versus the piousness of Lent, rum versus whiskey, people living life to the fullest and enjoying fine meals right next to where we store our dead. Such is life in the Crescent City.

ON PROHIBITION

The tricky thing about researching Prohibition, which also conversely makes it enigmatic and exciting, is that so little recorded information is available. The only records remaining, for the most part, are those of the raids and arrests, which seemingly are the rare exceptions in a city that otherwise got away with a great deal of subversion. I also noticed, pleasingly, that all reports of arrests during Prohibition are by federal agents—the members of the New Orleans Police Department seemingly paid no mind to the coffee cups and flasks in waiters' aprons that so many restaurateurs and customers later admitted were commonplace throughout the 1920s. Just know that the information included in this book is merely what was available, but rest assured that every restaurant included that was open between 1919 and 1930 doubtlessly kept *les bon temps rouler*-ing, so to speak.

ON LAGNIAPPE

A disclaimer from a guilty food writer: When I studied journalism at Loyola University, my mentor, Michael Guisti, who advised our student paper, *The Maroon*, of which I served as senior staff writer and later managing editor, taught me that accepting anything more than a cup of coffee as a gift from a source was unethical. Although I chose each of the included restaurants completely independently from any communication with them, and certainly independently from any free food, it is *impossible* to interview more than a dozen chefs and restaurateurs in New Orleans and say no to every complimentary appetizer, meal and beverage unexpectedly placed in front of you. The driving force of the restaurant industry is hospitality, and for those interviewed for this project, it runs in their blood. So I hope my former advisor, as well as you, my reader, will understand that sometimes in New Orleans a crab ravigote *is* the equivalent of a cup of coffee. While I cannot deny enjoying these crudités from some of the city's most famous hosts and hostesses, I promise that my coverage of them is in no way affected by my gluttony.

ON CLIMATE CHANGE

The science behind the majority of climate change research points out that New Orleans could quite possibly be underwater, at least partially, within another century. Much of the barrier island chain protecting New Orleans from gulf storms was lost to Hurricane Katrina, and scientists say that with hurricanes growing in intensity, we can almost definitely expect tangible effects on the city of New Orleans by the year 2100. While I certainly hope this research is inaccurate, it seems gravely remiss not to at least consider the possibility. Several of the restaurants featured in this book have celebrated full centennials of continuous business. It would be a sad thing if some were unable to meet that milestone, or unable to make another century, due to environmental factors beyond their control. Katrina proved that whatever happens, the individuals who keep these restaurants running will do everything in their power to continue to serve their city.

ON ACCURACY

New Orleans historians often seem to place more emphasis on the "story" aspect of the field than the research. While there is a great deal of information available about some of these restaurants, some of it is conflicting and much of it is unsourced, but inevitably, it is almost always interesting. I have done my best at separating the fact from the fiction, but it is still New Orleans, so I hope it is entertaining as well. I think the restaurateurs of years past, knowing their flair for drama and style, would understand.

That said, in all of my extensive research required to write this book, doubtless some fact or several have been reported in error. If you find this is the case, I would so appreciate it being brought to my attention (alexandrakennon@gmail.com).

Notes

Chapter 1

1. Roy F. Guste Jr., *Antoine's Restaurant Cookbook* (New Orleans, LA: Carbery-Guste, 1979).
2. Meigs O. Frost, "Master's Famed Dishes Are Linked with City's Name," *Times-Picayune*, September 16, 1934.
3. Paul Freedman, "Antoine's Haute Creole," *Ten Restaurants that Changed America* (n.p.: Liveright Publishing Corporation, 2016).
4. David S. Shields, *The Culinarians: Lives and Careers from the First Age of American Fine Dining* (Chicago: University of Chicago Press, 2017).
5. Guste, *Antoine's Restaurant Cookbook*.
6. Freedman, "Antoine's Haute Creole."
7. Guste, *Antoine's Restaurant Cookbook*.
8. Freedman, "Antoine's Haute Creole."
9. Ibid.
10. Guste, *Antoine's Restaurant Cookbook*.
11. *Times-Picayune*, "Birthday Cake for Mme. Alciatore: Venerable Hostess of Antoine's Celebrates Her 85th Anniversary," August 14, 1917.
12. *Times-Picayune*, "Good Livers Glad that Antoine's Still Holds Forth Like Beacon Light," November 2, 1902.
13. Antoine's Restaurant, "History of Antoine's," https://antoines.com.
14. *Times-Picayune*, "Alciatore-Roy," April 1, 1894.
15. Conversation with Rick and Lisa Blount, interview with author, December 11, 2018.

16. Freedman, "Antoine's Haute Creole."

17. Ibid.

18. Antoine's Restaurant, "History of Antoine's."

19. Frost, "Master's Famed Dishes Are Linked."

20. Conversation with Rick and Lisa Blount.

21. Guste, *Antoine's Restaurant Cookbook*.

22. Conversation with Rick and Lisa Blount.

23 Arthur Hardy, "Carnival Visit from Duke and Duchess of Windsor in 1950 Still a Historical Highlight," *New Orleans Advocate*, February 17, 2015.

24. Freedman, "Antoine's Haute Creole."

25. Antoine's Restaurant, "History of Antoine's."

26. Roy L. Alciatore, *Souvenir Du Restaurant Antoine* (New Orleans, LA, 1940).

27. Ibid.

28. Freedman, "Antoine's Haute Creole."

29. Conversation with Rick and Lisa Blount.

30. Freedman, "Antoine's Haute Creole."

31. Guste, *Antoine's Restaurant Cookbook*.

32. *Kreol Magazine*, "Roy F. Guste Jr: Traditional Cuisine Expert Recounts Great-Grandfather's 19th Century Culinary Prowess" (October 13, 2017).

33. Freedman, "Antoine's Haute Creole."

34. Todd A. Price, "Antoine's CEO Once Told He'd Have No Future There," *Biz New Orleans*, January 26, 2015.

35. Conversation with Rick and Lisa Blount.

36. Ibid.

37. Howard Witt, "Part 1: Antoine's Next Course," *Chicago Tribune*, October 16, 2005.

38. Conversation with Rick and Lisa Blount.

39. Ibid.

40. Ibid.

41. Freedman, "Antoine's Haute Creole."

42. Conversation with Rick and Lisa Blount.

43. Conversation with Rich Lee, interview with author, March 12, 2019.

44. Conversation with Rick and Lisa Blount.

Chapter 2

1. Poppy Tooker, *Tujague's Cookbook: Creole Recipes and Lore in the New Orleans Grand Tradition* (Gretna, LA: Pelican Publishing Company, 2015).

2. Tujague's Restaurant, "Tujague's History," tujaguesrestaurant.com/history.

3. Gwendolyn Knapp, "A Legendary New Orleans Restaurant, 160 Years in the Making," *Eater*, September 2, 2016, https://www.eater.com/2016/9/2/12736732/tujagues-new-orleans.

4. Thomas Kelly, "Speaking of Food," *Times-Picayune*, November 1, 1925.

5. *Times-Picayune*, "Tujague's 100th Year Is Marked," July 15, 1956.

6. *Times-Picayune*, "Changes Being Made in Old Restaurants: Tujague's Son-in-Law Sells Restaurant to H. Begue's Bartender and Associate," January 19, 1916.

7. Tooker, *Tujague's Cookbook*.

8. Podine Shoenberger, "Film Stars Easy to Handle, Says Visiting Director," *Times-Picayune*, February 23, 1935.

9. *Times-Picayune*, "Orleanian Seized by Raider After Serving Absinthe," April 7, 1931.

10. Shoenberger, "Film Stars Easy to Handle."

11. *Times-Picayune*, "Bond Is Awarded for National Contest," April 3, 1956.

12. Tooker, *Tujague's Cookbook*; Knapp, "Legendary New Orleans Restaurant."

13. *Times-Picayune*, "Up and Down the Street," July 17, 1956.

14. *Times-Picayune*, "Tujague's Cat Missing," October 28, 1955.

15. *Times-Picayune*, "Up and Down the Street," July 17, 1956.

16. *Times-Picayune*, "Tujague's Owner Dies," May 16, 1975.

17. *Times-Picayune*, "Tastes of New Orleans," January 11, 1981.

18. Susan Langenhennig, "Steven Latter, Owner of Tujague's Restaurant, Dies at 64," *Times-Picayune*, February 18, 2013, https://www.nola.com/dining/2013/02/steven_latter_owner_of_tujague.html.

19. Ian McNulty, "Is Tujague's 'America's Oldest Neighborhood Restaurant?' Sizing Up the Legacy of a French Quarter Legend," *New Orleans Advocate*, May 10, 2016.

20. Conversation with Mark Latter, interview with author, November 8, 2018.

21. Tooker, *Tujague's Cookbook*.

22. Conversation with Mark Latter.

23. Conversation with Thomas Robey, interview with author, November 8, 2018.

24. Conversation with Mark Latter.

25. Conversation with Thomas Robey.

26. Conversation with Mark Latter.

27. McNulty, "Is Tujague's 'America's Oldest Neighborhood Restaurant?'"

28. Conversation with Mark Latter.

29. McNulty, "Is Tujague's 'America's Oldest Neighborhood Restaurant?'"

Chapter 3

1. Allie Mariano, "1862: The First Cup at Café Du Monde," *Times-Picayune,* April 21, 2017.
2. Peggy Sweeney McDonald, *Meanwhile, Back at Café du Monde: Life Stories About Food* (Gretna, LA: Pelican Publishing Company, 2012).
3. Mariano, "1862."
4. Ibid.
5. Maria Muro, "Brewing Up Success," *New Orleans Living,* January 28, 2009.
6. McDonald, *Meanwhile, Back at Café du Monde.*
7. Muro, "Brewing Up Success."
8. Mariano, "1862."
9. Jennifer Larino, "The Untold Story behind How Cafe Du Monde Stands Ended up in Japan," *Times-Picayune,* October 6, 2014.
10. Café du Monde, "Locations," cafedumonde.com.
11. Muro, "Brewing Up Success."
12. McDonald, *Meanwhile, Back at Café du Monde.*
13. Mariano, "1862."
14. Muro, "Brewing Up Success."

Chapter 4

1. Richard Campanella, "The Turbulent History behind the Seven New Orleans Municipal Districts," October 9, 2013, https:// www.nola.com/ homegarden/2013/10/new_orleans_seven_municipal_di.html.
2. Brennan and Brennan, *Commander's Palace New Orleans Cookbook.*
3. Anne Cutler, "Famed New Orleans Restaurant 'Commander's Palace' Discovers Century-Old Secret," WGNO, November 23, 2015.
4. Conversation with Ti Martin, interview with author, December 11, 2018.
5. *Our House Stories,* "Emile Commander—Before the Palace," July 24, 2013.
6. Jim Fraiser, *The Garden District of New Orleans* (Jackson: University Press of Mississippi, 2012).
7. *Times-Picayune,* "Emile Commander, Whose Restaurant on Washington Avenue Was a Landmark, Dies in Wales," August 28, 1906.
8. *Times-Picayune,* "Prohibition Raids Uncover Brewery: Beer, Whisky, Gin, Mash, and Absinthe Confiscated by Agents," October 27, 1923.
9. Ibid.
10. Brennan and Brennan, *Commander's Palace New Orleans Cookbook.*

11. *Times-Picayune*, "Commander's to Open Doors at 5 P.M. Today," September 18, 1948.

12. *Times-Picayune*, "Soft-Shell Turtle Now Being Served; Come and Get It, Says Frank Moran," April 18, 1946.

13. *Times-Picayune*, "Commander's to Open Doors at 5 P.M. Today."

14. Lucius Beebe, "Commander's Palace in Holiday Magazine," *Times-Picayune*, March 16, 1951.

15. *Times-Picayune*, "Commander's Noted 71 Years for Excellent Food & Wonderful Service," July 12, 1951.

16. *Times-Picayune*, "Restaurant Loot Is $550 in Liquor," April 22, 1952.

17. Kerry McCaffety, *Etouffee, Mon Amour: The Great Restaurants of New Orleans* (Gretna, LA: Pelican Publishing Company, 2002).

18. *Times-Picayune*, "Death Claims Restaurateur," September 24, 1966.

19. Jack Du Arte, "Commander's Palace Born Again Restaurant," *Times-Picayune*, August 7, 1977.

20. Brennan and Martin, *Miss Ella of Commander's Palace*.

21. Ella Brennan and Dick Brennan, *The Commander's Palace New Orleans Cookbook* (New York: Clarkson Potter/Random House, 1984).

22. Ella Brennan and Ti Adelaide Martin, *Miss Ella of Commander's Palace* (Layton, UT: Gibbs Smith, 2016).

23. *Times-Picayune*, "Brennans Buy Commander's," May 31, 1969.

24. Du Arte, "Commander's Palace Born Again Restaurant."

25. Brennan and Brennan, *Commander's Palace New Orleans Cookbook*.

26. Conversation with Ti Martin.

27. Brennan and Brennan, *Commander's Palace New Orleans Cookbook*.

28. Brennan and Martin, *Miss Ella of Commander's Palace*.

29. Jack Du Arte, "Holiday Awards Gathering Success in Food City, N.O.," *Times-Picayune*, October 3, 1976.

30. Dickie Brennan and Steven Pettus, "Oral History Interview with Dickie Brennan and Steven Pettus," interview by Mark Cave, via the Historic New Orleans Collection, April 8, 2010.

31. Du Arte, "Holiday Awards Gathering Success."

32. Brennan and Martin, *Miss Ella of Commander's Palace*.

33. Victor William Geraci and Elizabeth S. Demer, *Icons of American Cooking* (Santa Barbara, CA: Greenwood, 2011).

34. Du Arte, "Holiday Awards Gathering Success."

35. Brennan and Martin, *Miss Ella of Commander's Palace*.

36. Geraci and Demer, *Icons of American Cooking*.

37. Du Arte, "Holiday Awards Gathering Success."

38. Geraci and Demer, *Icons of American Cooking*.
39. Ibid.
40. Brennan and Martin, *Miss Ella of Commander's Palace*.
41. Ibid.
42. Ibid.
43. Gwendolyn Knapp, "Emeril Lagasse Looks Back on the Restaurant that Started It All," *Eater*, March 27, 2015.
44. Ibid.
45. Ti Adelaide Martin and Jamie Shannon, *Commander's Kitchen* (New York: Broadway Books, 2000).
46. Ibid.
47. Regina Schrambling, "Jamie Shannon, 40, Chef Who Embraced Creole Cuisine," *New York Times*, November 30, 2001.
48. Ibid.
49. Brennan and Martin, *Miss Ella of Commander's Palace*.
50. Conversation with Tory McPhail, interview with author, December 7, 2018.
51. Brennan and Martin, *Miss Ella of Commander's Palace*.
52. Conversation with Tory McPhail.
53. Ibid.
54. Ibid.
55. Brennan and Martin, *Miss Ella of Commander's Palace*.
56. Ibid.
57. Ibid.
58. Micheline Maynard, "New Orleans Loses a Restaurant Queen as Ella Brennan of Commander's Palace Dies at 92," *Forbes*, May 31, 2018.
59. Conversation with Ti Martin.
60. Ibid.
61. Ibid.
62. Martin and Shannon, *Commander's Kitchen*.

Chapter 5

1. Joseph Maselli and Dominic Candeloro, *Italians in New Orleans* (Charleston, SC: Arcadia Publishing, 2004).
2. Judy Walker, "A Scoop of History—A Century After It Opened, Angelo Brocato Still Makes Ice Cream the Old-Fashioned Way," NOLA.com, July 28, 2005.

3. Sarah Roahen, "New Orleans Eats/Guardians of Tradition," Arthur Brocato, Angelo Brocato's Ice Cream and Confectionary, Southern Foodways Alliance, February 17, 2007, www.southernfoodways.org.

4. Ibid.

5. Errol Laborde, "Understanding Brocato's," *New Orleans Magazine* (August 2005).

6. Roahen, "New Orleans Eats/Guardians of Tradition."

7. Walker, "Scoop of History."

8. Ibid.

9. Roahen, "New Orleans Eats/Guardians of Tradition."

10. Angelo Brocato's, "About Us," angelobrocatos.com.

11. Roahen, "New Orleans Eats/Guardians of Tradition."

12. Conversation with Arthur Brocato, interview with author, January 24, 2019.

13. Ibid.

14. Ibid.

15. Ibid.

16. Ibid.

17. Adam Nossiter, "Spumoni Fills a City's Void, and Its Belly," *New York Times*, October 1, 2006.

18. Conversation with Arthur Brocato.

19. Ibid.

Chapter 6

1. McCaffety, *Etouffee, Mon Amour*.

2. Shields, *Culinarians*.

3. Ibid.

4. Shields, *Culinarians*.

5. Leon Galatoire, *Leon Galatoire's Cookbook* (Gretna, LA: Pelican Publishing Company, 1994).

6. Melvin Rodrigue and Jyl Benson, *Recipes and Family History from the Time-Honored New Orleans Restaurant* (New York: Clarkson Potter Publishers, 2005).

7. Ibid.

8. Ibid.

9. *Times-Picayune*, "Half-Million Left by Jean Galatoire," October 2, 1919.

10. Ibid.

11. Rodrigue and Benson, *Recipes and Family History*.

12. Ibid.

13. Ibid.

14. Ibid.

15. Marda Burton and Kenneth Holditch, *Galatoire's: Biography of a Bistro* (n.p.: Garrett County Press, 2011).

16. Brett Anderson, "Throwback Thursday: Galatoire's Fires a Waiter—and Its Customers Revolt," *Times-Picayune*, April 28, 2016.

17. Galatoire's Restaurant, "History," Galatoires.com.

18. *Times-Picayune*, "Galatoire Fire Damage $75,000," January 5, 1956.

19. Arthur Nead, "David Gooch—Galatoire's," *Tulanian*, November 29, 2004.

20. *Times-Picayune*, "Gabriel Galatoire, Restaurateur, Dies," October 6, 1944.

21. Rodrigue and Benson, *Recipes and Family History*.

22. Ibid.

23. Ibid.

24. Conversation with Melvin Rodrigue, interview with author, March 20, 2019.

25. Ibid.

26. Ibid.

27. *Galatoire's Restaurant, Celebrating 100 Years*, menu (New Orleans, LA: Galatoire's Restaurant, 2005).

28. Rodrigue and Benson, *Recipes and Family History*.

29. Mary Foster, "Galatoire's Restaurant Sells Majority Interest," *Boston Globe*, December 10, 2009, Boston.com/business.

30. Conversation with Melvin Rodrigue.

31. Todd A. Price, "Galatoire's Hires Avant-Garde Chef Phillip Lopez," *Times-Picayune*, August 26, 2018.

32. Conversation with Philip Lopez, interview with author, April 1, 2019.

33. Conversation with Melvin Rodrigue.

Chapter 7

1. Michael Mizell-Nelson, "The History of the Poboy," Oak Street Poboy Festival, http://www.poboyfest.com/history.

2. James Karst, "The Messy History of the Po-Boy," *Times-Picayune*, September 4, 2016.

3. Michael Murphy, *Eat Dat New Orleans: A Guide to the Unique Food Culture of the Crescent City* (New York: Countryman Press, 2015).

4. Parkway Poorboys, "Parkway History," https://parkwaypoorboys.com/about/parkway-history.

5. Blake Pontchartrain, "Blakeview: A Brief History of Three Longtime Po-Boy Purveyors in New Orleans," *The Gambit*, November 5, 2018.

6. Conversation with Jay Nix, interview with author, Tuesday, October 23 2018, at Parkway Bakery and Tavern.

7. Parkway Poorboys, "Parkway History."

8. Conversation with Jay Nix.

9. Conversation with Justin Kennedy, interview with author, Tuesday, October 23 2018.

10. Conversation with Jay Nix.

11. Conversation with Justin Kennedy.

12. Conversation with Jay Nix.

Chapter 8

1. Justin A. Nystrom, *Creole Italian: Sicilian Immigrants and the Shaping of New Orleans Food Culture* (Athens: University of Georgia Press, 2018).

2. Bret A. Clesi, "The Arbreshe and Contessa Entellina," Contessa Entellina Society, 1976.

3. Poppy Tooker, *Pascal's Manale Cookbook* (Gretna, LA: Pelican Publishing Company, 2018).

4. Ibid.

5. Ibid.

6. Brendan McCarthy, "Carlos Marcello: The Times-Picayune Covers 175 Years of New Orleans History," *Times-Picayune*, January 29, 2012.

7. Tooker, *Pascal's Manale Cookbook*.

8. Ibid.

9. *Times-Picayune*, "Liquors Delivered Promptly to Homes Day and Night by Manale Restaurant and Bar," December 10, 1936.

10. Tooker, *Pascal's Manale Cookbook*.

11. Erin Z. Bass, "What's a Manale, Anyway?" *Deep South Magazine* (April 9, 2015).

12. Tooker, *Pascal's Manale Cookbook*.

13. Ibid.

14. Bass, "What's a Manale, Anyway?"

15. *Times-Picayune*, "Pascal's, Manale's—One and the Same," June 8, 1944.

16. Tooker, *Pascale Manale Cookbook*.

17. Ibid.

18. Ibid.

19. Ibid.

20. Tooker, *Pascal's Manale Cookbook*.

21. Conversation with Mark DeFelice, interview with author, February 13, 2019.

22. Judy Walker, "Pascal's Manale Shares Family Cookbook—but BBQ Shrimp Recipe Still a Secret," *New Orleans Advocate*, October 10, 2018.

23. Op cit (DeFelice interview with author 2019).

24. Conversation with Thomas "Uptown T" Stewart, interview with author, January 31, 2019.

Chapter 9

1. Patricia Heintzelman, National Register of Historic Places Inventory— Nomination Form: Mayor Girod House, United States Department of the Interior, July 15, 1975.

2. New Orleans Public Library Website, "Administrations of the Mayors of New Orleans: Nicholas Girod," October 7, 2002.

3. Shannon Selin, "Nicolas Girod and the History of Napoleon House in New Orleans," *Imagining the Bounds of History*, blog, 2012.

4. New Orleans Public Library Website, "Administrations of the Mayors of New Orleans."

5. Mikko Macchione and Kerri McCaffety, *Napoleon House* (New Orleans, LA: Cheers Publishing LLC, 2006).

6. Ibid.

7. Conversation with Chris Montero, interview with author, October 10, 2018.

8. Ibid.

9. Ibid.

10. Macchione and McCaffety, *Napoleon House*.

11. Ibid.

12. Conversation with Chris Montero.

13. Macchione and McCaffety, *Napoleon House*.

14. Ibid.

15. Ibid.

16. Heintzelman, Nomination Form: Mayor Girod House.

17. Joan Kent, "'Mr. Joe' Celebrates Life at 100," *Times-Picayune*, July 29, 1985.

18. *Times-Picayune*, "Joseph Impastato, Owner of Napoleon House, Dies," December 14, 1985.
19. Conversation with Chris Montero.
20. Ibid.
21. Todd A. Price, "Napoleon House Sold to Ralph Brennan; Impastato Family Ends 101-Year Run," *Times-Picayune*, March 31, 2015.
22. Conversation with Chris Montero.
23. Price, "Napoleon House Sold to Ralph Brennan."
24. Conversation with Ralph Brennan, interview with author, October 25, 2018.
25. Ibid.
26. Ibid.
27. Conversation with Chris Montero.
28. Price, "Napoleon House Sold to Ralph Brennan."
29. Conversation with Chris Montero.
30. Conversation with Ralph Brennan.
31. Conversation with Chris Montero.
32. Ibid.

Chapter 10

1. *Times-Picayune*, "Deaths," May 31, 1948.
2. Kit Wohl, *Arnaud's Restaurant Cookbook* (Gretna, LA: Pelican Publishing Company, 2005).
3. Ibid.
4. *Times-Picayune*, "Arnaud's Restaurant Doubles Facilities," January 17, 1939.
5. *Times-Picayune*, "Court Declines to Quash Charge Against Arnaud," January 21, 1933.
6. Arnaud's Restaurant, "Lagniappe," https://www.arnaudsrestaurant.com/about/lagniappe.
7. Wohl, *Arnaud's Restaurant Cookbook*.
8. *Times-Picayune*, "Arnaud's Restaurant Doubles Facilities."
9. Ibid.
10. *Times-Picayune*, "Arnaud's Large Seating Capacity Takes Peak-Hour Crowds in Stride," March 6, 1947.
11. *Times-Picayune*, "Cat Saved After Ten Days," September 24, 1946.
12. *Times-Picayune*, "Deaths."
13. Arnaud's Restaurant, "Lagniappe."

14. Ibid.
15. Conversation with Katy Casbarian, Arnaud's Restaurant, interview with author, October 17, 2018.
16. Arnaud's Restaurant, "Lagniappe."
17. Wohl, *Arnaud's Restaurant Cookbook.*
18. Arnaud's Restaurant, "Lagniappe."
19. Wohl, *Arnaud's Restaurant Cookbook.*
20. *Times-Picayune,* "Arnaud's Restaurant Announces Dress Up Night Each Saturday," September 7, 1961.
21. Wohl, *Arnaud's Restaurant Cookbook.*
22. Arnaud's Restaurant, "Lagniappe."
23. Wohl, *Arnaud's Restaurant Cookbook.*
24. Conversation with Katy Casbarian.
25. Arnaud's Restaurant, "Lagniappe."
26. Ibid.
27. Conversation with Augie Spicuzza, Arnaud's Restaurant, interview with author, October 17, 2918.
28. Wohl, *Arnaud's Restaurant Cookbook.*
29. Brett Anderson, "Archie Casbarian, Owner of Fabled Arnaud's Restaurant, Dies," *Times-Picayune,* January 11, 2009.
30. Conversation with Katy Casbarian.
31. Wohl, *Arnaud's Restaurant Cookbook.*
32. Ibid.
33. Ibid.
34. Anderson, "Archie Casbarian."
35. Conversation with Tommy DiGiovanni, Arnaud's Restaurant, interview with author, October 17, 2918.
36. Wohl, *Arnaud's Restaurant Cookbook.*
37. Ibid.
38. Arnaud's Restaurant, "Lagniappe."
39. Anderson, "Archie Casbarian."
40. Conversation with Katy Casbarian.
41. Ibid.

Chapter 11

1. Brenda Maitland, "Broussard's," *Country Roads* (January 28, 2014).
2. Evelyn Preuss and Gunter Preuss, *Broussard's Restaurant Cookbook* (Gretna, LA: Pelican Publishing Company, 1996).

3. Ibid.

4. Maitland, "Broussard's."

5. Ibid.

6. Preuss and Preuss, *Broussard's Restaurant Cookbook.*

7. Ibid.

8. *Times-Picayune*, "Restaurateur Dies; Rites Set," February 7, 1966.

9. Preuss and Preuss, *Broussard's Restaurant Cookbook.*

10. Ann Benoit and the Preuss family, *Broussard's Restaurant & Courtyard Cookbook* (Gretna, LA: Pelican Publishing Company, 2012).

11. Ibid.

12. Preuss and Preuss, *Broussard's Restaurant Cookbook.*

13. Ibid.

14. Ibid.

15. Ibid.

16. Benoit and the Preuss family, *Broussard's Restaurant & Courtyard Cookbook.*

17. Conversation with bartender/server Rita Pastrano, interview with author, March 14, 2019.

18. *NOLA Defender*, "Broussard's Reopens After $1M Renovation," September 20, 2013.

19. Maitland, "Broussard's."

20. Conversation with Chef Jimi Setchim, interview with author, March 14, 2019.

21. Ibid.

22. Conversation with Rita Pastrano.

23. Katherine Sayre, "Creole Cuisine's Family Approach Nets Restaurant Success," *Times-Picayune*, May 10, 2016.

24. Conversation with Chef Jimi Setchim.

Chapter 12

1. Leah Chase, *The Dooky Chase Cookbook* (Gretna, LA: Pelican Publishing Company, 1990).

2. Dooky Chase's Restaurant, "History of Dooky Chase's Restaurant," dookychaserestaurant.com.

3. Chase, *Dooky Chase Cookbook.*

4. Pat Mitchell and Leah Chase, "An Interview with the Queen of Creole Cuisine," lecture, TEDWomen, New Orleans, LA.

5. Dooky Chase Foundation, "About Us," http://dookychasefoundation.org/about.

6. Dooky Chase Foundation, "About the Owner: Edgar Lawrence 'Dooky' Chase Jr.," https://www.dookychaserestaurant.com/about/owner.

7. Chase, *Dooky Chase Cookbook*.

8. Carol Allen, *Leah Chase: Listen, I Say Like This* (Gretna, LA: Pelican Publishing Company, 2002).

9. Chase, *Dooky Chase Cookbook*.

10. Dooky Chase Foundation, "About Us."

11. Chase, *Dooky Chase Cookbook*.

12. Allen, *Leah Chase*.

13. Conversation with Leah Chase, interview with author, April 10, 2019.

14. Allen, *Leah Chase*.

15. Ibid.

16. Ibid.

17. Chase, *Dooky Chase Cookbook*.

18. Ibid.

19. Jessica B. Harris, "Leah Chase: The Queen of Creole Cuisine," *Garden & Gun* (August/September 2018).

20. Allen, *Leah Chase*.

21. Ibid.

22. Chase, *Dooky Chase Cookbook*.

23. Allen, *Leah Chase*.

24. Chase, *Dooky Chase Cookbook*.

25. Harris, "Leah Chase."

26. Conversation with Leah Chase.

27. Chase, *Dooky Chase Cookbook*.

28. Conversation with Leah Chase.

29. Allen, *Leah Chase*.

30. Chase, *Dooky Chase Cookbook*.

31. Casey Ferrand, "Dooky Chase's Restaurant Played Key Role in Civil Rights Movement," WDSU, July 3, 2013.

32. Allen, *Leah Chase*.

33. Conversation with Leah Chase.

34. Allen, *Leah Chase*.

35. Ibid.

36. Conversation with Leah Chase.

37. Allen, *Leah Chase*.

38. Ibid.

39. Ibid.

40. Dooky Chase Foundation, "About Us."

41. Chase, *Dooky Chase Cookbook*.

42. Allen, *Leah Chase*.

43. Ibid.

44. Ibid.

45. Ibid.

46. Ibid.

47. Dooky Chase's Restaurant, "History of Dooky Chase's Restaurant."

48. Allen, *Leah Chase*.

49. Sharon Litwin, "Restaurateur Leah Chase Also an Avid Art Collector," *Times-Picayune*, September 13, 2011, https://www.nola.com/nolavie/2011/09/post_27.html.

50. Allen, *Leah Chase*.

51. Ibid.

52. Ibid.

53. Ibid.

54. Kim Severson, "In New Orleans, Knives, Forks and Hammers," *New York Times*, August 23, 2006.

55. Allen, *Leah Chase*.

56. Conversation with Leah Chase.

57. John Pope, "Gumbo Tradition Lures the Holy Thursday Faithful to Dooky Chase's Restaurant," *Times-Picayune*, April 1, 2010.

58. Conversation with Leah Chase.

59. *Nourish*, "Gumbo 101 with Leah Chase," July 3, 2018.

60. Allen, *Leah Chase*.

61. Chase, *Dooky Chase Cookbook*.

62. Megan Hill, "Leah Chase's Hometown: Madisonville, Louisiana," *Country Roads* (February 29, 2012).

63. Conversation with Leah Chase.

64. Chase, *Dooky Chase Cookbook*.

65. Allen, *Leah Chase*.

66. Dooky Chase's Restaurant, "History of Dooky Chase's Restaurant."

67. Leah Chase, *And Still I Cook* (Gretna, LA: Pelican Publishing Company, 2003).

68. William Grimes, "Edgar Chase Jr., Purveyor of Creole Cuisine, Dies at 88," *New York Times*, November 23, 2016.

69. Conversation with Leah Chase.

Chapter 13

1. Hermann B. Deutsch, *Brennan's New Orleans Cookbook* (Gretna, LA: Pelican Publishing Company, 1961).

2. Ibid.

3. Ibid.

4. Ibid.

5. Jimmy Brennan and Ted Brennan, *Breakfast at Brennan's and Dinner, Too*, 3rd ed. (New Orleans, LA: Brennan's/Quebecor Printing Book Group, 1994).

6. Deutsch, *Brennan's New Orleans Cookbook*.

7. *Times-Picayune*, "Brennan Taken by Death at 45," November 5, 1955.

8. Brennan and Martin, *Miss Ella of Commander's Palace*.

9. Brennan and Brennan, *Breakfast at Brennan's and Dinner, Too*.

10. Brennan and Martin, *Miss Ella of Commander's Palace*.

11. Deutsch, *Brennan's New Orleans Cookbook*.

12. Ibid.

13. Brennan and Martin, *Miss Ella of Commander's Palace*.

14. Krewe of Bacchus, "Our History," http://www.kreweofbacchus.org/about-bacchus/our-history.

15. Conversation with Ti Martin, interview with author, December 11, 2018.

16. Brennan and Brennan, *Breakfast at Brennan's and Dinner, Too*.

17. Brennan and Martin, *Miss Ella of Commander's Palace*.

18. *Times-Picayune*, "You Only Think You've Dined at Brennan's," July 21, 1974.

19. *Times-Picayune*, "Brennan's Is Sued," April 10, 1976.

20. Jack Du Arte, "Famed Brennan's Is Now Top-Flight Restaurant," *Times-Picayune*, June 27, 1974.

21. Doug MacCash, "Brennan's Restaurant Family Feud Continues with Management Coup," *Times-Picayune*, June 14, 2013.

22. Ibid.

23. Gwendolyn Knapp, "Brennan's Brennans Face Off in Court This Week," *Eater New Orleans*, May 13, 2013.

24. Conversation with Ralph Brennan.

25. Ibid.

26. MacCash, "Brennan's Restaurant Family Feud."

27. Ibid.

28. Conversation with Ralph Brennan.

29. Todd A. Price, "Ella Brennan, for the First Time in 40 Years, Visits Brennan's," *Times-Picayune*, November 28, 2014.

30. Doug McCash, "Ralph Brennan Unopposed in Purchase of Brennan's Restaurant Name," *Times-Picayune,* July 8, 2014.
31. Kenny Lopez, "Turtles on Parade: The Slowest Second Line at Brennan's," WGNO, March 12, 2015.
32. Todd A. Price, "Former Brennan's Restaurant on Royal Hires Slade Rushing of MiLa as Its Top Chef," *Times-Picayune,* June 10, 2014.
33. Ibid.
34. Conversation with Slade Rushing, interview with author, October 10, 2018.
35. Op cit (Ralph Brennan interview with author 2018).
36. Ibid.

About the Author

Alexandra Kennon grew up in the small town of St. Francisville, Louisiana, just a short drive north of New Orleans. After graduating from the Louisiana School for Math, Science and the Arts, she moved down the Mississippi River to attend Loyola University in New Orleans, and the Crescent City's eccentricities and debauchery suited her so well that she has since proudly called it home. In addition to writing about Louisiana's rich history, cuisine and culture, Alexandra leads tours of her beloved city and acts for the stage and screen—one of her proudest credits is originating roles in two Tennessee Williams one-act plays for the Tennessee Williams Literary Festival in New Orleans.

Printed in the USA
CPSIA information can be obtained
at www.ICGtesting.com
LVHW020712191223
766853LV00005B/27